The UK Maharajahs

The UK Maharajahs

Inside the South Asian Success Story

Ram Gidoomal

with David Porter

NICHOLAS BREALEY
PUBLISHING

LONDON

First published by
Nicholas Brealey Publishing Limited in 1997

36 John Street
London
WC1A 2AT, UK
Tel: +44 (0)171 430 0224
Fax: +44 (0)171 404 8311

17470 Sonoma Highway
Sonoma
California 95476, USA
Tel: (707) 939 7570
Fax: (707) 938 3515

http://www.nbrealey-books.com

ISBN 1-85788-188-5

British Library Cataloguing in Publication Data
A catalogue record for this book is available from the
British Library.

Printed in Finland by Werner Söderström Oy.

Contents

Preface   vii

Dedication   xi

Introduction   xiii

PART ONE: SETTING THE SCENE   1

   Chapter 1: The UK South Asians   3

   Chapter 2: Reasons For Success   33

PART TWO: PORTRAITS OF THE MAHARAJAHS   55

   Chapter 3: Out of India: Gulam Noon   57

   Chapter 4: Out of Africa: Manubhai Madhvani   75

   Chapter 5: Maharajahs of the Diaspora   85
      Azad Shivdasani   86
      Kumar Datwani   100
      Bharat Desai   107

Chapter 6: Against the Odds: Berjis Daver   119

Chapter 7: Law and Law-givers   129
His Honour Judge Mota Singh, QC   130
Dina Dattani   135

Chapter 8: The Next Generation   143
Shami Ahmed   145
Jayesh Manek   155
Chai Patel   162

PART THREE: CHALLENGES FOR THE FUTURE   169

Chapter 9: Identity and Self-expression   171

Chapter 10: And Now For the Bad News   177

Chapter 11: A Helping Hand   195

Chapter 12: Building Success on Success   215

Appendix   237

Further Reading   251

Notes   255

Index   263

Preface

This is not an all-inclusive book of every single UK Maharajah and I am using the term Maharajah to include not only people of wealth, but also people of power and influence – both within the South Asian community and in mainstream British life.

As with every such book, we will all have our own views on who should or should not be included. As it is not possible to include everyone who might qualify, my choice is bound to offend some people and I do feel how painful it must be to have one's favourite Asian personality omitted from this gallery.

My motivation for writing this book stems from my conviction that minority communities, who have contributed greatly to UK plc, are poised to take on a bigger role in British mainstream life. Britain is a multicultural society. I find it encouraging how many are seeing the positive aspects of ethnic diversity as an asset rather than a liability. There are sadly some, like Lord Tebbit, who still think about multicultural Britain as a negative phenomenon, though I was heartened by the muted response to his comments at the 1997 Tory Party Conference in Blackpool.

1997 was a particularly poignant year for all South Asians as it marked the fiftieth anniversary of Indian Independence as well as the twenty-fifth anniversary of the expulsion from Uganda. I would like to take this opportunity to thank the UK government of the time and the British people for accepting us, especially those who did their best to make us foreigners welcome in their midst.

After these many years, an increasing number of Asians in the UK, particularly those born here, have begun to see themselves as British Asians with a role to play and a loyalty to their country that they wish to express.

I am convinced that there is a shift in social attitudes reflected in the popular response to the recent tragic death of Diana, Princess of Wales. This shift of attitudes provides an opportunity to harness the goodwill and accelerate the pace of change to bring about the fairer and more just society for which she clearly felt a need to strive in her lifetime.

Perhaps it was an aspect of this shift of attitudes that Prime Minister Tony Blair was expressing when he said in his address to the Labour Party Conference in Brighton:

> I want the twenty-first century to be the century of the radicals.
>
> We cannot be a beacon to the world unless the talents of all the people shine through. Not one black High Court judge; not one black chief constable or permanent secretary. Not one black army officer above the rank of colonel. Not one Asian, either. Not a record of pride for the British establishment. And not a record of pride for the British Parliament that there are so few black and Asian MPs.
>
> I am against positive discrimination. But there is no harm in reminding ourselves just how much negative discrimination there is.

Brave words, indicating strong intentions. Asians wait to see how soon they will be translated into actions, though the UK Maharajahs themselves have a responsibility and a key part to play in bringing to reality the vision outlined by the Prime Minister with the following words:

> Now make the good that is in the heart of each of us serve the good of all of us. Give to our country the gift of energy, our ideas, our hopes, our talents. Use them to build a country each of whose people will say that 'I care about Britain because I know that Britain cares about me'.

ACKNOWLEDGEMENTS

The idea for this book came following discussions with my friends Professor Prabhu Guptara and Kumar Datwani, and the encouragement of Dr Raju Abraham.

My grateful thanks:

To Prabhu Guptara for his constant willingness to discuss new ideas and to read and re-read the material as it developed.

To David Porter for his help in this project and also for the very significant part he played in the preparation of the lecture that I delivered at the Royal Society for the Encouragement of Arts, Manufactures and Commerce on 5 March 1997. I am also grateful to his wife, Tricia Porter, who has spent hours transcribing interviews and trying to decipher cross-cultural accents!

To Deepak and Celia Mahtani, Sheena Carey and Shalini Gidoomal, for helping with research.

To Auntie Lakshmi (Shivdasani), for all her support and encouragement to Sunita and me over the years.

To those who agreed to be interviewed and have given up precious time in very busy diaries to meet with me. Their interest, input and encouragement have been invaluable.

To all those who read the manuscript (many during their summer holidays) and provided very helpful comments – Sunder and Kamud Advani, Anuradha Basu, Vivian Brown, Lord Meghnand Desai, Spinder Dhaliwal, Peter Elsom, Raj Loomba, Christopher Lucas, Chatru and Jyoti Manglani, Lal and Nirmala Panjabi, Contessa Bina Sella, Usha Prashar Sharma, Linbert Spencer, Shailendra Vyakarnam.

To my colleagues who released me of most office commitments so I could focus my time and energy on this book.

To my children Ravi, Nina and Ricki for their patience with my absorption in this new project. And to my wife Sunita who not only looked after home and office, but also spent hours transcribing interviews at short notice and always against impossible deadlines – even on her birthday!

And to all members of my extended family for their love, support and encouragement. The pulling together of family has brought us from the corner shop to where we are today and I am grateful to God for all my family.

Dedication

To those of my extended family who are no more on earth, but whose memory lives on. They have influenced me and encouraged me and inspired me in my entrepreneurial activities.

From my family:
Gagandas Dayaram Gidoomal, my biological father
Naraindas Dayaram Gidoomal (Daddy), my uncle
Vashdev Naraindas Gidoomal (Vinod), my youngest brother
Vishni Dayaram Gidoomal (Ama), my grandmother.

And from Sunita's family:
Tirath Tekchand Shivdasani (Dad), a director of the Inlaks Group
Vishni Tirath Shivdasani (Mum), her mother
Indurkumar Hassaram Shivdasani (Uncle Indoo), founder of the Inlaks Group
Sunder Khushiram Advani (Uncle Sunder), a director of the Inlaks Group.

Introduction

Forget the much-massaged public statements of the political parties, alternately prophesying boom and bust for the UK economy, depending on whether or not they happen to be running it at the time. There *is* a tiger economy in Britain, a wealth-creating economy of fast and accelerating growth.

It's an economy within an economy. The business tycoons who are at the cutting edge of that economy are hardly household names, though the goods and services they produce are. When we read about the community from which they come, it's usually in media reports of social deprivation and possible threats to the smooth running of UK plc.

'Tiger' and 'Maharajah' are current buzzwords in business and economic discussions, and they're entirely relevant to this book. For we're talking about the UK South Asian business economy. 'South Asia', in my use of the term, comprises the seven countries of the Indian subcontinent: India, Pakistan, Bangladesh, Nepal, Bhutan, Sri Lanka and the Maldive Islands. Like anything else to do with that sprawling, multi-nation, multi-people-group segment of the earth's land surface, the subcontinent is a mixture of extremes. And the UK South Asian population closely reflects those extremes.

It is a population at a point of change, often painful change. In the experiences of small businesses in London, Leicester, Bradford and other centres with large numbers of South Asian residents, values and business practices that have been sacrosanct for many centuries are being questioned and sometimes superseded. At the same time great financial empires are being built, and behind the scenes power and influence are developing alongside wealth.

I am a businessman and a South Asian myself – a British Indian from Kenya; my family originally came from Pakistan. I worked for many years with the multinational Inlaks Group, and a few years ago left to develop a wider portfolio including public sector, charity work and community work among South Asians. Much of that work has involved sitting on boards and committees of organisations and agencies that target the ethnic minority communities and try to solve the problems that many of them face as they attempt to manage change in a bewilderingly complex financial world.

This book is inevitably built around the Maharajahs, the UK counterparts of the Tatas, Birlas and Ambanis and other South Asians who are part of the worldwide Asian wealth club.[1] But it also asks some hard questions which will emerge as we go on. To set the scene before we start, here are some news stories taken at random:

❑ The attendance of Perween Warsi (together with singer Frankie Vaughan and actor Michael York) at Buckingham Palace to receive the MBE from the Queen. You probably haven't heard of Mrs Warsi. You will have, if you are in catering in the Midlands. She started selling food from her kitchen ten years ago and now heads a £35 million company, S & A Foods in Derby.[2] She is also a member of the President of the Board of Trade's Advisory Group on Competitiveness. **Similar stories can be told all over the UK, where South Asians have built small businesses into major companies.** (You'll read about some of them in this book.)

❑ The announcement that the 121-year-old Cullens grocery chain – once bigger than Sainsbury's – was to be taken over by the Patel brothers, who already own the Europa Foods convenience store chain and Hart's the Grocers. The group began as a newsagent's shop in North London less than twenty years ago.[3] In 1996 its profits exceeded £60 million. **Like Mrs Warsi's, the story of the Patels is one of classic UK South Asian entrepreneurial success.**

❑ A feature on Tony Hussain, a Scottish-born Indian who lives in Dundee, and spends his mornings in his food business making naan bread for supermarkets, his evenings working in his Indian restaurant in Dundee, and his afternoons making multimillion-pound movies. This last venture was launched after showing a visiting Indian film director around Scotland. Hussain's company finds Scottish locations for Indian film makers. He also acts in the films – a 'spare-time' activity: 'I don't get paid for it … I do it because I want to promote Scotland.' The British Film Commission has warmly welcomed the new company, and the Scottish Tourist Board is not at all displeased either.[4] **South Asians have an aptitude for hard work.**

❑ News that Amartya Sen, Professor of Economics and Philosophy at Harvard University, has become Master of Trinity College Cambridge, an appointment that is in the gift of the Prime Minister. He is the first Indian academic ever to become head of an Oxbridge college. Other people who had been considered for the Mastership included ex-Foreign Secretary Douglas Hurd and Nobel Prize-winner James Mirrlees.[5]

❑ The long-running BBC1 television soap opera *EastEnders* already features several South Asian story lines, dramatising many of the issues we will be considering in this book. For example, the on-going saga of Sanjay and Gita Kapoor (played by Deepak Verma and Shobu Kapoor) and their struggles to develop their market stall into a clothing empire – with the sometimes unwanted co-operation of Sanjay's mother – is typical of many real-life dramas being played out today in South Asian family businesses.[6] **South Asians and South Asian themes are common on British TV.** For example the role of Milly (Amita Dhiri) and other characters in the BBC2 legal drama series *This Life*.

Within the main text of the book I have included various brief items on a wide cross-section of leading UK South Asians who have achieved senior positions, national and international influence and/or personal and corporate wealth. **Many of them are quite unknown to the general public – and they don't seek publicity.**

A sober counter-theme (which I shall be exploring in the pages that follow) emerges from publications like Tariq Modood and

Richard Berthoud's *Ethnic Minorities in Britain: Diversity and Disadvantage*.[7] Such studies show that, in general, being a member of an ethnic minority is like being the world's second-largest car hire firm – you have to try harder. For example, according to Richard Berthoud, Pakistanis and Bangladeshis who gain university degrees stand exactly the same risk of poverty as do white people without any qualifications at all.[8] **The UK South Asian community has not consistently prospered.**

But I haven't written this book only to celebrate some major South Asian achievers. I want to analyse how the South Asians as a community contribute to the UK, and to show where unexpected influence as well as wealth exists. I shall describe some of the factors that currently pose a threat to the South Asian community, the areas of vulnerability and the strategy that should be (and sometimes has been) embarked on to prevent a catastrophe for UK South Asians and for UK plc.

In this year of the anniversaries of Indian and Pakistani independence and of the expulsion of the Ugandan Asians, I propose a celebration – and sound a warning.

In **Part One**, I provide an overture, setting out the main characteristics of the South Asian community under three headings: their ethnic background, their position in UK society, and the characteristics of South Asian family and business life. I discuss in Chapter 2 some of the reasons that have been suggested for the success of the South Asian community in the UK.

In **Part Two**, I look at a number of UK Maharajahs, each of whom is chosen to reflect a part of the diversity of this extraordinary enterprise culture and wealth-creating economy. There are stories of great wealth and also of influence; some are textbook examples of South Asian entrepreneurial success, some depart radically from the usual traditions and methods. These 'case studies' are based on personal knowledge of, and extensive interviews with, the people they feature. I am grateful to them for their contribution.

In **Part Three**, I consider some of the themes that emerge from the first two parts. It is a discussion of present opportunities and present minefields, of future possibilities and of future policy. In this part, I discuss some of the ways in which the South Asian community is being supported by government and other agencies, but I also point out a few of the great many other things that could and should be done to secure continued prosperity and benefit to UK plc. I argue that the causes of vulnerability may well lie in previous success.

In the Appendix, I have included lists of organisations and media active in UK South Asian affairs, and a selective reading list.

Part One

Setting the Scene

'The South Asian community of Britain ... is now in excess of 1.5 million strong; a highly successful wealth-creating community, with an estimated disposable income of around £5 billion. It is a community that we cannot, indeed must not, ignore; a community which makes an invaluable contribution to UK plc.'

John Savine, former Chairman, SOLOTEC[1]

1

The UK South Asians

'This is not merely the story of an individual, but the autobiography of a generation.'

His Excellency Dr L. M. Singhvi

I stepped out of the plane into a clear Scottish afternoon and crossed the
tarmac of Aberdeen Airport towards the terminal building. It was a beautiful sunny day in 1986, and I was full of anticipation. It was my first visit
as Managing Director of Highland Seafoods; I'd come from Geneva to
tour the factory that the Inlaks Group, my employers, had acquired. I had
not had the job for long. Originally an Englishman had been chosen to
head up the Scottish operation, but a late change of plan now meant that
he had been posted to London and I was sent to Scotland.

At the meeting point I scanned the group of people waiting and saw the
firm's chauffeur holding up a placard. Soon I was in a comfortable car
speeding away from the airport, the open sea on one side of the road, the
lush countryside of Aberdeenshire on the other. The Production Director
– a tall, rather dour man – pointed out local landmarks as we headed for
Inverbervie. We turned down a precipitous cliff road and suddenly there
the factory was: tucked away in the attractive estuary landscape, a curl of
smoke from the salmon-smoking plant lazily ascending into the blue sky.
We came to a halt in the car park in a space satisfyingly labelled 'Managing Director'.

We went inside. A number of key staff had been assembled to greet me formally; a kind of welcoming committee. They looked nervous and tense, as well they might. Two hundred people knew that the change of owner-ship meant they were about to lose their jobs. They didn't know that we planned to re-employ them immediately. I began to shake hands, moving down the line.

Something peculiar was happening as I greeted my new Aberdeen workforce. The bristling suspicion that had greeted me as I walked in was evaporating. When I was introduced to each staff member as the new Managing Director, barely suppressed hostility turned to welcoming smiles. I would have thought that my job title would have identified me as one of the enemy, but here I was being warmly welcomed.

I wondered about it for a while but was soon absorbed in a tour of the factory. I knew very little about seafood. Inlaks was a niche corporation with interests all over the world and expertise in a wide variety of markets. In Nigeria I'd overseen all imports for trading operations for Inlaks; in Geneva we dealt with an extensive range of activities from investment management to group personnel. But this was my first specialist appointment.

At the next factory, however, a similar thing happened: initial hostility, dis-appearing when my new colleagues discovered that I was the new Managing Director they had been told was coming; then warmth and co-operation.

Several months later I had my feet firmly under the desk and knew my way around. I was no longer a stranger in Scotland and felt myself among friends. I was glad that my employers had decided I was the one who should have the Scottish job. But I was still puzzled by the odd reception I'd had on my arrival. Eventually I tackled the Production Director who had greeted me on my first day, and asked him to explain.

'When I arrived here, everybody was so suspicious of me when they knew I was coming, and then gave me such a good welcome when they saw me. What was going on?'

He hesitated for a moment, then smiled.

'To be absolutely frank, Ram, we hadn't heard of the change of plan. We still thought we were going to get an Englishman...'

I began to understand the football slogans I'd seen in my Scottish trav-els: 'We support Scotland – and every team that plays England'!

Racial mistrust is much the same whatever the races involved. Unfamiliarity and lack of understanding form a major factor. British schools have only recently begun to teach children about the lives and beliefs of ethnic communities in the UK. They do it because lack of understanding leads to suspicion, to ridicule and to hostility – on both sides. So I want to begin by talking a little about the South Asians whom I shall be discussing.

Almost all of them are British citizens. Most growth in the ethnic minority population in the next few years won't come from new immigrants but from births among those already in Britain. As we shall see, immigration legislation over the past few years has slowed the rate of immigration down to a trickle.

The UK South Asians come originally from the seven countries of the Indian subcontinent: India, Pakistan, Bangladesh, Nepal, Bhutan, Sri Lanka and the Maldives. They are people who belong to many races and people groups, many religions and many social backgrounds. The largest of the seven countries is India, which gained independence from Britain in 1947 and is today the world's largest functioning democracy. It's a vast country and the statistics are bewildering.

INDIA

❑ The population is around 955 million growing at 2.3 per cent annually. By AD 2020 India will be the world's most densely inhabited country with almost 1.3 billion people (though China will still have the largest population).

❑ 4,600 people groups speak 1,652 languages, of which 33 are spoken by at least 100,000 people.

❑ There are four major religions – Hinduism, Islam, Christianity and Sikhism – and hundreds of minor ones.

❑ The caste system, an important element in the majority Hindu population, contains around 6,500 social divisions.

Some of the most ancient peoples in the world made their home in the subcontinent. For example, I am a Sindhi. My people originated in Sind in the Indus Valley in North India, now part of Pakistan. Many followed the Sufi religion (most Sindhis living in Pakistan today are Muslim, although my own family was part of the minority Hindu community). A highly developed civilisation, living in homes with sophisticated bathrooms and efficient drainage systems, inhabited Sind in the third and fourth millennia BC; in 1924 archaeologists discovered plentiful ancient Sindhi artefacts including superb jewellery made of precious stones and metals.[2]

Yet the long history of India and its peoples has not been a settled one, even in modern times. In 1947 the Partition of India between Hindu and Muslim left the Sindhis among the worst sufferers on both the Indian and Pakistani sides of the new border. Many became stateless; when the Sind province became part of West Pakistan, the Hindu Sindhis became a 'diaspora' or scattered nation whose homeland had disappeared. Some stayed on under Pakistani rule. Others, as had the Jews, the Armenians, the Romanies and many more before them, became exiles and wanderers throughout the world.[3]

Like many other Sindhi families, the Gidoomals settled in East Africa where my father and other family members developed major trade enterprises and lived comfortably in a palatial home. But our travels were still not over. In 1963 Kenya gained independence from Britain. The British had ruled since 1895 and had strongly influenced economic and cultural life. By contrast, the new regime of Jomo Kenyatta was strongly African nationalist. Kenyan Asians holding British passports were increasingly marginalised. Pro-African policies were introduced, there were increasing restrictions on work permits for non-Kenyans, and trading licences were refused for many non-Kenyan citizens. By 1966 we had little choice but to become impoverished refugees again. We came to Britain.

My father arrived at Heathrow Airport in 1966. By the next year, when I and the rest of the family joined him, 500 Kenyan Asians were arriving every week. The British government was temporarily in a quandary. Urgent legislation was clearly needed to control an escalating situation. But if it were announced that legislation was being drafted, the flood of refugees might turn into a tidal wave as immigrants tried to get in before the doors closed.[4] And if legislation were delayed, there were many voices in Britain that would complain bitterly that the government was going soft on immigrants. We were among the lucky ones. Soon entry to Britain would become much harder.[5]

My father brought £2,000 with him – the most that each household was permitted to take out of Kenya. It was the equivalent of £20,000 in 1997 money; the average house price in 1966 was £3,850. He bought a newsagent's business in Shepherd's Bush, London, with a four-roomed flat above it in which fifteen members of the Gidoomal family made their home. Two thousand pounds was more capital than many in Britain possessed (though it was not a large sum to share between fifteen people) and we were not the only ones living in cramped housing. It was quite a new experience for my family, however. We had left behind large business interests throughout East Africa, a wealthy lifestyle and a palace that had been our home.

I'll be talking more about my family's experiences later. For the moment, it's enough to make the point that we were just one family in a global South Asian diaspora. In Uganda too, thousands of Asians were expelled, though this time not because of economic and nationalist pressures but following the frightening threats and horrific deeds of Uganda's tyrant president, Idi Amin. And South Asians spread still farther afield: there are significant South Asian communities in Canada, Australia, South Africa, Indonesia, mainland Europe and many more countries. It is estimated that 18–20 million or more make up a huge diaspora that has increasing influence, power and wealth.

The largest concentration of South Asians in any single country is in the UK. There are around 1.5 million settled in Britain. Leicester is the second largest Indian city outside India. The only city with a larger Indian population is Durban in South Africa. Most UK South Asians live in what is known as the M1/M6 corridor, stretching from Lancashire in the North West down to Kent in the South

East. This includes the two main South Asian population centres, the West Midlands and Greater London.

It was not an arbitrary choice. The 1958 *Concise Oxford Atlas* shows the major British population centres occupying roughly the same corridor, with only a few differences reflecting, for example, the rise in importance of Southampton. The immigrants simply located themselves in the main population centres. This is not surprising in view of the fact that the first post-war immigrants were invited to Britain to work in specific jobs and were initially warmly welcomed by a country at that time still recovering from a war that had taken its toll on the labour force.

The first post-war immigrants were Jamaicans, who arrived in 1948 to answer the call of the country they had served in wartime. Over the next ten years the number of Jamaicans and other 'West Indians' in Britain gradually increased. Some came because British companies had recruited in their home countries. A 1956 London Transport advertising campaign brought 3,787 Barbadians over twelve years. In 1966 further campaigns were launched in Trinidad and Jamaica. Other organisations such as the British Hotels and Restaurants Association recruited skilled workers in Barbados. Many came to work as London Underground staff, bus conductors and hospital orderlies.

Somewhat later, when it was clear that the West Indian influx was insufficient to meet the labour needs of post-war Britain, substantial immigration from South Asia followed. Before the War very few people from the Indian subcontinent were resident in Britain (even though immigration from South Asia had begun in the eighteenth century) and those who were tended to be in the élite classes. But in the 1950s, again with encouragement from Britain, rural workers from India and Pakistan began to arrive. By the end of 1958 there were around 55,000 Indians and Pakistanis in the UK and around 125,000 West Indians. They came by invitation and they came by right. The 1948 Nationality Act entitled Britain's colonial (and ex-colonial) citizens to British citizenship and the right of residence in Britain.[6]

They were early and optimistic days. The first immigrants were warmly welcomed by the British press and government spokesmen (though the general public was not nearly so welcoming as were the media, and the trade unions' welcome was also cool). The gap between that welcome and the tense and hostile attitude towards immigrants that existed when my family came to Britain a couple of decades later is a wide and depressing one.

Among the 1.5 million South Asians now living in Britain are a large number of Britain's million Muslims and most of the 800,000 British Hindus and Sikhs. Numerically it is a community that can't be ignored. One-and-a-half million, after all, is the number of people living in Northern Ireland; it's the number of Jews currently living in Europe; it's the number of Arabs living in the occupied territories.

Very strong links exist between Britain and the countries of South Asia and the subcontinent: 50,000 Asians come to Britain each year to study, and many thousands of UK citizens in their turn visit South Asian destinations. There are links through organisations such as the British Council and the BBC World Service. The Indo-British Partnership has seen trade rise by over 50 per cent in both directions since 1993. UK trade with Pakistan (which has the highest average GDP growth in South Asia in the last fifteen years) has risen almost 50 per cent in four years. A new generation of British entrepreneurs of Asian descent is revitalising the flow of commerce. Companies like National Grid and ICI are winning business in South Asia's most liberal and deregulated economy. Today National Power is leading work at the Hub river on Asia's biggest private power project.[7]

The UK South Asians, then, are a community linked by their ethnic origins in a common subcontinent. Despite the huge extent of that subcontinent, they share some social and other characteristics. A people in diaspora, they have retained a stronger sense of visible community than have some other scattered peoples.

SOUTH ASIAN ENTREPRENEURISM

It would be quite wrong to argue that everything is rosy in the UK South Asian garden. But in this book I will be looking at a great deal of success (proportionally much more than might be expected), achieved by what has historically been regarded as a disadvantaged minority.

In at least one area the South Asian community has been immensely and visibly successful – the corner shop. If the British are (to quote Napoleon's famous misquotation of a comment by Adam Smith) 'a nation of shopkeepers', then at the outset we must concede overwhelming superiority to the British Asian community. They are shopkeepers *par excellence*. As the 1980s came to an end it was estimated that almost two-thirds of all UK independent retail outlets were Asian owned. Many recent studies of Asian businesses have provided similar statistics.

Yet focusing on retail success alone is misleading. Today's UK South Asians are involved in a very wide range of business, professional and other activities. Quantifying the results is difficult, as very little research has yet been published. But the gross product is remarkable. One has to go back to 1992 to find it spelled out. South Asian Development Partnership and SOLOTEC (South London Training and Enterprise Council) joined forces to produce a UK South Asian population report. It described the Asian population as 'the £5 billion corridor' – a figure, for example, that is considerably more than the earnings from the current government's one-off windfall tax. The report was based on the 1991 Census, which for the first time requested ethnic information.

The contribution of immigrants in general to national prosperity has often been pointed out. The 1990 Labour Force Survey found that some 25 per cent of foreign residents were in professional or managerial jobs or were employing other people, compared with 22 per cent of British citizens. Recent immigrants tend more often to be self-employed than British-born people (16 per cent compared with 12 per cent) and their children tend to stay in education longer than do the children of British-born parents. In the case of asylum seekers, a far higher percentage have higher educational and professional qualifications than in a similar sampling of the majority population.

A pilot research project carried out for Business Link London South Ltd by Tradeways International focused on Croydon, where 20 per cent of businesses are run by people from the ethnic minorities. Indians represent 5 per cent of Croydon's population yet are responsible for 10 per cent of business start-ups. Of male entrepreneurs 6.6 per cent are Pakistanis, 9.7 per cent Indians and 14.9 per cent Bangladeshis. Over half of Croydon's South Asian businesses expect growth in 1997.

Britain is also acquiring skilled workers at other countries' expense. For example, of the 52,040 foreign-born doctors, dentists and nurses (23 per cent of health-service employees) working in Britain in 1994, a significant number were trained abroad.[8] One can only speculate gloomily on the devastating consequences for the national economy if some extreme British nationalists had their way and every member of the immigrant communities left tomorrow.

Comparisons between the contribution to UK plc made by the 1.5 million UK South Asians, and that which might be expected from a 1.5 million sample of the majority ethnic population, show that the South Asians perform consistently better.

This is apparent in broad social indicators. Proportionally more Asians own their own houses than do members of the majority ethnic population. Originally many lived in ghetto areas; today they are making inroads into the wealthy leafy suburbs. South Asians, too, are increasingly to be found in the Institute of Directors and in London clubs. Indeed, prestigious Asian clubs are being set up, like the Durbar Club and Baroness Flather's Asian Conservative Club in the House of Lords. And in July 1997, Kamlesh Bahl, Chair of the Equal Opportunities Commission, achieved a remarkable double. She was made a CBE – and also became the first woman ever to be admitted to the Law Society Wine Committee!

There are direct benefits to be seen as a result of South Asian entrepreneurism, for example to local economies. The large ethnic minority community in Dundee, Scotland, includes many successful entrepreneurs who came to the city and settled with their families. Mosques and other ethnic facilities began to appear as the community grew. Several years ago Keillers, the famous marmalade manufacturer, was facing bankruptcy. The company was bought by a local Pakistani entrepreneur, who thereby not only rescued local jobs, but also protected a part of Dundee's heritage. Keillers, like Coopers of Oxford, made its city celebrated on the nation's breakfast tables; thanks to a South Asian entrepreneur and some useful government back-up, it was able to go on doing so.

Similar stories can be told in many UK cities where South Asian business start-ups have revitalised local communities. Where new businesses take over ailing or moribund organisations and turn them round, they keep a community amenity going. Where separate new businesses are started, the local economy is frequently boosted and even saved from collapse. Whether by closure prevention or by injecting new enterprise, UK South Asians have been responsible for the revitalisation of many local communities.

This can also be argued the other way round. In Hammersmith a branch of Tesco opened in competition with the local Asian and ethnic small businesses. One by one whole rows of shops have closed. What was until recently a living, vibrant community is now dying. You could call it a defeat for the Asian business community in Hammersmith – and so it is; but it also demonstrates what that community's presence was achieving. When the Asians left, the neighbourhood declined. They must have been contributing *something* that was important for social growth.

COUNTING WEALTH

'Books of lists' are always popular; 'rich lists' especially so. For example, the *Sunday Times* annually lists the wealthiest people in Britain and charts the rise and fall of millionaires; *Eastern Eye*[9] has done the same for the UK Asian community. There is a great deal of wealth to be listed; among the UK South Asians are some who are immensely rich and many who are very prosperous indeed.

Rich lists are fun, but highly misleading. Some people who head such lists do so on the basis of estimates by the compilers, or of the published accounts of companies. But this ignores factors such as debts and entailments that reduce the book value of the company, or the compilers may be unaware of changes in the individual's situation that reduce his or her personal wealth. This is often the case when South Asians are listed, because – as we shall see – the ownership of wealth within an Asian family business is frequently hard to pin down. Applying the methods of the stock market, FTSE index and other ways of identifying who the Maharajahs are, and what they are worth, makes most published listings very unreliable. Gulam Noon, whose name appears in the rich lists, is very sceptical of them indeed:

> The lists of Asian millionaires that are compiled can be grossly exaggerated in some cases and undervalued in others. It is difficult to assess the assets and liabilities of private companies owned by family members, and one cannot apply the principles of multiples of public companies to assess the value of family concerns. I would be cautious in evaluating, for example, the figures mentioned in the *Eastern Eye* list of Britain's richest Asian 100.[10]

So you won't find in-depth treatment in this book of some whose names are usually mentioned when rich South Asians are being discussed. For example, Lakshmi Mittal normally heads the list. An Indian from Calcutta, he wholly owns the steel company Ispat, valued at £1.5 billion. Ispat's plants are in Trinidad and Tobago, Mexico and Ireland. His relocation of corporate headquarters from Jakarta to London's Berkeley Square is very recent. His base is in London but his great wealth has been created elsewhere. Similarly, the Hinduja brothers are Indians based in London; they are noted philanthropists and backers of huge projects like the Concordia High Technology Park near Peterborough. Their wealth from oil and trade is around £1.1 billion; but their major areas of activity are in India and the Middle East.

I have interviewed, and discuss in this book, some of the 'big names' where they illustrate important themes: for example, Gulam Noon is almost a textbook example of the classic entrepreneur, and Manubhai Madhvani's story illustrates some key points about the role of UK Asians in present-day East African affairs. But my interest is much more in the people who are not in the headlines. I'll be talking about South Asians who are little known but control enormous global interests, such as Azad Shivdasani who is head of the Inlaks Group, the vast family business with interests ranging from tea estates in India to aluminium processing in Africa, and with several thousand employees worldwide. I'll be talking about major national business figures such as Chai Patel, founder of Court Cavendish, one of Britain's largest independent care providers. I'll be talking about some UK South Asians who occupy positions of surprising influence and power in Britain – not many are aware that until very recently a South Asian was Chairman of Ladbroke, a hugely profitable betting empire, and an influential member of government thinktanks both in the gambling industry and in Training and Enterprise Councils. And I'll be talking about the up-and-coming generation, including Shami Ahmed, the fashion tycoon, and Jayesh Manek, the brilliantly intuitive investor.

Some of the wealthiest UK Maharajahs have benefited the larger UK economy. Many made fortunes by acquiring dying companies and turning them around – saving, and creating, jobs. Lord Swarj Paul, owner of Caparo Steel, has invested in economically depressed areas like South Wales. As an example of these I'll be talking about the Madhvani family, who have successfully recreated their pre-1970 dominance of Uganda, building on an economy ruined by years of turmoil – and opening up many possibilities of renewed UK/Uganda trading links.

I'll also be discussing people like Bharat Desai, founder of Syntel; people whose business activities in the UK are only part of a truly global enterprise. Such enterprises reflect the way that trade frontiers are disappearing and new relationships between countries and communities are developing, as the communications revolution and the growth of the Internet redefine the notion of a catchment area.

For many of the 1.5 million South Asians resident and working in the UK, the fact that they or their parents were British citizens and held British passports was what brought them here, as other countries expelled them and looked to the UK to take care of them. The twenty-five years since the Asian exoduses from Kenya and Uganda have shown that the benefits have been mutual. Here is Manubhai Madhvani, reflecting on his feelings in the anniversary year:

> There is gratitude. Especially gratitude to Sir Edward Heath, whose government authorised our entry when we had nowhere to go. What I should like to say to him now is: 'Thank you. We are grateful we were permitted to live in your country. And I would want to say to you that we have not been a burden to you. We have prospered – and our prosperity has benefited Britain.'[11]

FAMILY AND BUSINESS

So let us continue this overture to our main theme by asking: what are the characteristics of South Asians as individuals, as families and as business people?

The individual

There are two main categories of UK South Asians: those who came to Britain from East Africa, and those who came from the subcontinent. It has only recently been recognised that the two groups differ significantly in such areas as manner, accent and articulation. Social background is often markedly different. East African Asians have usually done well in Africa and have retained their middle-class background and ease in dealing with the majority population. Manubhai Madhvani points out that a typical Asian storekeeper in Kenya would have been grocer, mechanic, spare-parts dealer and much more to the white farmers he served, and would have prospered in that situation.

Asians from the subcontinent, already identifiable by their different accents, usually have a different background. Indians usually come from big towns and are familiar with the urban environment, and are typically professional and modern. Pakistanis and Bangladeshis usually come from a rural environment. There is therefore a difference between their approaches to life, aspirations and expectations.

The UK Maharajahs – those who have achieved wealth, power and influence – tend to come from the East African Asians. But there is also a strong Indian 'establishment', including such people as Lord Bagri, Baroness Flather and Lord Paul, who have made it into the UK establishment. Out of the five Asians in the House of Lords, four are from the Indian subcontinent and have lived in Britain for some years. The fifth, Lord Dholakia, is from East Africa.

What all the UK South Asians share, wherever they originate from, is a willingness to work hard. Most South Asian entrepreneurs are prepared to work long hours, to put up with difficult working conditions in order to make the business prosper, and to sacrifice home comforts and leisure for the sake of deferred benefits. Kumar Datwani, a South Asian entrepreneur whose substantial business interests cover three continents, sums it up like this:

When it comes to closing time the staff don't drop everything, down tools and go home. They stay on to finish what they're doing and only then do they leave. They aren't doing it because they get paid overtime … they don't. They aren't doing it out of some kind of concern for the honour of the family or filial duty, though that may have something to do with it. They are doing it because they are motivated to do it, and that is why so many Asian entrepreneurs succeed.[12]

There is a further dimension that shapes a great deal of the entrepreneurial attitude. Most of the South Asian religions have a high ethical content, teaching values of integrity, responsibility, hard work and filial respect. Many in this community regard success in business as a family duty. For example, many Hindus have a deeply ingrained sense of *dharma*, of doing one's duty, that is reinforced in the temple and Hindu literature. And as virtue brings its rewards, success as a religious obligation often becomes a religious blessing.

The family

A South Asian is aware of his extended family from the day he is born.

One of my strongest childhood memories from Kenya is the meal times, when thirty or so members of my extended family ate together. It was a different system to Western family meals. The children all ate together, all the uncles were served by the women, and the women didn't eat until the men had been served. But we all ate as one extended family, sharing the meal that had been cooked in three kitchens in neighbouring apartments.

When we came to Britain there were fewer of us living close to each other, but we kept the old tradition. Every day ten or twelve of us sat down to dinner, and on Sunday members of the family living farther away joined us so that our numbers swelled to thirty or forty. I grew up knowing all my uncles well, and they knew me, as our extended family bonded and grew together.

If you asked me to explain the unique nature of South Asian business, I would point you to those meals, for it was there that I built up, as naturally as growing, the relationships that would serve me well throughout my business career. When I needed to do business with one or other of my uncles many years later, we each knew exactly who we were dealing with. Either he trusted me or he didn't. Maybe I was the naughty one who never paid up. Maybe I was the one with a good track record for honesty. Whichever it was, he knew. And I knew him. It was a family relationship. Even if a youngster had a reputation for being a little irresponsible with money, he was still employable. One just watched over him more. He was family.

The concept of family is crucial in South Asian business. It extends even beyond the extended family and into the workplace (I'm speaking particularly here about East African Asians, though you can see this also in Asians from the subcontinent.) In a factory employing a hundred people, the employees will work hard and be prepared to work long hours if necessary because they regard themselves as part of a family. One reason why many businesses see the debate over minimum wage as unlikely to have much impact on South Asian businesses is that many of them practise profit sharing. Employees know that whatever the weekly wage is, at the end of the year their share of the profit will lift their annual earnings well above the average wage.

Obviously, British South Asian businesses will comply with whatever legal requirements are imposed, but in the best of them the employees are unlikely to see the introduction of minimum wage controls as an important breakthrough. Of course there are bad businesses in every community and the sweatshop is a peculiarly Asian corruption, one that has to do with non-responsibility to those outside the circle of family, caste and religious group. But I am talking specifically about Asian businesses in the UK, under European legislation. And I believe that the culture of the extended family gives South Asian business a natural tendency to a generosity of heart and a conviction that the staff are a family.

But let's return to the 'family business' in the other sense, that of a business founded and run by members of a particular family. In the West, an entrepreneur will set up a business, will perhaps employ members of the family and will draw a salary from the profits, out of which they will provide for their immediate family. If the company grows to a certain size, the next step will be to go public with a share flotation, ensuring that control is retained by a majority shareholding, which need be little more than 50 per cent of the stock. South Asian businesses are different.

First, it is the case in very many Asian families that **the whole family owns the business**. It is considered quite usual for some members of the family to be devoting long hours to the company, for other members who are not directly involved to be equal partners, and for retired and elderly family members to have equal influence in determining company policy and decision making. The family owns the company and owns its financial assets corporately. The young enterprising entrepreneurial teenager who identifies his untapped niche market and goes for it is not primarily securing wealth for himself (though that often follows), but is providing for his family.

Linked to this is the profound respect that Asians have for older family members. In the West, families are nuclear and two generational; the typical 'father and mother and 2.4 children' exist as a self-contained unit (even that well-worn tag needs to be modified today: the figure is nearer 1.7 children now). In South Asian society, families include at least three generations and are thus 'extended families'. There is considerable filial piety. A son reveres his father or his father's memory and 'honouring one's father and mother' is a basic value. For example, my own father died when I was four weeks old, but my uncle, whom I grew up to regard as my father (and refer to as my father throughout this book), took his place and became the head of the family, making all the decisions. When he died, I was sixteen. In such a situation the mother will look to the oldest son, or all the sons working as a team under the oldest son's leadership. If there are no sons, it will fall to an uncle or a cousin to take on the responsibility. That is why a son is so important to an Indian family, because he will one day take over; and if his father dies when the son is a minor, an older male relative will be appointed to act on his behalf to act as a kind of regent until the boy comes of age.

It will always be a male relative. That does not mean that the mother in a South Asian family is undervalued. On the contrary, she is often in charge of running a large household, which in the sub-continent will frequently involve managing a staff of servants and their pay. She will certainly pay the family bills, out of a budget supplied by the father – I remember my own mother each month settling accounts with the doctor, the schools and so on. It was my mother who made decisions on furnishing and decorating the family home;

in many ways, watching how she ran things was part of my own edu-cation in managing a business. Family roles were clearly delineated. Foreign travel, buying a car, investments – those were matters usu-ally handled by the men in the family. There was, too, an under-standing that my father ran the office and my mother the household.

Although this is a typical South Asian model, there are some variations. For example, not all Asian families are as large as the Gidoomal family! And there are quite a few families in which the wife is the one definitely 'wearing the trousers'. But by and large my experiences were typical.

There are several implications for business. One of the key issues currently affecting Asian business in the UK is that of succession, which is as important in business as in families – the oldest son suc-ceeds to the headship of the family business, regardless of his com-petence – and I will be looking at that in later chapters. Another is determining the extent and limits of competence. For example, dur-ing the war my father, then in his twenties, traded in silk. He imported from Japan to Mombasa and sold mainly to the Indians in the army. His customers included officers' wives and the families of Indian labourers brought in by the army to build the railway. It was a lucrative business. At its height, my father's Mombasa Silk Empo-rium had around eleven ships on their way to Mombasa loaded with silk. The profits easily covered the occasional ship lost by enemy action. He made bolder and bolder decisions, and the older uncle who was supposed to be giving him counsel and guidance just sat back and let him do it, for he was making millions for the family.

In the end my father made one bold gamble too many. The Mom-basa Silk Emporium crashed and the huge wartime profits were lost. The business had to rebuild from the beginning because of a failure to make the right decisions at the right time, to institute control pro-cedures, to monitor expenditure against returns – a situation that has many resonances in Western business today (the Nick Lee-son/Barings Bank story has some particularly close similarities). It is also one that is repeated in many South Asian businesses every year because of the reluctance of Asian family businesses to institute professional staff accountability procedures and (especially) performance monitoring and evaluation by outsiders.

But the system has many successes too. Decision-making responsibility is not gained by rising up a hierarchy, as is the case in most businesses in the majority ethnic population. It is given because the person is known to the family and has proved himself or herself by accurate decisions and imaginative planning in a limited capacity. When one has established a good track record, one is given a longer rein. That in turn forces development of skills and professional maturity, which in turn brings further responsibility.

In my own growth as an entrepreneur in a South Asian family business, a key factor was that I knew at any particular time what my own competence and expertise were considered to be. For example, I was once involved in a dramatic opportunity to sell a consignment of chickens to a country whose borders were, the company learned (through one of those efficient grapevines that every entrepreneur knows), about to be closed to foreign imports. We managed to charter a ship, buy the frozen chickens, get them loaded, rush the paperwork through, get the ship to the port of entry and complete all unloading and paperwork just before the deadline expired. Of course we made a killing – because the locals knew that these were the last cheap chickens they were going to see for a while. But in the course of this I had to commit large amounts of Inlaks money and take a crucial decision involving chartering a ship for a million dollars, the highest figure we had ever paid to charter a vessel.

I would normally have consulted other directors. Unfortunately I was the only director not on holiday, and contacting the others would have taken valuable time. Yet I had no qualms about authorising the expenditure, because financial dealings were, when necessary, carried out on trust and the details dealt with in due course. It was a situation directly arising from the extended family and the knowledge that its members had of each other over the years. The family knew me and I knew the family. So there were no bottlenecks in the corporate structure that might have kept the deal hanging while other directors were consulted. I did my deal.

Because the family is such an important core element of the company, few South Asian companies choose the route that many other companies do: eventually to go public and issue shares. To do so would be to invite a large body of non-family investors to have a say in the running of the company. If the reason for floating the company is to recapitalise, a South Asian family business would rather look for alternative funding, either within the extended family or within the larger South Asian community. If neither of these approaches succeeds, the family may even sell the company outright and retire from it, either to live off the proceeds or start again.

One of the most difficult aspects of South Asian business for people joining the company from outside the community is the relative lack of interest in professionalising. Additionally, in decision making a high importance is placed on the opinions of family members who are either not directly involved in the day-to-day running of the business or are simply not involved at all. The outside accountant may well find that more weight is carried by the opinions of a respected elderly uncle in Mumbai than by his own, experienced and qualified though he may be.

In companies of any size the most important executive body is the family council. Generally speaking this is one of the key differences between South Asian business administration and Western-style board meetings.

Cultural factors

The accountant knocked at the door of the office. It was six o'clock on a Saturday evening. When the meeting had been requested, he hadn't asked for a more convenient time. The Pakistani family that ran the small London publishing house didn't automatically stop work at five o'clock or even six. Saturday meetings were common; once he'd even been summoned on a Sunday to discuss a late VAT claim.

It seemed that nobody was going to answer the door, so he pushed it open. He went into the deserted reception area and rang the bell on the desk. Still no sign of life. He sat down and reached for one of the glossy magazines provided in the waiting area; he began to read.

He'd worked his way halfway through the pile of magazines and the clock had almost reached seven before voices sounded in the corridor and an apologetic director came in: 'It was good of you to wait.'

But why had the accountant waited, faced with such a lack of the usual courtesies? Accountants' time costs money and there had been no sign that anybody was in the building at all. Nobody had even arrived to offer him a cup of tea. Wouldn't it have been simpler to have written the meeting off and gone home for his disrupted evening meal?

He'd stayed because he was himself a South Asian and was familiar with Islamic culture. He'd worked out very quickly why there was nobody to meet him. The fast of Ramadan was ending and today was the fast breaking, a day of special prayers and festivities, focused on the end of the fast at sunset. The family had miscalculated the time their fast would end; they had still been praying and so it was quite impossible for them to attend to him, still less offer him food or drink. So the accountant waited, where a non-Asian accountant might well have given up and perhaps even lost a client.

Religion dominates much of South Asian business life as well as everyday life. Just as Hindu society is deeply characterised by the caste system, and the Islamic day is interrupted by frequent set prayers, so members of the majority population doing business with South Asians will often find, like the accountant described above, that religion is an important factor in many routine business matters, even when for some individuals concerned the religion may be more a matter of habit than of piety.

Different religions affect business in different ways. For the Hindu, everything is integrated. God is in your books and in everything you do. For example, my brother owns a newsagent's shop, and his conversation is punctuated by phrases such as 'By the grace of God' and 'Thank God'. Everything is God driven. In Manila I met a Hindu businessman who, like me, had become a follower of Christ. He asked me to pray with him, to consecrate his account books. He was no longer a Hindu believer but he still felt the strong need to find a Christian equivalent to what he had done as a Hindu businessman.

Many South Asians make a practical separation between their faith and their work. 'Practical', because they are often devout worshippers in the mosque, or temple, or church. It would be a mistake for business people from the majority population to assume that because religion is not all pervasive in a particular Muslim, Hindu or Sikh office, it is not important. I employed a first-generation Muslim in my own office and we had to respect (and it was right to respect) the fact that he prayed five times a day, fasted and so on, though Islamic teaching allows a fairly broad 'time band' for each of the five prayer times, so it is usually possible to minimise disruption.

The extended family is another cultural factor, and a very powerful one in business, especially for entrepreneurs.

For example, when we set up our newsagent's in Shepherd's Bush we funded it from the extended family. When my father wanted to extend his own business and needed more funding, he knew of a friend in Manchester from whom he could borrow money. That friend in turn was able to borrow money from the account of a family in Hong Kong. A neighbour of ours in Shepherd's Bush ran a grocers: my father respected him, so when our neighbour wanted to buy a second shop and asked my father for a loan, we were able to lend to him from the funds generated by our own family business which had been enabled to grow by loans from Manchester and Hong Kong. So cash flowed from Hong Kong through Manchester and on to Shepherd's Bush to my father and on to our neighbour.

There were certainly interest rates, but they were not extortionate. Bills of exchange called *hoondees* were issued; they were the instrument we used in our own private financial circle to control and to honour our debts. Each had payment dates and maturity dates – it was an effective system that by-passed any conventional UK financial systems. It was certainly not a black economy, but it was a way of surviving in an alien hostile environment, where the bank manager was unfamiliar with one's track record and background. The man in Hong Kong, before releasing the money, would have asked the man in Manchester: 'To whom is this money being lent? What is their name?' And when he had his answer he would have said: 'Oh

– that's a good family. Even though my money is going to them through intermediaries I know it's safe now. I'm confident I will be repaid.'

Business people from the majority population who observe this happening might think it would work against them – a close protectionist circle working in its own interests against outsiders. But it is also a form of insurance against being let down, and outsiders should be encouraged by it. A South Asian businessman is less likely than others to cheat you or to abscond with your money. The reason is less because of any high moral code than because of the practical realities of being dependent on an honour system and the reputation of your family if you are to succeed in business. A South Asian who defaults on a loan, embezzles his company's money or absconds with it not only brings great disgrace on his extended family, but also affects their credit rating within the Asian business community and can wreak havoc on networks of trust established over many years.

An English property dealer in North London had made a deal with an Asian who then refused to pay. There was a large bad debt in the making. But a deputation from the Asian's community came to her very quickly: 'Please don't worry. We will assume responsibility for this debt and you will be repaid every penny.' That is a very typical way of solving such a problem. Honour and reputation must be rescued. It was in the community's interest to make sure that the property dealer was fully satisfied, because if she was not, the whole community would be blacklisted, not only by the property dealers but also by the rest of the South Asian business community.

Hence the great pressure on young South Asians to protect the reputation of their family by maintaining their own business integrity. Of course there is, as in every community, the occasional 'bad apple'. But bad apples are comparatively rare in the South Asian community. A financial scandal will mean not only that the family will be stigmatised in business but also that it will be impossible to make good arranged marriages; the family will be like lepers. It's a truly global punishment, for if you go as far as Hawaii, and you want to deal with other South Asians, you will still have to invoke family relationships. At that point you are drawing on your family's reputation; you are calling on trust. There is a strong family 'glue' that extends far beyond the immediate family home. So failure to deliver in London can have very widespread repercussions.

A similar situation arises with divorce. One reason fewer arranged marriages fail than do other marriages is that an arranged marriage is a commitment of the extended family. When I began a friendship with Sunita who is now my wife, an uncle telephoned me: 'You're going out with an Asian girl from a reputable family. Declare your intentions – or cut off the relationship!'

It was more than a relationship. Bigger issues were at stake. Families were involved, trade networks, financial obligations. So if one marries and then divorces, much is affected. What happens to your debts? What about business partnerships with your spouse's family? What about the various business relationships that will have been formed between members of your family and of your spouse's? The consequences of an Asian divorce, quite apart from the personal tragedy of a broken marriage, can be similar to those of one's bank foreclosing. Most South Asians literally cannot afford divorce, even though many do divorce and then have to live with the disastrous repercussions.

A very good illustration of what I have been saying is the typical South Asian wedding invitation. It makes a much bigger statement than 'This boy is marrying this girl'. The phrasing is not the Western convention of 'The father and mother are pleased to invite you...', but 'The father and mother, on behalf of this family, that family, this community...' It is rather like a Council of Reference or a Board of Trustees, or a corporate entity. Which, in an Asian context, it is. For example in my Sindhi community there's a word *bradiri*, which means 'community'. It's not just the Gidoomal family inviting you but the Gidoomal *bradiri*. It's the community extending the invitation, so you had better make sure you are there unless you have a very, very good reason to be absent. Even being away on a business trip abroad is sometimes not an adequate reason if you are close to the family.

Marriages to non-Asians are not encouraged, but when they do happen the family will also look carefully at the non-Asian. They will want to know the background and, most of all, the family. In all discussions about proposed marriages, the first question always asked is, 'Is the boy from a good family?' The second question is usually, 'Is he from a family of comparable financial standing to our own?' If the answer is 'No', marriage is still possible, though there will be problems. And the family will then be looking for integrity and honesty in the boy to the same degree that they would expect such qualities from a boy from the Asian community.

That is why the UK South Asian business community, founded on the extended family concept, can operate on the same basis of trust that can be seen in markets and town squares in the subcontinent itself, where large sums of money and consignments of goods are traded and the deal confirmed by a handshake or a promise.

NEW CHALLENGES, NEW OPPORTUNITIES

The world of the approaching millennium is a very different one to that of the 1970s, and some of the assets that the South Asian community are able to contribute are only now beginning to be fully realised as the world shrinks and new communications bring everybody closer together. For example, Asian businesses often source stock through their direct connections abroad. So they cut down labour costs and cut out unnecessary middlemen. The result is that competition with indigenous British industry is intensified – and prices are forced down, to the benefit of customers. Bulk buying, direct importing and other practices are all examples of the global diaspora being turned to commercial profit.

There are advantages too in the competition for global trading. Organisations like the Indo-British Partnership facilitate trade. Trade agreements worth £5 billion were signed as the result of negotiations between the then Prime Minister John Major and the Prime Minister of India. There are other trading links as well, such as those between Britain and Pakistan. The Department of Trade and Industry's South Asian Advisory Group meets regularly to advise on and facilitate the development and monitoring of trade. Concorde has visited India several times, taking British trade delegations to promote UK exports to India.

London is a preferred centre of business for many South Asians, including those who are not based in Britain. For example, when the Inlaks Group's head office was in Geneva, few of our Nigerian personnel wanted to visit us there. They were unfamiliar with the language and they found Geneva a boring city. They much preferred London, with its cosmopolitan atmosphere, its thriving business world, its colourful and entertaining social life. And Britain benefited in numerous ways, from the hotel industry through to bank charges.

NEW DOMESTIC MARKETS

The retail businesses in which so many of the first generation of South Asian immigrants invested are no longer the main area of UK South Asian success. But in retailing, nevertheless, the South Asian community has moved with the times and provided stimulus and competition to retailers in the majority population. The traditional facilities of the ubiquitous Asian corner shop – longer hours, convenience shopping, 'corner supermarkets' and other innovations – are still there, and existing businesses must rise to the challenge or lose out. Nidish Amin, manager of the Patel family's Hart's the Grocer branch in Gloucester Road, London, says: 'Gloucester Road wouldn't be as it is now, without us. In fact Hart's *is* Gloucester Road. The bank opened late because of us, and now everything is open.'[13]

Over the years, the Asian advantage has been eroded. Others have not been slow to cash in on South Asian initiatives. Many non-Asian businesses stay open late, and some of the business areas in which UK South Asians have been most successful are now being taken over by white businesses with massive capital. However, part of the South Asian genius has been the ability to keep one step ahead of the opposition; they can still often give the competition a run for its money. There are South Asian pharmacies, for example, that have installed healthcare professionals who administer basic tests and measurements. You can have your blood pressure checked, your heart rate monitored and your medicine administered. It's similar to the apothecaries you find in some Eastern European countries, where there are tables with water flasks and glasses at which you can sit and take the first dose of the medicine which has just been dispensed. Of course, there is no intention of replacing the GP's surgery, but it's an attractive way of avoiding long queues for the treatment of minor illnesses.

Such innovations are really a fight back against the competition from the large multiples and supermarkets. They draw on some traditional qualities of South Asian trading. My brother runs a shop in Chiswick. He knows all his customers by name and they come to him because they know him personally. In so many urban and rural communities, loneliness is a major issue and one that is getting worse. There will always be people who will shop at my brother's in preference to a supermarket. Sainsbury's is an excellent store, but the staff don't have time to chat with you as they go about their duties. My brother does.

CHANGING TIMES, CHANGING MARKETS

Another characteristic of today's minority ethnic business is its diversity. Some new opportunities have emerged from traditional South Asian enterprises. For example, ethnic food is an exploding market today. An ingenious Homepride TV advertising campaign for ethnic food brilliantly illustrates the presence of Asian culture in Britain and the integration that is happening at least at the culinary level: Asians with Glaswegian accents (the adverts imply) eat Homepride Asian food because it's so good that even Asians enjoy it. In the major supermarkets, you can buy food that Gulam Noon would be happy to eat at home. The Patels' Europa stores offer an extensive range of ethnic foods that are popular far beyond the ethnic communities. Essex girls munch bhajis, take-away Tandooris operate in the heart of Welsh Wales and home cooks in the majority white population, who not so long ago had only a couple of brands of pre-mixed curry powder to choose from at the grocers, now have a bewildering selection of Asian spices and ingredients available in every supermarket.

A flourishing diverse minority ethnic market is good news for majority population business interests, for there are many ways in which this profitable area can be tapped. Video companies, for example, are now realising that Asians watch a great many videos, and are seeking to exploit this market. That's not surprising when you consider the sheer size of the Indian film industry. Let me suggest to the video chains – keep track of the ten top Asian videos, and arrange to have them displayed in your outlets. Asians who never came in before will hear that they are available, will hire them and will be exposed to all the other things you have to offer as well.

And here's another suggestion. Video outlets in Asian areas usually sell an ethnic product called *paan* – betel nut and other delicacies and juices all rolled up in a green leaf. South Asians love to eat *paan* after dinner. If a mainstream video outlet stocks it as well as the current top ten Asian films, Asians are twice as likely to shop there – they will come in to collect a video and to stock up on *paan*.

After-dinner delicacies have kept quite a few South Asian businesses afloat! *Paan* and its tasty derivative *paan* liqueur are what an Indian family may choose to round off a meal in an authentic Indian restaurant. But one observant restaurateur noticed that British people like to eat after-dinner mints. Suppressing his natural horror that anybody would want to do such a thing after a wonderful Indian meal, he created a highly profitable line of 'After-Curry' mints, and now markets them to restaurants.

There are a number of companies already exploring ways of tapping the ethnic market, often very ingeniously. British Telecom, for example, launched a 'Call Home' service with cheap rates on Asian festival days, and advertised the service strategically in Hindi on Sunrise Radio. Another example is WH Smith, which stocks religious greeting cards for Muslim and Hindu festivals. It charges a premium price and has reached a market that otherwise would not have been identified.

MODERN TECHNOLOGY

Manufacturing businesses have joined retail businesses in the roll of Asian success. In Manchester, Shami Ahmed runs the Legendary Joe Bloggs. In Peterborough, Meera Taneja's Musquaan Trading prepares Tandoori chicken for sale in Tesco's. Walk down London's Tottenham Court Road or the Edgware Road (both of them hubs of the thriving computer and hi-fi markets) and you will be in the retail territory of such business empires as Vashi Tulsiani's Audio Marketing, Jessa Razahussein's Watford Electronics, Humayan Mughal's Akhter computer group. Go further afield, to Northampton for instance: there you will find Ashok Taylor's Leisuresoft, whose sales of computer games touch £40 million per year.

This thriving trade, undreamed of in the 1970s, began long before the Bangalore phenomenon and the global village that Bharat Desai's Syntel exists to serve. It started with the Hong Kong phenomenon. South Asians with Hong Kong links realised that South Asians there were engaged in the electronics trade. The Far Eastern manufacturing countries that specialised in electronic, photographic, hi-fi and computer products – all of them countries near to Hong Kong and South Asia – were a promising source of new trading networks. They first negotiated contracts with the Canary Islands, where Asians dominate the electronic and new technology retail industry, and then drew on their connections in the region to facilitate setting up operations in London. In fact, the families who today run the electronics stores up and down London's Tottenham Court Road and Edgware Road have family connections in the Canary Islands, with Spain and Spanish territories (which are also countries with a strong investment in electronics) and Hong Kong. On the other hand, a London shop is often a spin-off from one in Asia, where a family member has taken on the task of opening up a branch of the business in Britain. The parent business might be British or foreign based, but in either case there is a contribution to British prosperity.

This chapter has outlined the kind of success which South Asians in the UK have achieved and the characteristics of the typical South Asian family and business. Before we look in Part Two at some individual stories, Chapter 2 will consider the foundations and motivations on which this success has been built.

2

Reasons For Success

'The earliest Asian shops were all grocers. These required, one, less capital and two, more labour ... Also, these shops had another function to perform in the early years. They were places where Asians could meet fellow Asians, get to know about who was going back home, and, if possible, send money back through them. People did not mail money, or use banks.'

A Pakistani newsagent in Oxford[1]

What is behind the prosperity of this entrepreneurial and business community that forms the backdrop of Britain's wealthy and influential mini-tiger, billionaire economy-within-an-economy? Researchers have tended to adopt one or other of two theories; and a third has been suggested by some of those interviewed for this book.

SURVIVAL TACTICS?

The first theory argues that South Asian business success is a survival mechanism, the only option open to immigrants in a country where historically they have been socially, financially and culturally disadvantaged. Like immigrants all over the world, the British South

Asians who have come to Britain in recent years came with very little, to settle in a society whose attitudes, legislation and sympathies were stacked against them.

It was a very different situation to the euphoria that surrounded the first arrivals in the 1950s. Stringent controls from the 1960s onwards have slowed immigration to a trickle, and the immigration legislation of those years shows a clear trend, often driven by understandable fear – for example, when the Kenyan and Ugandan Asians began seeking to enter Britain in ever-increasing numbers. A possible relaxation of the pattern of increasingly strict immigration legislation and controls was indicated in 1997 when the incoming Labour government proposed to change the onus of proof for relatives wishing to join families in the UK; one of the first initiatives of the new government was to relax the 'Primary Purpose Rule' that had required immigrants marrying British partners to prove that the primary purpose of the marriage was not to secure entry to Britain.[2]

The 1991 Census found that 47 per cent of the UK ethnic minority population had been born in Britain. It was forecast that the minority ethnic population would double in size in the next twenty years. But this would not be because of large numbers of immigrants entering the country; it would be the result of births within the ethnic minority communities. Today, nearer 70 per cent of the ethnic minority population was born in Britain, so the prophecy looks sound.

However, British unease with immigrants hasn't always been fuelled by concern that the UK and its people might be unable to absorb sudden influxes. There has also been a great deal of prejudice and resentment, discrimination on the basis of colour, religious intolerance, cultural rejection and much more. So, the theory goes, to keep their heads above water in a sea of negative attitudes, legislation and sympathies, many South Asians have indeed striven for business success purely in order to survive.

Published research on why Asians choose to become self-employed tends to support this. A study conducted as long ago as 1978[3] compared 300 Asian small retailers and 300 white businesses in Bradford, Leicester and the London Borough of Ealing. It found that one major reason was that Asians did not want to be condemned by racial discrimination to permanent low-status employment. The survey showed that 20 per cent of Asian owners were graduates, as opposed to only 3 per cent of white owners. A later study in 1990–91[4] again asked why Asians become self-employed: 178 Asian owners, 54 Caribbean and 171 white owners were compared in a number of locations throughout England:

> Over a quarter of ... Asian respondents gave 'push' factors such as unemployment, underemployment, job dissatisfaction and/or blocked opportunities as their principal business entry motive ... Their entry into self-employment is seen as a 'damage limitation' exercise to avoid unemployment.[5]

Let me illustrate these theoretical findings by making reference again to my own family story. I'm not claiming that our experiences are unique – quite the opposite. They are typical of many British Asian families; a point made by the Indian High Commissioner in London, His Excellency Dr L. M. Singhvi, at the launch of my book *Sari 'n' Chips*[6]: 'This is not merely the story of an individual but the autobiography of a generation.'

Rich and penniless

We arrived in Britain from East Africa under-capitalised and with all the odds stacked against us. My father travelled ahead in 1966 to prepare for the rest of the family's arrival, bringing with him the £2,000 he was allowed to take out of Kenya – a small sum compared to the wealth he left behind.

Arriving in Britain then was a very different matter to how it had been for immigrants entering Britain in the 1950s. Then, notwithstanding the difficulties that the early immigrants were to experience, there had at least been a warm welcome from the government, and housing and jobs waiting. In the 1970s, the numbers made emergency measures necessary; many spent their first weeks in a transit camp.

Some were lucky. An Asian clergyman in Uganda was so saddened by the treatment of the Asians in his country that he contacted the church in Britain about a particular family that was being expelled. When the family arrived at Stansted Airport, there was a message on the paging system: 'Will the family of Mr Solanki please go to Information.' They found someone waiting for them who took them to a house where they were accommodated for a few weeks while another house that had been specially bought for them was prepared. From the day of their arrival they had the use of a car. There were many similar acts of kindness and support. Leaders of the Asian community already in Britain co-ordinated strategies to get the new arrivals out of the camps and into the community, and to set up effective lines of communication.

In the camps were people with a wide range of skills and backgrounds. There were business people and professionals, but also carpenters, masons, shopkeepers and others with many more talents. In addition, a large number of the people who were arriving already had family links in Britain. So, either because they had marketable skills or because they had family members in the UK, many were met at the airport and taken directly into the South Asian community. They were helped by families, friends, neighbours, contacts.

Thousands were virtually penniless; but many, like my father, arrived with something more valuable than capital. They arrived with a heritage of Asian community, with a wealth of contacts and associates; and most of all they arrived with a name. Their riches lay in the bank of cultural and family and community networks on which they were able to draw, because their families were known in the community.

Building a business

My father and many like him are a good illustrations of the fact that, though succeeding in business was the obvious way out of his difficulties, his success was due to more than the survival motive.

Making his base with other Asians living in London, seeking their advice and carefully considering the options open to him, he invested his small capital in a newsagent business in Shepherd's Bush, West London. Over the next twelve months the rest of the family arrived.

His £2,000 was quickly spent on the lease of the business and its goodwill, and on rent and basic necessities. That left no funds for buying stock and no cushion against a slow start or a bad trading week. So he was dependent on increasing the number of customers coming into the shop and thereby raising the volume of sales. But more sales meant re-ordering. Most retailing suppliers operate on the basis of credit. By the time my father had been in business for several months suppliers knew he was reliable in paying his bills and that he was a good credit risk – an essential reputation to have if the business was to expand. But at the beginning, when he was a stranger in London with no previous dealings with the suppliers, it was the South Asian community who stood as guarantors and enabled him to get credit and by-pass the usual barriers into business: credit reference, credit checking, obtaining an overdraft facility. They did this because of the network, the extended family, the fact that Gidoomal was a name that was known.

It was the same for the Shahs, for the Patels, for the East African Asians who came to Britain already known to the community they were joining. The main investment was in shops. Some only had enough capital to buy a news kiosk at a station or a roadside newsstand, but through the network of South Asians already in Britain they were able to obtain stock on credit and to borrow enough to pay their rent while they were starting out. There is no doubt that the reason so many South Asians are successful retailers and shopkeepers today is that their community gave them a flying start and enabled them to hit the ground running.

Not everybody went into retailing. Some in the professions, finding it impossible to break into British practice, set up as lawyers, accountants and so on in their ethnic communities. Dina Dattani's story (p. 135) tells of some of the frustration such people experienced.

Other immigrants used their previous work experience in new and ingenious ways. I know of a man who came to Britain as a university student from East Africa, before the Asians were expelled. He gained a first-class degree in electronic engineering and joined Ferranti, where he quickly realised that at that time in the company's history there was a 'glass ceiling' beyond which he was not going to progress. One reason was that Ferranti were handling Ministry of Defence contracts, and there were limits to how much a foreigner could be involved at a senior level. He received a tempting offer from a relative in Kenya who owned a thriving video and audio tape duplicating business. Would he set up a video duplicating plant for him in London? Having done the same thing for Ferranti and also for Rank Xerox, he agreed immediately, and set up a huge duplicating facility in West London that is still in production today.

The next step was to set up on his own account. Like most Asians, he had been a regular saver all his life; he now had capital and the confidence of his suppliers. Soon he had bought a unit on a London industrial estate (today he employs over a hundred women there). His first major contract was with the BBC, whom he had been pursuing for years. Eventually his chance came: the Corporation had a desperate need for video duplication and its regular suppliers couldn't handle it. Like any good businessman he was ready to seize the opportunity. When he delivered, the BBC said to him, 'You're good. Your price is better, your quality is better, and you deliver earlier than the rest. Where have you been hiding?'

'I've been here all the time,' he said. 'Just waiting…'

Fear and resentment
Outside the warm, welcoming and supportive South Asian community, many white British people feared and resented people like us. Two years earlier, Smethwick had become a new byword for ethnic distrust when the local council had approached the Ministry of Housing for funding to buy up houses in the town, to prevent coloured immigrants from moving in. The Ministry, mindful of the impending Race Relations Bill that contained a specifically anti-discrimination clause, refused; but tempers ran high in Smethwick. In November 1964 the Commonwealth Immigrants Act had been

renewed, and between 1,600 and 2,000 entry vouchers were being granted to heads of families. Housing Minister Richard Crossman noted the change of mood. 'We have got to control the rate of immigration into this country – we can't digest the numbers who are now arriving in the West Midlands … Hugh Gaitskell and George Brown opposed the Tory Immigration Act lock, stock and barrel only three years ago. The atmosphere has changed since then!'[7]

By 1965 some ministers, including Crossman, recognised that fear of defeat at the polls was forcing them to become illiberal and to close the doors further at a time when labour was in short supply. In the 1966 General Election, immigration was a major voting issue in the Midlands, and the Labour Party victory was due, in part at least, to the recent strengthening of controls. The majority in Britain opposed immigration, and the result showed it. This is not to say that the matter was resolved without frantic efforts. Britain's special envoy Malcolm Macdonald embarked on fruitless negotiations with Kenya's president Jomo Kenyatta, who flatly refused to control the numbers of Asians coming to Britain. The situation called for politics which Prime Minister Harold Wilson described as 'postponed decisions'[8] – accurately, for recommendations and white papers had been put on one side for a long time and the growing threat ignored.

In 1968, a year after I had arrived in Britain with the rest of my family, two years of government inaction ended with crisis legislation. At the same time, Enoch Powell was beginning his public campaign against large-scale immigration, in which he was to warn that Britons would soon be 'strangers in their own land' and that there would be 'rivers of blood'. Powell found many sympathisers among ordinary men and women.

We had arrived in Britain just before the doors began swinging shut, and some time still before what the British press perceived as the second great influx of East African Asians in 1972 brought a flood of Ugandan Asians to Britain, and the doors later closed tighter still.

So one common characteristic can be observed among many British South Asians, and indeed among immigrants to Britain in general. **South Asians have usually arrived in Britain either as a relatively cheap labour resource or as refugees from difficult home situations, and are usually very under-capitalised. Without the extended family and the networks, most South Asians would never have survived.**

Making a mark

There was a sizeable Asian community in Shepherd's Bush. We bought our shop there because selling was the only thing that the Gidoomals were good at, and we needed to eat. We sold what our neighbours needed, working long hours, doing almost everything ourselves to avoid hiring (and paying) staff. Regardless of age or sex the whole family worked in the business. We began to prosper.

But our first successes were not merely because we were working hard. My father was a talented entrepreneur, used to looking at situations and exploiting potential that other people had missed. Our shop was typical of most of the Asian shops belonging to our extended family and to other members of the local community; we supplied many of the home comforts such as food and trinkets that Asians could not find in English-speaking shops. From this obvious (and profitable) playing to our strengths, we went on to take a long hard look at local leisure patterns and working hours. Many of our neighbours were regulars at the Bingo Hall. What happened when the Bingo Hall closed? Crowds emerged, often wanting to pick up a snack for supper or a pint of milk on their way home – at the very time that the shops were closed.

We made sure we were open.

Many Irish people lived in the area. Perhaps because we too were strangers in a strange land, we noticed a market for Irish newspapers and Irish cigarettes.

We stocked up. We even learned a little Gaelic.

None of the other retailers in our area offered such services. News spread quickly. Business became brisk. Of course, we charged premium prices! We were offering something worth paying a little extra for. We had identified a niche in the market, and many people were willing to pay to have that niche filled.

It was a characteristic of the whole local South Asian entrepreneurial community. An Asian neighbour, like us, ran a newsagent. When I began travelling regularly to South Asia on business, I didn't buy my tickets from the travel agents. I bought them from my Indian newsagent friend. He had spotted the number of local Indians needing to travel to the subcontinent and had begun chartering planes. He was a pioneer of the low-cost, basic amenities bucket shop!

So a second characteristic common to most British South Asians can be identified: **South Asians are skilled at identifying niche markets and unexploited trading opportunities. They have to be, for in a competitive society slanted against immigrants, being good is not enough: you have to be better.**

'Thanks – but no thanks'

My father turned his small business round, increasing its turnover fourfold within a very short time. Before long we owned several shops.

It was all done by hard work, it involved a lot of sacrifice and it was very much an Asian-style initiative. Although government initiatives existed, designed specifically to help people in my father's position – even in those early days of the beginnings of strict immigration controls – he preferred to go to Asians already in London and even Manchester for help, and to arrange what finance he needed through family links. It was to him a matter of pride – *izzat* – but it was also an ethical choice. He would not consider going to the state or to professionals outside his people group, preferring to draw on the help of his own people when setting up his business.

We shall see later in this book that reluctance to make use of funding opportunities and sources of business help is the reason for some of the problems which UK South Asian businesses face today. It is a reluctance that goes back a long way and to a large degree is a consequence of the situation in which early immigrants found themselves.

Many from East Africa had, only months or even weeks previously, seen the fruits of years of successful business wiped out. These were money and assets that not only had paid for a comfortable lifestyle, but were also intended to provide for retirement and old age. The money had disappeared by government decree. The South Asians had arrived in Africa as settlers and refugees; they had contributed massively to the economy of their adopted country; and now that country had thrown them out. No wonder many of them were unwilling to trust governments, banks and official agencies ever again. Some simply kept their money under the bed. Many (with a more businesslike eye to maximising their resources) went to banks like Grindlay Ottoman which had links with overseas financial institutions. Those who had accounts with the Colonial Dominion Overseas Bank found that they were easily able to open accounts with Barclays. Others made arrangements with friends and relatives already in Britain to use the banking facilities they had set up.

High street banks were slow in setting up procedures to deal with the new arrivals. Even as recently as six years ago I took my mother to her local high street bank in Southall to arrange an account for her. It was astonishing that in an area like Southall, which has an extremely high Asian population, the staff – certainly the senior staff – were around 50 per cent Caucasian and could not help her with her requirements. She didn't know how to write a cheque (which says something about Asian families: such matters tend to be left to the husband or sons) and I had to teach her and show her all those things that you would expect a bank to show a new customer as a matter of course. But they couldn't speak her language, they didn't understand her culture. When we got home she was very distressed and wondered if she would ever master this complicated process. I was quite angry that a bank that was thriving on the local community wasn't providing basic services to meet local needs at the grassroots, customer-to-bank level.

Today, there are not many Asian bank managers but their number is increasing. Most banks and most branches have Asian staff at reasonably senior levels such as assistant manager, who are there to provide some cultural input to the senior manager in decision making. In some branches serving large ethnic minority populations, particularly in busy areas like Wembley, there are Punjabi-speaking bank managers.

The Midland Bank runs a South Asian Business Unit, 'specifically set up in order to understand and respond to the business banking needs of customers from South Asia'. It has offices in Birmingham and in the City of London. So far as personal banking is concerned, a Non-Resident Indian Desk in the Leicester Belgravia branch offers a wide range of sterling and rupee non-resident accounts with facilities for customers to open accounts with the Hong Kong and Shanghai Bank in India. Staff are able to speak a wide variety of languages of the Indian subcontinent, and though the branch is in Leicester it can offer banking services to customers throughout the UK.[9]

In the early days of Asian immigration, hardly any of this was happening. It wasn't simply a matter of handling the practicalities of paying money into a bank and making withdrawals as needed. Banks are lending institutions as well as depositories for money. Here too the new arrivals ran into great difficulties. Few South Asians were able to get unsecured loans. From the banks' point of view they were displaced persons with a small capital of £2–3,000 and no business experience in Britain – a distinctly bad risk. Matters would have been very different if more banks had sought the opinion of those who knew the Asians from colonial and expatriate experience. As Sir Garry Johnson, Chairman of the National TEC Council, observes: 'We really missed a trick in not allowing the Hong Kong South Asians to come to Britain. If they achieved for Britain a tenth of what they have achieved for Hong Kong, the revival in the UK economy would have been quite something to see.'[10]

When the refugees arrived in the 1960s and 1970s, there were no procedures in place to evaluate and assess the quality of the human resource that had descended so unexpectedly on Britain. Today countries such as America and Canada have a points system, by which immigrants can be assessed for their potential value to the host economy. But even without such procedures (which do admittedly contain the potential to become virtual means tests, thus excluding some genuinely needy cases), the heritage that Asians arrive with is a great and often untapped asset.

So here's a third characteristic: **many South Asians – for example, many from East Africa – take pride in being self-sufficient, often choosing not to take up state funding sources and preferring instead to utilise family and ethnic relationships.**

An alien in a foreign land for the second time in his life, my father survived, like so many others did, by entrepreneurism: by making the best of a bad start, by finding a niche and exploiting it, by sheer hard work, and by the support, expertise and financial help of his fellow South Asians. It was a survival mechanism and it worked.

SUCCESS GENES?

A second theory that is often suggested as the explanation for South Asian success is that it's an ethnic trait. People will tell you that there's a 'success gene' built into South Asian people that will make them tend to succeed. Being born South Asian and inheriting the Asian cultural, social and other background is, they will assure you, actually a recipe for success. It's in the blood. After all, there do seem to be a lot of successful South Asian shopkeepers, don't there?

It might seem that this theory too is borne out by my family's experiences. We fit the pattern that has been identified in research undertaken by Race for Opportunity, an initiative supported by a number of major sponsors including British Airways: that the Asian communities are more affluent than other minority communities, and predominantly white collar. We conform, if you like, to the stereotype of the industrious affluent South Asian.

If you are looking for ethnic traits, education is a good starting place. Asians are the largest minority in British education. In some schools they make up the largest ethnic group. The Asian presence is by no means confined to inner-city schools in areas with large immigrant populations. In South London's prestigious Dulwich College, for example:

Boys from ethnic minorities make up about 35 per cent of the College population. For instance, there are currently 40 Patels in the College which is just over twice as many as the combined number of Smiths and Jones. They all rub shoulders very happily with overseas boys from Africa, the Far East, and increasingly from Eastern Europe.[11]

King Edward's School, Birmingham, is a direct grant independent day school, 40 per cent of whose 825 boys are Asian. In 1997 the captains of both Oxford and Cambridge University cricket teams were former pupils of the school. Both were Asians: Mark Wagh captained Oxford and Anurag Singh Cambridge.

The children of ethnic minorities tend to stay in education longer, and many go on to higher education where they have a proportionally higher representation than does the white population. South Asians also lead the ethnic groups in their rate of qualification. (For example, out of around 70 entrants annually to the UK Shell Graduate recruitment programme, 5 per cent are UK South Asians and a number of South Asians are also recruited directly from South Asia itself.[12])

South Asians are prominent in the medical professions, too, and particularly so in dentistry: the British Dental Association estimates that approximately one-quarter of the dental profession is made up of minority ethnic individuals. Half the entrants into dental schools are from a minority ethnic background, predominantly a South Asian one. It has been estimated that minority ethnic individuals will form approximately half of the dental profession within 15 years. This contribution to dentistry is a much higher percentage than is the case in general medical practice.[13] Also, an unpublished paper by three researchers at Birmingham University's Business School found that Asians constitute 15 per cent of registered pharmacies in the UK (the calculation was based on a surname count, so the real figure could well be higher).[14]

It should be said that the Barclays Review found that black businesses lead the field in vocational training. Over 60 per cent of black small business owners and managers have undertaken vocational or practical training as opposed to only 41 per cent of Asians.[15] But Modood and Berthoud[16] suggest that the mean figure is very much a South Asian majority, even in vocational training, indicating that their larger sample had a closer correlation to the true national figure.

That is not surprising when you look at what proportion of the ethnic minority population does in fact go on to higher education. Around one-eighth of all British university students are from ethnic minorities, more than double their representation in the overall population – and this has been achieved despite the fact that there are no British 'affirmative action policies' comparable to those that have pushed up numbers of non-white students in the United States. Consequently the proportion of qualified people from the UK ethnic minority populations is bound to rise. This does not mean that disadvantage does not exist in the South Asian community; far from it. Obtaining a job after qualification often means getting to know the right people, which may be a lengthy process. And ethnic minority students still tend to go to the newer universities (the former polytechnics), while many large employers continue to recruit from the older, mainly white, universities.[17]

However, the findings of the Fourth National Survey of Ethnic Minorities[18] confirm the proportionally higher rate of further education. There are more ethnic minority students, both men and women, in full-time further education than there are students from the majority ethnic population. Indians and African Asians head the list, followed by Pakistanis and Bangladeshis. The survey presents some very impressive statistics which can be summed up like this:

Looking at participation by qualification levels shows where the real difference between whites and ethnic minority people is ... It is when we look at those with a GCSE or higher qualification who were continuing in (or had returned to) full-time education that we see a degree of minority commitment quite different to whites.'[19]

So when I obtained the required examination results to enter Imperial College to read physics, and later went on to do postgraduate research, I was by no means an exception in British Asian society. When (finding physics not to my long-term liking!) I moved on to use the six languages and extensive business skills I had acquired from my family to enter the international group which my extended family ran, that was typically Asian too.

Does all this mean that success was written into my DNA because of the subcontinent my family came from?

I don't believe it does. There are two reasons. First, I think that ethnic stereotypes are unhelpful and also unrealistic. If South Asians are born with an inbuilt 'success gene', why are so many British South Asians experiencing poor living standards, unemployment and social disadvantage? Secondly, I don't believe that it is necessary to invoke a success gene to explain why so many South Asians have been successful in business. It's fair to say, and statistics of British retail ownership and entrepreneurial success rates bear it out, that Asians do have a knack of successful entrepreneurism and running businesses that work. And it is in the nature of emigration that, where people have voluntarily sought their future in a foreign land, they will tend to be unusually talented and resilient. But far more important than any supposed ethnic trait is the heritage of networks that South Asians possess. This brings us back to those characteristics of the South Asian family and business that I discussed in the last chapter.

A heritage of networks

From my immediate and extended family, I have inherited certain characteristics I share with other South Asians – I enjoy cricket, for example, and I am good at coming up with solutions and using lateral thinking – but by far the most important thing I have inherited is that family structure itself. I have already suggested that this heritage is a common factor in a great deal of the UK South Asian community. Let us now look at what it provides.

It is a heritage of networks. Simply by being born into a South

Asian family, most South Asian entrepreneurs have inherited trusted access to a whole community of people. At its core are the financiers, those South Asians with money who are prepared to lend. Because of that wide-ranging network of families, raw young businessman can talk to them with confidence and on an equal social footing. They are willing to lend or trade without requesting the usual guarantees and references. A penniless immigrant just arriving in Britain from the subcontinent or from East Africa will find people willing to lend them money. Gulam Noon, for example, first arrived in Britain to try to launch his Indian sweets business. He had very little money in his pockets. Exchange controls were in force, he had almost no disposable cash; his considerable business capital was blocked in India and there was no guarantee that he would be able to cover any losses he might make in Britain. But he was able to secure financial cover through the network of Indian businessmen already resident in Britain, and that enabled him to begin to build his immensely successful Noon Products plc.

The networks exist globally. I have travelled widely on business trips to Manila, to Bangkok and elsewhere, and there was always a network in place to enable rapid familiarisation, capital if needed, introductions to local business people. For example, I took a young Asian from Birmingham to meet some people in Oxford with whom we were going to do some community visiting. I knew the Oxford team very well, and anticipated being able to make useful introductions and put him in touch with a new circle of people. But I was very taken aback when the Oxford group discovered that my friend from Birmingham originated from the same village in the Punjab that they did. As soon as they knew he came from Jullunder, and recognised his family name and realised they knew who his parents were, it was as if I wasn't there any more. He was instantly welcomed and accepted, and they were able to talk as intimate friends. I, as a non-Punjabi, could only sit on the fringe and join in as and when I could. And when we all went community visiting, he was immediately embraced into the local families, because he was part of the network. His name, family and home village were enough to guarantee immediate acceptance.

And in the new world in which South Asians are living today, the diaspora of the first wave of immigrants, the scattered families of the subcontinent, has itself become a network. Previously distant markets offer to a new generation of South Asians enticing opportunities for prosperous trading. As the map of Asia and the Far East changes, and the new tiger economies of countries such as Singapore begin to challenge those like Hong Kong and Japan that previously dominated the financial world, strong trading links are being developed that benefit not only individual businesses but also the UK as a whole.

There's a two-way benefit. UK South Asian businesses are a gateway for Britain into the developing tiger economies of Asia; for example, in Britain there are many small to medium-sized businesses that are technology based and there is a tremendous opportunity to export those technologies (for example, computer numerically controlled machine tool technology, front-line water filtration technology and car spares) to the new tiger economies where they are often desperately needed. The problem is how to carry them across the cultural gap. Here there is an opportunity for British companies to use UK South Asians as consultants, as non-executive directors, on advisory boards, in trade fairs, as trade delegates and in many other ways where their expertise and familiarity with Asian culture will be invaluable.

In the other direction, Asian businesses find that their contacts and new businesses in the UK are a gateway into Europe; and often there is an opportunity for British firms to establish relationships of mutual benefit – again, making use of the UK South Asian community's expertise.

And South Asian success in the UK is only part of the success that is being achieved by the South Asian diaspora worldwide, in such places as Dubai (for example Jumbo Electronics, Chabbria), the diamond capital Antwerp (Gujeratis, Shahs), in South Africa and in the USA (Bose Corporation, Syntel) and in Hong Kong (Harilela).

Role models

Asian society, with its extended family basis and its emphasis on certain basic values, is a natural environment for role models to be sought and imitated by younger generations. This is especially so in sport, a rich source of role models in any culture and, for ethnic minorities, often one way of breaking out of the ghetto.

South Asians have many role models around the world, and nearer home they have their parents and grandparents – intuitively there are lessons to be learned, examples to be imitated; it is an upbringing that almost conditions them towards success. Add to that a natural ability to fight against barriers (one that is seen in many immigrants, who have to struggle to gain a footing alongside the host community) and an upbringing that encourages business success to rub off on to the younger generation, and we may well have the origin of the notion of a South Asian 'success gene'.

Let me illustrate this with an example from my own family. My son Ravi leads a band called Thirst. They decided to make a cassette to launch themselves at a concert. He didn't come to me for help, but used his network of connections. He hired his younger sister to play cello, booked some other musicians, had rehearsals, and even found a friend who was willing to give them a free day in a recording studio. He'd watched a similar process five years ago when I was setting up a fusion music cassette. He saw how we did it and used our experience, only he did much better; he got his studio for free! That was the role model and the networks. But he also showed ingenuity and determination to overcome obstacles. He went to the same copying company I had used, and when he got their quote for the job realised that there were VAT implications. So he telephoned an uncle who runs a company and asked if he would handle the order so that they could reclaim the VAT; his uncle agreed. There was only around £80 involved, but Ravi had already grasped some entrepreneurial principles.

When he took the cover artwork to the printer he discovered that colour separation hadn't been allowed for. This meant there would be delays and further expense, so he took the job back and worked out a solution with another (and cheaper) print shop. Having surmounted all the obstacles he took delivery of 250 cassettes in time for the concert.

I didn't teach him how to do it. But I watched him on the telephone, turning up the address books, making use of contacts and connections – and I realised that he had grasped the process for himself. He's learned as I learned, from father and uncles and others. Listening to them talk, seeing what they did, observing who was willing to lend money, who could be of help in business. Entrepreneurism is often caught, not taught; and the extended family, the key unit of South Asian life, is a proven incubator of business success.

So it is not a matter of a 'success gene' that is bound to bring success where others fail, but of having an appropriate background for success. Most South Asians bring to the UK business experience and business connections that have made them prosperous in their home countries. When they arrive in the UK and find themselves in a situation of economic and social deprivation, they attempt to reverse the situation, drawing on their extended family in their new country and in their home country, just as they would have attempted to reverse any business setback at home.

This is particularly true of Asians coming from East Africa, though I am aware of several cases of Asians from the subcontinent who have successfully rebuilt businesses that collapsed when BCCI went into receivership.

That is not to say that there aren't some characteristics of success that many South Asians possess. Just as many English are naturally reserved, French people are often chic and many Welsh people have a talent for singing, you find many South Asians who are motivated by problems, rather than letting problems throw them into abject despair. Bharat Desai, the founder-President of the multinational, multimillion-dollar Syntel corporation, who arrived in Britain in 1997 to make a major inward investment in computer services (p. 107), acknowledges that the issue is not simple:

It's partly genetic, I'm sure. If you look closer you may want to ask: is it genetic or environmental? And in answer to that I'd have to say that environment is a very large factor. But then it can't be the whole story, because if it were then everybody who had the same environment would be equally able to become an entrepreneur, which plainly isn't so. Human beings are very complex creatures.

The UK South Asian success is not a freak result of a resilient response to setbacks. It's neither a bunker reaction nor a genetic fingerprint, enabling South Asians to keep their heads above water in an unfavourable and alien society. Yet in my opinion, both of the theories we have considered contain some elements of truth. Of course many South Asians succeeded because they had to. But the value of the extended family network, which ensures that from the beginning the South Asian entrepreneur has available contacts and sources of business help that by-pass the red tape and paperwork of the conventional money channels, is that it fosters the tradition of prosperity and business initiative that features in the stories of most of the successful entrepreneurs in that community. This book contains stories that amply illustrate both aspects.

They also illustrate a third factor, one that has been suggested to me as I have talked with a wide range of South Asian business people and read the literature of South Asian entrepreneurism.

KNOWING THE ROPES

An Englishman who had spent many years working with Indian companies gave grudging approval to what he'd seen of the Indian style of doing business. 'Clever people,' he said. 'Lots of red tape in India, it's a very bureaucratic society. If you want to make progress in business and achieve your targets you have to know the ropes. There's always a way round the paperwork. Those Indian business-men were brilliant at dodging past the forms and the phone calls. Not usually actually *criminal*, mind you. But they certainly knew how to make life easy for themselves and they wouldn't stand to be bogged down by the system.'

He was right. In the countries of South Asia, attitudes to banks and local government are usually much more informal than is often the case in the UK. Asian businessmen won't be put off by the bank manager's crowded diary: they will go and sit in the outer office until he gives in and sees them. A great deal of business is done on trust, the paperwork eventually catching up with the brief conversation in a bar or the deal struck at a relative's birthday party.

South Asians rarely take no for an answer. They are very good at finding out how the system works and living with that system, but they use it to maximise their profits. They often may not have the same level of ingenuity and skill in the boardroom, but when it's a matter of money making, of business survival and riding out crises, they excel at finding ways round paperwork and cutting out inter-mediaries. In dealing with banks, for example, they quickly identify who are the real decision makers and try whenever possible to by-pass the counter clerk and the cashier and go straight to the man-ager. South Asians often invest considerable time and resources in building up a good relationship with their bank manager.

I have a relative who is a good example of this. Over the past thirty years he has wined and dined a succession of bank managers, and I'm constantly amazed by the credit facilities that he persuades them to extend to him. He has no GCSEs, he hasn't been to college, but he is a very successful businessman. So he isn't deceiving the bank; he has a proven track record, and the bank knows it's backing a winner. My relative's problem is that he isn't a paperwork person. Asking the bank for help involves filling in complicated forms, mak-ing a case for funding, creating a business plan and profit and loss predictions. And that is where his long investment in building up relationships with his bank pays off. When he takes the bank man-ager to dinner, before long the manager agrees not only to fill in the forms but to prepare the whole application.

When the South Asians came to Britain they encountered innu-merable laborious rules and regulations and promptly devised ways of minimising bureaucracy just as they did in Asia. My relative learned from watching his extended family. Those from outside the Asian community who observe that bank transactions, planning applications, trading licences and other administrative paraphernalia are often dealt with much more speedily than happens in the majority population are often amazed. They watch with some astonishment as business proceeds more quickly – yet quite legally – than might otherwise be expected.

This third characteristic of the South Asian community is yet another example of turning disadvantage to advantage. My relative has not been through college, yet his bank manager is happy to do the paperwork. Why? Because my relative's business is profitable, he pays his bills on time, his suppliers don't have to wait for their money, his capital expenditures are justified, he is clearly a good risk.

We have seen so far who the UK South Asians are, how they came to Britain and some of the reasons for their success. Underlying that success are tensions and problems that have already begun to emerge in our discussion, and to which we must turn in Part Three.

But first, let us meet some of the UK Maharajahs.

Part Two

Portraits of the Maharajahs

3

Out of India: Gulam Noon

'I hope that in my lifetime the words "ethnic minority" will be dropped.'

Gulam Khaderboy Noon entertains visitors in his Southall office around a magnificent table. It's a solid sheet of thick glass supported on four heavy silver pedestals, intricately worked in traditional Indian style. His visitors sit in luxurious leather armchairs of unmistakably Western design, like the large, tidy desk on the other side of the office. East and West are attractively blended, as in the assortment of framed photographs that line the windowsill.

Business has clearly made G. K. Noon (whose clothes have the same elegant, understated opulence as his office décor and whose car bears the number plate N1 GKN) a seriously wealthy man. Eat a meal on a British Airways flight to India and it will be Noon's food you enjoy. Pop into Sainsbury's for an off-the-shelf oven-ready Indian meal and you'll find his products on display. The frozen meals you buy in Somerfield, the poppadums on the shelves in Waitrose – Noon again. He supplies over two million chilled and frozen meals a month to the supermarkets. And if you are so fortunate as to eat as

Noon's guest in the elegant managerial suite at the Southall factory, served by quietly attentive Indian hostesses from Noon's own staff, the food you eat will have been cooked in the same building to Noon's demanding specifications. He has made his fortune by insisting on only selling food that he is prepared to eat himself. And he is a demanding gourmet.

If being a Maharajah means possessing wealth, Noon amply justifies his place among this selection. But I want to look at his story in some detail, because it is also a classic tale of successful entrepreneurism; we shall find many echoes of the themes we have already discussed.

Like the majority of entrepreneurial success stories, this one starts in financial hardship, in an Indian family situation; in Noon's case, the family had been prosperous but through the death of the breadwinner had fallen on difficult times.

RISE AND DECLINE OF AN EMPIRE

Bombay (modern Mumbai), the commercial capital of India, is a startling mixture of extreme wealth and extreme poverty. You can walk through the biggest slum in Asia and wander straight into districts whose residents pay some of the highest rents in the world for their housing, all within the city boundaries.

Noon's grandfather began his food empire in 1898. Queen Victoria, Empress of India, had celebrated her jubilee the year before. The Queen's printers had produced a sumptuous volume for the occasion that included illustrations of Bombay's public buildings and its 'native houses'.[1] The public buildings were 'probably the most daunting group of official buildings in the Empire', according to one modern historian:

Here in three great blocks the Establishment of the Bombay Presidency was concentrated, celestially removed from the chaos which, out of sight beyond Esplanade Road and the Victoria Terminus, ran indescribably away to the north.[2]

In this jewel of the British Empire, Gulam Khaderboy Noon's grandfather opened a confectionery shop.

Family Obligations

Noon – his mother chose the nickname for him; today he is 'Noon' to family, friends and some of the most prestigious names in food manufacturing – was born in 1936. His father came from nearby Rajasthan, where the family still owns property, but moved to Bombay when he took over the running of the family business. When Noon was born, the family owned two shops and had endowed two hospitals. But when he was only eight years old his father died – possibly of grief, for Noon's eldest brother had died six months earlier.

The death of his father turned his life upside down. It was a devastating personal tragedy and much was now expected of him. Noon was not the oldest surviving son, but when he was old enough he would be expected to work in the family business. His main duty now was to equip himself to do so. A cousin came to Bombay to take over the role of head of the family, for the sons were all still of school age. It was a classic situation of the South Asian extended family in bereavement. The primary issue was to support Noon's mother, and thus to generate enough income to provide for the needs of the family.

Noon's training, like that of most South Asian entrepreneurs of the period, was practical rather than academic. At school he never became a star pupil, though he was a good sportsman. But after school finished for the day he was more likely to be in the family shop than practising at the nets. All the family members had to do their share, of course, but Noon needed no prodding.

The family accountant gave him some basic business training and persuaded him to get up at six o'clock every morning to take accountancy lessons. By the time he had finished secondary school, Noon was sure he didn't want to go to university. He was going to enter the family business. His family situation made it imperative – but in any case, it was the only thing he wanted to do.

Noon's childhood was typical of many who grew up in South Asian family businesses, especially those where the main bread-winner died young or the family arrived as immigrants in a foreign country. The usual days off, holidays and small comforts that most working people enjoy are out of the question. Everybody in the family pitches in and helps. Some who might have been considered too old to have to work unpack stock late in the evening. Younger members of the family act as delivery boys. In many Asian businesses child labour is not an issue; either your family has worked for long enough to make it unnecessary, or your youngsters take their turn in the storeroom and behind the counter because that is the only way of ensuring that the business will succeed as soon as possible.

A good example of a British South Asian family in this situation is that of Laxmishanker Pathak, who was born in a poor family in India that later emigrated to Kenya. There they set up a samosa and sweets business catering for the Indian community. In 1956 the Pathaks moved to London, where the only job offered to Laxmis-hanker was cleaning the drains in Camden. He decided instead to start again in the business he knew best: sweets and savouries.

> His beginnings were modest. His family all played a part. They helped to make the delicacies in the kitchen of their rented house, the children setting to work once they had returned home from school. As his business gradually grew Pathak was able to buy shops to sell his wares, first in Euston in 1958 and then another in Bayswater in 1961.[3]

It took Pathak just twenty years from arriving in England with £5 in his pocket to heading 'one of the most successful privately owned businesses in Britain, commanding annual profits of £2 million'.

A FIVE-YEAR PLAN

Noon was a quick learner. When Jawaharlal Nehru, the first prime minister of independent India, announced that India was going to have a five-year plan, Noon decided that the family business was going to have one too. He learned from anybody who had things to teach him. 'Fortunately all my friends were better educated than I was,' he says modestly. His remarkable mother had insisted that Noon help out in the shop every day. That had given him plenty of opportunities to pick their brains and try out their suggestions along with his own ideas.

The five-year plan worked. The business grew quickly. Noon was driven by a single motive: to improve the family's standard of living and secure a good income for them all. Caring for his mother was the most important factor in his plans. For himself, he had a simple ambition: he wanted a car. When he drew his first hundred rupees salary from the company he bought a bicycle. He was on his way.

He'd joined the business in the early 1950s. By 1962 he was able to modernise the main shop premises. He installed air conditioning, at that time almost unheard of in small shops. His rivals thought it a waste of time buying top-quality furniture and fittings; Noon hired one of the best architects he could find and remodelled the premises. Over the door, the family business name was proudly displayed: Royal Sweets. Some of his friends remarked that it looked more like a jewellery shop than a sweet shop. It certainly looked like a palace. The new premises were a huge success. Noon looked for bigger challenges. His next step was to set up a factory. Traditionally, confectionery was made in a small area in front of sweet shops. Noon realised the advantages of a separate manufacturing operation and bought a local small factory.

The most important person he had to win over to his plans was his cousin; not so much out of respect for any superior business wisdom and experience, but because his cousin's support as head of the family was vital. He took some persuading that the usual 500 square feet was inadequate and that 5,000 were required, but Noon managed to convince him. Business took off. Noon renovated the other shop and opened two more.

FROM MANAGER TO ENTREPRENEUR

Noon's first foray into independent entrepreneurism was a risky property deal. The first Royal Sweets shop was located in an apartment block, a large building of about seventy tenements completely encircled by roads. The tenancies were rent controlled and ground rent was payable to the government. When Noon decided he was going to buy the block, even the owner tried to discourage him.

'All I take in rent goes in maintenance.'

'What's the purchase price?'

The owner told him.

'I'll buy it,' said Noon. He was just twenty-five years old.

'You're a very brave young man,' said the owner. 'The tenants will chew your head off.'

Noon problems were closer to home. 'Just don't tell my cousin,' he said. 'I'll give you a deposit now and sort it out with him. And I'll get our solicitor to start the paperwork.'

His mother was the first to be convinced, and she then helped to persuade Noon's cousin.

The purchase established Noon as the head of the business and made the family financially secure. The building had been managed badly, and with some strategic changes it began to show a profit almost from the beginning. Noon discarded his cycle and bought a motorbike. Soon the family was able to move to a larger, more comfortable apartment and even buy a car.

The experience gave him enormous confidence and he began to look for fresh challenges. So far his plans had succeeded and his family was once more comfortably off. But it worried Noon's business sense that all his eggs were in one basket: Royal Sweets. The next step had to be diversification, to spread the risk in order to profit from several markets.

A chance meeting with an acquaintance in the paper-recycling trade gave him his opportunity. 'Let me know if you hear of any business opportunities,' he said.

'Why don't we work together in the paper trade?' was the reply.

So with Noon's financial and business skills and his friend's expertise in the paper industry, Paper, Print and Products was launched. Noon had to convince his cousin of the soundness of diversifying away from the family's traditional business, but by now his cousin was confident in Noon's ability and was happy to stand aside and watch the profits arrive. The new business did very well and is still making money for the family in Bombay.

Noon had fulfilled his family obligations. He had carried on the business that his father had bequeathed to the family and it was prospering. An income had been provided for each member of the family. His mother and his cousin were installed in apartments befitting their status in the family; the oldest son lived with his mother, fulfilling the obligation of care that goes with being an oldest son in an Asian family. Noon himself was living in comfortable style in an apartment of his own, and had finally been able to achieve his ambition and was driving a small Fiat car. And still the business grew. A construction company was the next diversification and there were more to come.

Outside business, Noon's interests were also diversifying and expanding, another classic characteristic of successful South Asian entrepreneurs, who often become prominent in community affairs. For Noon, road safety was his chosen interest; before long he had become President of the Indian equivalent of British ROSPA (the Royal Society for the Prevention of Accidents). He became secretary of the powerful confectionery trade organisation, and in 1968 was appointed a justice of the peace. For many people it would have been enough; Noon had hardly begun. 'I was doing well commercially. I was doing well socially. I was involved in many other organisations. There was a lot of fire in my belly! I began to feel that Bombay wasn't big enough. And I found myself – an uneducated Bombay man! – thinking that I should be going off somewhere else. I told my family that I was going to England.'

None of the Noon family had ever been to the UK.

FRESH FIELDS

Royal Sweets had recently acquired a small canning facility. Noon decided that canned sweets were going to be his secret weapon to conquer the UK market. He took his samples to Britain.

An Asian arriving alone in London, as we have already seen, is not on his own. The extended family and the global connection network ensured that there were plenty of people to help him and introduce him to the British market. Commercially the trip was a disaster. Noon did very little business. Canned sweets were not an attractive product to English buyers. But Noon had discovered a new love in his life: England. 'I came here and I liked London, I liked England, I liked the culture, I liked the people. I was absolutely madly in love with England. I said, "I must come and live and work here. I must do something here."'

His friend Taherbhai Suterwalla rented an apartment in Bombay in the same building that Noon lived in. TRS, the Suterwalla company, is run today by Taherbhai's five sons and is worth £25 million; but even in those early days Taherbhai was establishing himself as a pioneer in the ethnic branded food industry. Taherbhai Suterwalla warned him it might not be easy: 'You'll not be able to take any money out of Bombay.' It was no more than the truth. The fact that Royal Sweets was financially as solid as a rock made no difference; strict exchange controls were in force. But Noon's reputation, track record and family were security enough. 'Any time you want to set up business in England, I'll help you with the finance.' It was a generous gesture, coming from somebody who knew Noon well and probably realised that this ambitious young man would be one of his strongest competitors.

Noon went back to India with great plans forming in his mind. In 1970 he put the management of the Bombay companies into the hands of his brother, and returned to England to set up a Royal Sweets factory in Southall, West London. With the promised financial backing (Suterwalla's sons became partners in Royal Sweets, providing the necessary cash investment to enable Noon to start up afresh) and slowly overcoming some resistance from British tastes unused to Indian sweets, he began to build up the business. His main customer base was the small Asian communities in England at that time.

But the availability of venture capital wasn't in itself Noon's big break. Royal Sweets was transformed into a major success by the activities of a bullying, dangerously unstable tribal chief in another continent altogether: Africa. In troubled Uganda, struggling with an economy plunging ever deeper into disaster, President Idi Amin decided that the time had come to expel the country's non-Africans. Suddenly London was crowded with Asians, hundreds and thousands of them, arriving by every plane and longing for some reminder of the culture they had been forced to leave behind. Now there were lots of customers for the Indian delicacies that Noon was selling. By the end of his first year in Britain, he had franchised nine shops in Leicester, Bradford and London.

Royal Sweets made quality its main criterion. Noon looked hard at the way Indian sweets were usually packaged: sold in a brown paper or plastic bag, crudely overprinted. Manufacturers paid little attention to making their products look attractive. But from the beginning Noon used his experience of the paper industry to package his product in attractive cardboard boxes, like quality chocolate. This attention to detail was practical as well as visually pleasing. For example, there's an Indian sweet called Ras-malai that is a great favourite with South Asians. It's a very sticky, messy delight. Before Noon opened his shops, Ras-malai was sold in aluminium foil containers or plastic bags that rarely reached customers' homes intact. Noon's Ras-malai was of superb quality, naturally; but he was reluctant to change its consistency for something more manageable. He travelled as far afield as Norway to find the answer: vacuum packaging. He studied Norwegian techniques and decided to use them.

New Products, New Opportunities

Noon was building a characteristically entrepreneurial success: quality product, a niche market identified, innovation (in packaging) and a desire to expand and grow. In 1976 Noon broke new ground again, adding a phrase to the English language when he took a savoury snack and turned it into a classic English nibble. 'Mixture' had been a collection of whatever came to hand, packed and sold as a sideline by some food manufacturers. Noon rethought the recipe, imposed his usual quality standards and put it into tempting packaging. It was a quality variation on a theme, a snack that fitted in well with the rest of the Royal line – but something wasn't quite right.

'It's the name,' he decided. 'We have to change the name.'

That was how 'Bombay Mix' was born. It was named after Noon's main trading company, Bombay Halwa. The name was an inspired choice. It was snappy, memorable, and before long had become a household name.

Bombay Mix came to be one of the company's biggest sellers, but Noon was thinking big in any case now. In 1979, he was sought out by the head of the Taj International Hotel Group, who was visiting London from the United States. He was impressed with the Royal Sweets factory and invited Noon to join him in a partnership with the Taj Group for a venture in New York.

Leaving the London operation in the hands of a general manager, Noon moved in 1980 to the United States, where he spent four years, backed by the Taj Group, running a company producing Indian sweets and food. The major change was that instead of cooking for small numbers, he was producing food now for 2,000 or more. He rapidly learned ways of bulk cooking without losing flavour, and of refrigerating food in a way that preserved its freshness and quality.

During the four years he commuted to London regularly, and found that the general manager and management team were doing a good job. But Noon was fifteen years ahead of his time; the Americans were not ready to buy Indian food in quantity. After four years – which, because of his research and study of bulk food preparation, were to prove invaluable later – he wound up his American business interests and came back to Britain. He lost no time in putting his new ideas into practice. When he heard that British Airways was looking for a supplier of Indian vegetarian meals, he bid for the contract and won it.

The Entrepreneurial Model

Bombay Halwa and its flagship brand Royal Sweets were thriving. The franchising now extended to 39 shops, and the staff had expanded to 66 to handle the BA contract.

Like most entrepreneurs, Noon had been blessed with a combination of natural ability and sheer luck. But it was hard work that had put him in a position to seize the opportunities with which luck presented him. Accountancy lessons at six in the morning had been hard work, but they gave him a grounding in business without which he could not properly have analysed the opportunities. He took calculated risks – the purchase of the apartment block might have gone very badly – but it wasn't leaping blindly into the dark. Most of his broad innovative strokes, such as the Scandinavian trip, were based on careful market research and identifying opportunities others had missed.

He was still pondering what he had learned in the United States and was looking to use it in the UK food retailing business. Gradually an idea began to form in his mind. The time was right for a high-quality ethnic food product to take the supermarkets by storm. He began to try out new cooking ideas, earmarked a factory site and began to research again. He bought numerous samples of pre-packed Indian food from the major supermarkets. He hated them. They were, he decided, uniformly dreadful. Insipid, flavourless, unattractively presented and badly packaged, they had no authentic qualities at all. Many dreary forkfuls later he made up his mind: 'This is terrible! It's just not acceptable. I'd never eat it by choice.'

Storming the Gates

Noon resolved that his food products were going to have better distribution than that of the small-scale suppliers who trudged round the Asian shops making hundreds of small deliveries. He intended to use a major distributor. The biggest frozen food company in Britain was Bird's Eye. Noon approached the company and went to its offices several times asking to show managers samples of his food products.

After a great deal of persistence a Bird's Eye senior brand manager became interested.

'Yes – we can do business. Where's your factory?'

Noon was unabashed. 'I haven't got one! But I'm ready to build.'

With Bird's Eye's guidance a 6,500 square foot factory was built and equipped to Bird's Eye specifications. Noon celebrated by renaming the company. It was 1988 and Noon Products plc had arrived.

He expected the first order to be in the region of £300,000 worth of product, with hopefully even bigger orders in the future. He'd calculated that the new operation would provide a management opening for his younger brother, and for his daughter, a qualified food and beverage manager then working for the Taj Group in India. They could run the new factory and he would go on with his confectionery business.

Confirmation of the order arrived from Bird's Eye. It was for £2.4 million.

The whole family joined the staff of 80 workers, toiling six days a week. The order was completed. Noon often had cause to be grateful that his instincts had led him to insist on the best-quality equipment. Day after day output was maintained, more than meeting the strict requirements that Bird's Eye had stipulated. On Sundays everybody snatched a day's respite, before hurling themselves back into the production flow on Monday morning.

One day Noon was summoned to the Bird's Eye head office. 'Why don't you keep production going on Sunday?'

'Are you kidding? I have to pay double time on Sundays!'

'We'll cover that. We're selling your products very fast. You must move on to seven days a week running.'

Noon did some sums in his head and mentally re-organised a few timetables. 'We'll do it.'

'YOUR INDIAN FOOD ISN'T AUTHENTIC'

David Sainsbury looked across his desk at Gulam Noon, who had come at Sainsbury's request with a small group of his senior executives to talk about possible contracts.

'We've seen your Bird's Eye products, of course. They're very good.'

The Noon executives nodded an acknowledgement.

'Mr Noon, I'd like you to give me your opinion of the Indian food we sell in Sainsbury's.'

Noon responded immediately. 'It's not authentic Indian food.'

David Sainsbury sat back in his chair. This was hardly the language he was used to hearing from people hoping to secure contracts from one of the country's leading food retailers. He thought for a moment. 'Can you do any better?'

Noon could, and a relationship was established with Sainsbury's that marked the beginning of Noon Products plc's rise to market dominance. The first contract was signed in 1989. Today Sainsbury's takes 70 per cent of Noon Products' output.

The contract with Sainsbury's was the fulfilment of an ambition that Noon had cherished since he had first arrived in London. He was now firmly in the mainstream of British business. British Airways was a dominant British company, Sainsbury's was one of the handful of leading British supermarkets. He had made the transition. 'A niche market's all very well, but I was looking for mainstream outlets.' Royal Sweets sold primarily to Asian customers, but Bombay Mix was as British as the pubs and restaurants which stocked it.

His share of the mainstream supermarket business increased even further. Waitrose became a client in 1989. Others included the Somerfield supermarket chain, Welcome Break restaurants and other leading retailers. The export side of his work also began to grow. Soon Noon Products' premises in Southall, close to Heathrow Airport, occupied five factory units and 30,000 square feet, together with further units for warehousing, cold storage, laboratories and other facilities.

DISASTER

It was a November evening in 1994. Noon was having some difficulty parking his car: the black tie charitable event at the Dorchester
had proved very popular. Back at the factory, 150 people were working on the evening shift. Noon, who took charitable matters very
seriously, was taking the evening off to support the Dorchester
event. He was still manoeuvring the car when his mobile phone
rang. By the time the brief conversation was over he was already
back on the open road, heading for Southall.

The factory was engulfed in black smoke. Flames were shooting
up into the sky. A large crowd watched in awe as several years' worth
of effort and several million pounds' worth of plant and equipment
blazed and disintegrated. Nobody trapped inside could have survived. Several firemen, their ladders silhouetted against the flames,
played hoses on to the furnace below. The water seemed to be having no effect at all. Noon had to shout to make himself heard.

'*Did they get everybody out?*'

A bystander pointed to a nearby group of people. Noon recognised his daughter and brother and the production manager. He
rushed over to them.

'Everyone's safe,' they told him. 'We counted everybody as they
came out. They're all accounted for. Nobody's injured, thank God.
Everybody's OK.'

'What happened?'

'The fire people won't go in. They say it's not safe, the smoke's too
thick.'

He understood. A few weeks before, two firefighters had died in
a factory fire. Now that all the workers had been accounted for it
would have been crazy to risk life further in an attempt to save what
was left of the building.

Noon, his family and workers stood and watched their factory
burn. Many of the staff had been with the company since the first
factory had been built and there was immense loyalty among them.
Most of them were weeping; all of them realised they were seeing

their livelihood going up in flames. Noon tried to console them. 'We'll build another factory, God willing. A better one. You'll see.'

By three in the morning the flames were under control and the devastated shell of Noon Products plc could be seen smouldering. Occasionally beams crashed down into the ash that had been the scrubbed, gleaming factory floor. An oily, grimy pall of acrid smoke hung over everything. Noon went home, peeled off his scorched evening finery and cried himself to sleep.

Noon candidly attributes the decisions he then made to his child-hood upbringing and the values he had inherited: 'the human values – how you relate to people: your brother, your sister, your supplier, the elderly people nearing retirement who still work for us in Bom-bay.' He'd always built supplier relationships on the values he'd been taught by his mother, routinely declining offers of large discounts from companies trying to persuade him to switch his account. Rela-tionships of trust and respect were all important. Now that disaster had struck, it was a policy that paid dividends. A procession of col-leagues, friends, suppliers and even rivals came to offer sympathy and practical help. Some whose accounts were now unlikely to be settled in the immediate future only asked, 'When are you re-start-ing? And what can we do to help?'

David Sainsbury was among the first to call. 'Don't lay your staff off. Send them to our head depot at Hayes and Wembley. We'll give them jobs. And when you're ready to go back into production we'll release them back to you.'

The bankers and other advisers were more cautious. 'There are 225 on your payroll. The first thing you must do is give them all notice. You'll cut your losses and when you want to restart you can rehire them.' Noon refused, insisting that nobody was to be paid off and all were to be retained on full pay. He began to look as far afield as Wales for temporary premises but found nothing. Then, discussing the prob-lem with his partners, it struck him that Bombay Halwa Ltd maintained two plants. With the approval of his clients he converted one to a food factory. Production was restarted about a month after the fire, initially at 40 per cent of normal output and gradually reaching 80 per cent.

There were generous offers of money from colleagues, friends and individuals, like the wife of an Indian friend who approached him: 'Brother Noon, I have savings of £72,000. You can have it all.' Noon thanked her, saying he was glad to know it was there when needed. He didn't take up the offer, or any of the others. He didn't need to. The company was benefiting from years of goodwill, nobody was pressing for payment, extended credit was offered as a matter of course. When the insurance claim was settled, a factory site was made available to him by Metal Box; Noon's reputation ensured a quick sale and immediate possession.

In March 1995 Noon Products took possession of its present site on the Great Western Industrial Park in Southall. By August the building had been stripped and refitted with a mezzanine floor, sophisticated drainage and top-quality equipment.

Noon was back.

Fire is one of the biggest hazards in a food factory, and many factories have gone up in flames. But Noon's achievement in setting up temporary premises after three weeks and going into full production in less than eight months is very unusual. The re-opening was graced by the presence of the Indian High Commissioner. Noon, intoxicated by the emotion of the occasion, spontaneously announced a week's bonus to the 300-strong staff, and a string of food retailing celebrities contributed complimentary greetings to the glossy brochure that marked the re-launch.

THE KEY TO SUCCESS

Today, production at Noon Products plc is more than double its pre-fire levels. A second factory, opened in 1988, has led to the recruiting of 200 more staff. Noon's own-brand product launched in 1993 is selling strongly into retail outlets, and more initiatives are in the planning stages.

What accounts for all this success in a crowded and competitive market?

First is **commitment to quality**. Noon Products maintains its high standards consistently, day in and day out.

Second is **Noon's personal standards**. His whole business is founded on his refusal to manufacture anything that doesn't meet his criteria of quality and value for money. He still only produces food that he is happy to eat himself.

Third is **authenticity**. Noon's Executive Chef and Production Director, who share Noon's insistence on quality, maintain twenty-four hour quality control. The recipes are prepared with traditional ingredients and cooked with great care. Every spice is introduced at the correct point in the cooking, not, as is the case with some mass producers, mixed together and tipped in the pan at the start. In this Noon is like any dedicated chef: the only difference is quantity. Noon Products produce 70,000 to 80,000 frozen meals a day.

Fourth is **technology**, without which Noon could not have attained a fraction of what he has achieved. As a youngster in Bombay he installed air conditioning in his shop and equipped his first factory with the best equipment he could afford. He approached the task in Southall with the same attitude, and the factory is a model of high-tech cooking processes, often eyed covetously by rivals who would dearly like to have Noon's considerable technical knowledge and expertise.

Noon is well liked and admired in the South Asian community. As a young-looking and very fit sixty-one year old, he has acquired something of the status of elder statesman. His achievements in industry and his many charitable and welfare interests in Britain and India were honoured by the award of an MBE in the 1996 Honours List.

He had already received the accolade of the South Asian Community: in 1994 he was named Asian of the Year. Congratulatory messages accompanying the citation came from the then Prime Minister John Major, Michael Heseltine, President of the Board of Trade, the Indian High Commissioner, His Excellency L. M. Singhvi, and Paddy Ashdown, Leader of the Liberal Democrats and a personal friend of Noon's through their mutual commitment to liberal democracy.

One face in the glossy brochure would have given Noon – a life-long cricketer and passionate about the sport – particular pleasure: that of Imran Khan, Pakistani test cricketer and the first holder of the Asian of the Year Award.

4

Out of Africa:
Manubhai Madhvani

'We have prospered – and our prosperity has benefited Britain.'

Manubhai Madhvani is a tall man whose physical presence matches his status as a giant of industry. But there aren't many other clues in his office, a few yards away from London's Baker Street station, to remind you that the Madhvani family contributes around 10 per cent of Uganda's GNP and around 12 per cent of its tax revenue. The room is dominated by a world map, the desk behind which Mr Madhvani sits is a large one, and Baker Street is hardly an inexpensive place to set up an office. But there are none of the trappings of immense wealth (the Madhvani family has been estimated to be worth £140 million), and that comes as no surprise after you have talked with Manubhai, a softly spoken man who treats you with great courtesy and consideration. His devout Hindu faith emerges frequently in his conversation, and he speaks of the family's achievements with rather more wonder than pride – although he does permit himself a rare smile of satisfaction when he shows you a book he published of his own eloquent photographs of India.

The Madhvanis came to Britain when the Ugandan Asians were expelled in the early 1970s. The family already controlled a major business group in Uganda, known for producing sugar, beer, textiles, edible oil, safety matches, cardboard boxes, metal boxes, metal wire and tea, among other products. The group was founded in 1905 by Muljibhai P. Madhvani, Manubhai's father, and the anniversary of his death is commemorated each year. So is that of Manubhai's elder brother, Jayant Muljibhai, who by the time of his death in 1972 had become East Africa's leading industrialist; among his achievements was the building of East Africa's first steel mill. When Jayant Muljibhai died, Manubhai took over the running of the Madhvani group, which produced approximately half the sugar in the country and exported to neighbouring countries. The mainstay of its industrial complex was a 35,000 acre sugar plantation with one of the largest overhead water irrigation schemes in the world. But since the rise of Idi Amin the company had remained static and Uganda's economy had begun to shrink. From Amin's arrival, Kenya began to develop at Uganda's expense; for example, all Ugandan coffee was exported to Kenya.

Amin had resolved to expel the Ugandan Asians, but he did not realise what a valuable economic asset he was discarding in so doing. Jomo Kenyatta did. It is said that Amin was once invited as a head of state to a function in Kenya, where he was welcomed enthusiastically as the hero of Africa. The very pro-African Kenyans admired Amin for expelling the Asians. While he was there he sought out Kenyatta and said, 'It's very important you should do as I did. Throw your Asians out.'

Kenyatta was very wise. 'Let's sleep on it. Tomorrow morning we'll go for a walk.'

Next day he took Amin to a Shah shop (the Shahs are a Gujerati clan often involved in trading) and said to the proprietor, 'I want a cup for left-handers.'

'There's a cup there.'

'No, I want a left-handed cup.'

The Shah said, 'Let me go inside and check my stock.' So he brought the same cup back, but now turned around 180 degrees. 'Here is what you wanted.'

'Excellent!' said Kenyatta.

'But,' said the shopkeeper, 'it will cost you fifteen per cent more.'

Manubhai tells the story with a twinkle in his eye and a rumbling chuckle, but he speaks with great sadness of the terrible flowering of Uganda's ethnic tensions. How different it would have been, he reflects, if Amin had listened to Kenyatta, who considered the Asians to be undesirable but wasn't yet ready to expel them. Their particular brand of entrepreneurial skills and lateral thinking, their ability to create profit out of very little, was essential to growth. But Amin was pursuing disastrous policies. Uganda's economy dwindled inexorably. Every solution Amin tried failed. 'I believe that in the end, he made Asians the issue because it distracted attention from his brutal killing of over 300,000 Africans. It's for them I feel most sorry. Amin was an army man, a lance-corporal, and he saw everything as confrontation. While the world talked of Asians he got on with killing Africans – all intellectuals, Makerere graduates, doctors and so on.'

Apart from the dreadful human tragedy, the cost to Uganda's intellectual and professional life was incalculable. Manubhai himself was imprisoned by Amin in 1972. His crime? Being a brown businessman in Uganda. A deeply religious man, Manubhai joined with other Asian prisoners of various faiths to pray for the survival of the Asian community during Idi Amin's reign of terror, an ecumenical experience that affected him deeply and laid the groundwork for much of his later religious work.

Amin was thrown out in 1979, leaving Obote and other rulers of Uganda to decide what to do about the property of the Asians who had been expelled. Eventually, under pressure from the World Bank, they decided to give the confiscated property back. Not to do so would have been against the World Bank Charter. The major powers also demanded the return of the property. It took the courage of President Yoweri Museveni to pass the Expropriated Properties Act and invite the Asians back to Uganda. In 1985 President Museveni asked the Madhvani brothers to return to Uganda to help with the economic rehabilitation and reconstruction of a country that had been torn by strife and bloodshed. With the help of the World Bank and this unique partnership involving industrialists and businessmen from the private sector, President Museveni has made Uganda the darling of the international community in Sub-Saharan Africa. A key element in this revival was the Madhvanis, who single-handedly revived the sugar industry on which Uganda's economy depends. It was said that having a job with the Madhvanis was enough to get you into the country without a passport.

It was the first time that the World Bank had entered into a tri-partite loan agreement with a country and a family, the Madhvani group of companies. When the finances were agreed the Madhvanis restarted sugar production. Today output has passed the 70,000 tonne pre-1972 production level and is increasing all the time. In 1992 the Madhvani breweries, which had dwindled almost to nothing under Amin, were restored; half a million cases of beer are now produced each month. There are no overseas partners – it's not commercially necessary, and in Africa there is a preference for own-brand beer and some mistrust of Western brands. The business advantage over competitors who do work with foreign investors is that one doesn't have to pay large royalties.

The Madhvanis' pre-1972 steel and textile interests were also restored, though the steel industry needs a longer start-up period than most and it will be some time before output is back up. And it was decided that markets had changed dramatically in twenty years and that the textile interests they used to have would now have to be dropped.

SOUTH ASIANS IN THE UK

Manubhai is a British citizen and his share of the investment in Uganda may be considered to be a British Asian investment in that country. He is well aware of both the strengths of the UK South Asian community and the problems it is currently facing. He acknowledges the entrepreneurial success, the retail trading base and the strength of the family ties that ensured survival. But he senses that family ties are loosening, and acknowledges some of the disintegrating factors that we examine elsewhere in this book.

He also makes the point that there was very little competition in the early days. Asians replaced the Jews as successful small retailers. 'Asians, especially East African Asians (Indian Asians are slightly different) took over. Their boy would go to school in the morning, come back in the evening and then work at the till, and later do his homework when his mother would take his place at the till – it's a whole family system. In the process other relations came and joined them.'

But now things are changing. Manubhai thinks the biggest weakness of the UK South Asians is a failure to assimilate into the local situation. 'We made the same mistake in Africa. We haven't assimilated ourselves at the council level, in politics … someone asked me, why aren't Asians rising in society? But some of the blame must be taken by the Asians. My Jewish friends are very similar to us. There are between half a million and 600,000 Jews in this country. But there are thirty, forty of them – maybe more than that – in Parliament.'

For Manubhai, Asian influence is more important than Asian wealth. Conversation inevitably drifts to the very low and disproportionate level of representation at all levels; weak at local council level, at county level and higher, the South Asian voice is too little heard. He doesn't blame the political parties so much as the Asians themselves. The initiative and industry that enabled the community to overcome so many obstacles in employment and business have not been matched by similar efforts in the political sphere – and even in national business agencies and institutions.

He argues that what is needed most of all is for South Asians to change their thinking, and he sees today's younger generation as immensely encouraging.

Britain In the Millennium

The change in government following the 1997 General Election did not, in Manubhai's view, dramatically change either the situation or the responsibilities of the UK South Asian population. Asians are increasingly accepted in British society and it is their responsibility, he argues, to ensure that the process continues. Integration remains his favourite theme; like Gulam Noon, he looks forward to a future in which the country of your origin is of only secondary interest because your main identity is as a British citizen.

He's very dismissive of Asians who want to reduce the electoral process to the single issue of Asian identity. 'I'm asked what candidate best deserves our vote. I say, "Vote for the candidate who is best for us. If you want to vote Conservative, vote Conservative. If you want to vote Labour, vote Labour. Don't look for a brown candidate or one who comes from India. Those days are gone." ' True to his own advice he votes Conservative purely because he subscribes to Conservative values. He's reserving judgement on New Labour's relationship with industry and with the trade unions; it is early days.

But Manubhai is not worried about the future of Britain's involvement with traditional South Asian markets and the emerging economies of Asia. More important than any pro- or anti-Asian Labour policies, he says, are the shifts that are happening at the international level; the de-emphasising of the local dimension, the increasing role of facilities like EC loans, the fading of the old colonial backdrop. 'It doesn't really make a great deal of difference to Britain who is in power in India,' he says. 'The world is becoming freer, communication is better, everyone gets money from a different part of the world. It's something we have to live with.'

He is, however, an activist for UK South Asian involvement at every level, writing to Members of Parliament suggesting that more Asians should be recruited to Conservative Central Office and advising local committees and individuals on effective involvement. He urges that forums and round-table discussions should be organised and the feedback sent to the government. Well-publicised dinners with the Home Secretary will not, on their own, solve the problems; insist, he advises, that a forum be organised, with twenty or thirty people around the table, talking freely because no reporters are present. It's a tradition he remembers fondly from the days of

Margaret Thatcher, who used regularly to call Asians to meetings at 10 Downing Street. Manubhai was present. 'She would go on to do exactly as she liked, but at least we'd had the opportunity to talk with her!'

He makes the comment with his characteristic smile and deep rumbling laugh, but you sense that Lady Thatcher might well have found him a formidable guest. Certainly there were sharp words for the then premier on one occasion. A dinner had been arranged at Number 10 and an undertaking given that no reporters would be present. Manubhai was taken aback next day to find his presence at the dinner reported in the newspapers. He complained immediately to the Prime Minister. 'I told her, I didn't want it to be all over the papers that I had been meeting with Margaret Thatcher – that's a very Asian reaction. I said to her, "It's one of your people who did that, not an Asian!" '

Assimilation and Representation

Despite Manubhai's strong belief that the British South Asians' greatest ambition should be assimilation without loss of their cultural and ethnic heritage, he is sceptical about groups and committees that are specifically labelled 'Asian'. For example, in Margaret Thatcher's time an Asian Conservative Group was founded, but the name was soon dropped and the One Nation forum came into being. Manubhai approved but wants much more. 'We need to be on the inside track,' he says. 'We should be striving for representation on national societies, boards, forums and committees.' Mention a public function, thinktank or high-profile committee to him and he will immediately want to discuss ways of getting more South Asians on to it.

He's not planning a takeover of British society, nor South Asian dominance in every UK debate. It's a simple mathematical exercise. Manubhai has done the sums and come to the conclusion that South Asians are simply not represented in proportion to their numbers in the British population. Positive discrimination is no answer, but neither is ethnic marginalisation. 'There must be no more Asian Conservative Groups. We must fight against a certain tendency in ourselves to be individualistic, too.'

Ask Manubhai for an action plan as we enter the new millennium and he will push for discussions between UK South Asians, the politicians and decision makers; he will argue that they should be more evident in influential institutions like the Carlton Club; and that the South Asian community should be ready to take such opportunities as and when they arise by having people in it who are gifted, equipped and ready to take their place in such forums.

It's quite an agenda. But Manubhai Madhvani is somebody who might very well make it happen. At the time of the 1972 Asian influx he was already a leading figure in the British Ugandan Asian community, representing South Asian interests at the highest level. He was instrumental in filling the cultural gap between the British social services and the new influx of Asians they were trying to help. At a time of confusion and distress for the South Asians, he was an example of somebody who kept calm and helped to create the conditions for South Asians to settle in Britain. In the years since, he has been actively supporting the British Asian community in many, often unseen, ways.

Now, as South Asians face the bigger challenge still of integrating into British society and contributing their unique skills and insights to the larger UK economy, Manubhai may find himself playing yet another major role. It will not, however, be one restricted to business economics.

SPIRITUAL VALUES

Manubhai believes that the industrialist businessman cannot content himself with his economic contribution to society. He is morally obliged to make a direct and specific contribution in the area of spiritual and cultural values. 'In spite of an increasing level of material well-being in the world, I have noticed a growing spiritual poverty, a yearning for spiritual foods and a genuine path that would enable us to lift our minds and thoughts beyond basic and personal needs, to God, our fellow human beings and our spiritual destiny.' Putting this belief into practice, in 1994 Manubhai organised a Festival of Spiritual Unity in Roundwood Park in London, to which he invited spiritual leaders from all the major religions, some flown in from other parts of the world. For nine days they preached on various themes of religious unity to an average of 15,000 people a day.

For Manubhai it was the fulfilment of a twenty-year dream that had begun in a Ugandan jail. The festival was open to everybody. Free lunches were served to all (an estimated 360,000 chapatis were consumed) and a team of twenty GPs provided free check-ups and medical screenings as a further service.

'A picnic for nine days for 10,000 people', the festival was remarkably peaceful. During the ten days, with so many thousands in attendance, there was not one incident of violence or aggression that needed police attention.

5

Maharajahs of the Diaspora

In this chapter I want to look at three Maharajahs who have not only experienced diaspora but whose business world *is* the diaspora. I have chosen them because they represent a range of entrepreneurism. Azad Shivdasani inherited, managed and expanded an old-style entrepreneurial empire, operating in locations all over the globe. Kumar Datwani built his business in three continents, working with, for example, the large South Asian population in Hong Kong. And Bharat Desai is an entrepreneur of a different kind, one who could only have built what he has built in the world of the telecommunications revolution that has succeeded in binding most of the scattered world together electronically.

Are they UK Maharajahs? Certainly. Each of them has a major business commitment to Britain; two of them have homes in England, and the third, Bharat Desai, reflects the new cyberbusiness culture in which the location of your office or even your home no longer defines you as it once did. And the channelling of their business through Britain profits UK plc. Kumar Datwani's entry into UK property markets and Bharat Desai's establishment of a UK base both represent massive inward investment.

Let's look first at Azad Shivdasani, Chairman of the Inlaks Group. As I have mentioned in earlier chapters, I am a member of the Shivdasani extended family by marriage, and worked for many years with the Inlaks Group, the Shivdasani family business, trading internationally in a range of commodities and services. This is the Inlaks story.

Azad Shivdasani

'Forget about all those wonderful surveys, focus studies and all the rest. Get back in touch with the market. Go to the high street and have a look. Try and understand the product for yourself.'

In 1976 Azad Shivdasani completed his education (he studied at Harrow and Trinity College Oxford). His childhood was spent between the UK and Europe, with occasional trips to West Africa and India. By the time he had graduated from Oxford he had already been exposed to an array of cultures.

A characteristic of Azad and his generation of those of Indian origin brought up in Europe is their ability to operate in different worlds. Whether talking to a minister of a developing country, a European industrialist or someone leaning up against the same counter in a British pub, they seem at home and they relate.

The Shivdasani family is Sindhi in origin. Its business group, Inlaks, was established by Azad's father, Indurkumar (known to his friends as Indoo), who started his business career in Bombay in the mid-1940s and came to Britain after the partition of India.

Indoo had been involved in an unsatisfactory partnership and wanted to dissolve it. His partners negotiated the transfer to him of the company's Nigerian office as his share of the assets. When he went to Nigeria to examine his new acquisition he found he was the owner of an empty store, a shopfront, an empty warehouse and a staff consisting of a couple of bored Nigerian clerical assistants.

'How's business?' he asked hopefully.

'Sorry, Sir, there's nothing here. No goods. Nothing to sell.'

A less entrepreneurial man would have liquidated the lot and gone home to count up his losses. But Indoo decided that having come so far he might as well have a look around. It wasn't long before he noticed that a staple food in the region was a dried fish called stockfish. It was cheap, needed no refrigeration and was imported in huge quantities from Norway and Iceland. Two British companies dominated the industry. Indoo immediately began calculating how to capture the market.

It was a classic story in the Richard Branson/British Airways vein. The two large companies had become complacent and had been dictating ruthlessly to the Norwegians; working together as a cartel, they had quashed any attempt to raise the price they paid the Norwegians. In three weeks in Nigeria, Azad's father made himself into a walking encyclopaedia of stockfish. He familiarised himself with the various varieties and cuts and learned that timing was important; different stockfish products had to be sold in particular places and at particular times. He steeped himself in stockfish lore, then returned to the UK.

The break-up of the partnership and the trip to Nigeria had left the family with little money, and the gloomy news he brought back did not help matters. But one day he suddenly said to his wife, 'Let's go on a cruise. We can go up to the Arctic Circle, see the Northern Lights. We'll end up with a visit to Oslo.' Then, almost as an afterthought, he added casually, 'You know, I could even drop in and see those stockfish people, get to know them a bit.'

'We may as well go broke in style,' said his wife resignedly. Indoo booked first-class tickets for the cruise. They struck up a friendship with another couple on the ship. The husband turned out to be a distinguished Norwegian politician, whose brother-in-law was the country's biggest producer of stockfish. He undertook to arrange an introduction for the young entrepreneur.

In Norway Indoo duly met the suppliers and proposed that in return for paying a higher price he should be given a chance to compete against the British cartel. The Norwegians, impressed by his knowledge of stockfish and not slow to see where their own best interests lay, agreed.

Within about five years, he had 50 per cent of the market. The market for stockfish was large, so already at a young age Azad's father was successful. Soon he was trading internationally in a wide range of foodstuffs.

Indoo's headquarters were in Britain, first in Manchester and then in London. He was a cosmopolitan personality, who liked to spend time in Italy, France and Switzerland besides Africa and Asia. The business headquarters moved to Geneva during monetary export controls which cut international credit arrangements to an impossibly short period, forcing a relocation from London.

His attitude to his children was remarkably far sighted. Each was given financial independence at an early age. Indoo, however, had invested long years in building up a relationship of trust with his children. When Azad came down from Oxford in 1976 his father took him out to lunch and together they looked at the options. The outcome was that Azad abandoned his idea of spending a few years trying other things before considering entering the family business as the oldest son was expected to. He's not quite sure how his father managed it, but by the time the lunch table was cleared Azad had announced his intention of spending several years in the family business learning the ropes, after which he reserved the option of going off and working for himself.

The three years Azad spent working for his father were invaluable. For example, he was put to work in the Nigerian office. There he learned people skills in the real workplace. Sitting in a hot sales office in a Lagos railway compound, he made out invoices and collected payments for the commodities that the group was bringing in. He learned to negotiate with the tough Nigerian women traders who would turn up in colourful robes and carrying small children, counting out banknotes totalling large sums in any currency as he had the goods loaded on to their trucks. He learned to sense when claims for damaged goods were untrue, and at the same time he learned the wisdom of being fair when necessary, often giving a rebate if the company dropped prices soon after a client had bought a large consignment. 'On one occasion,' Azad recalls, 'I gave a concession to a dozen African lady traders who had come to petition me. We used to call them "Mamas" – and mind you, they were big ladies. They decided to show their appreciation by giving me a hug; we slipped, and the next thing I knew, they were all on top of me!' He was, he points out, learning hands-on judgement...

He spent some time working in the Geneva office, learning his way through the paperwork involved in international trade. Axioms were drilled into him – 'Never overlook a missing $10', for example (because if the books were out by $10, the discrepancy might actually involve $1 million). There were nights when Azad worked until 2 a.m. chasing a tiny sum that had gone astray. He couldn't go home until it was traced. 'It was the kind of training that the boss's son, and someone who was to become chairman at quite a young age, would not usually get,' he acknowledges. 'At the time, of course, I grumbled!'

Gradually he was given more responsibility. He was one of the first wave of businessmen in the mid-1970s dealing with mainland China, visiting there six times in three years. It was a curious experience; China was beginning to emerge from decades of economic isolation, and the customs procedures were cumbersome and tedious. 'It was the only customs border in the world where they gave you a four-course meal while they were searching the train.'

Azad's plans for the future changed sharply when in 1979 Indoo suddenly died. The London headquarters became the location of numerous meetings and discussions as the implications of this tragedy became clear. Azad was twenty-four years old, and had talked with his father only a few weeks earlier about leaving the family business and going off on his own. Now, as the oldest son, his duty was to take over the business.

TAKING THE REINS

Indoo had been a charismatic figure, hugely admired by many, the dynamic core of the group and the shaper of policy and future plans. Retirement had been far in the future and his death was quite unexpected. Azad took over the reins aware that much was expected of him. There was no shortage of people trying to test the new chairman, requesting promotion, bringing grievances, suggesting major changes in procedure and policy. Azad listened to them all, politely declining most with regret, but often realising that behind the complaint or request was valuable input. He embarked on a programme of improving staff interaction, making it possible to exchange ideas, visit each other's departments and improve communications.

The first five years of Azad's chairmanship were extremely successful. Demand for commodities in Nigeria was high and the work was stimulating and demanding. 'Looking back, I had to work long hours but it was probably one of the most fruitful and challenging periods in my whole life. In some ways it's a disadvantage having that kind of experience when you're young – because afterwards you're always looking for the same thing to happen again!'

He readily acknowledges that the successes of the early 1980s were the fruit of his father's work, though he takes credit for managing what had been bequeathed to him profitably at a time when other companies trading with Nigeria went to the wall. It was a ruthless market and margins were being slashed. Azad operated a very quick decision cycle, spending four months of the year in Lagos, keeping hands-on contact with the products the group was importing and distributing. Business was done mostly by telephone, based on trust. The Inlaks reputation meant that goods could be bought in large quantities by verbal contract and rapid advantage taken of shifts in the market and political moves. If word reached the office that sugar was about to be restricted, a telephone conversation secured the purchase of several shiploads of sugar, to be brought in speedily.

'The reason we were so effective is that the decisions were made fast. We had a clear focus and no identity problems. We were a trading company based mainly in Nigeria with buying offices all round the world.' The business relied heavily on local knowledge – what the competition was up to, what the suppliers were doing and who else they were supplying; they visited the ports and watched who was clearing what. Azad's intention was to know the market thoroughly and in detail, so that Inlaks was not only capable of trading profitably from day to day but was also well placed to make intelligent gambles.

'Of course it was a team effort. The core group of senior executives was maybe six to seven, they and myself made it happen. I took the big decisions and was involved in a lot of the daily detail but many important decisions were made by the core group. They were at that time our Nigerian MD, our Kano manager, the heads of our Geneva and London offices – my brother-in-law and our Industries MD, who together managed the early diversification into manufacturing – this group was, with myself, the command centre of the business. Then there was the next level of at least two dozen senior managers who were extremely important to our success. A good part of my job was making sure they all got on.'

The single dominating concept was integrity. People were treated well; suppliers or contacts who did Inlaks a favour were well rewarded, customers and clients were dealt with honestly and straightforwardly; and in what might have seemed a rather unworldly code of honourable conduct there was a certain hard-headed business thinking that served Inlaks well. 'All the good deeds we did were like credit marks in our bank of trust with our suppliers. It meant we could do those large transactions, sometimes get it right, and reap the rewards.'

CHANGING COURSE

When Azad took over Inlaks in late 1979 he had immediate ambitions to diversify into manufacturing and specialised services, both in Nigeria and other countries. He knew that good trading times could not last for ever, even though he intended to ride the wave while they continued.

'I talked about these ideas to my brother-in-law, Nicolo Sella de Monteluce, who had considerable experience in industry, and this helped to crystallise the strategy. The initial strategy was to manufacture products in Nigeria which we were already importing and selling. As long as we could match price and quality with a local product, we knew we could sell it, as we had the distribution channels.'

What happened next was explosive and headlong growth into new businesses. Between 1980 and 1984 Inlaks created eight new major concerns in Nigeria. New facilities and factories were being opened at the rate of one every six months. Most of this expansion was through start-ups. Only one was an acquisition.

In 1980 the Inlaks group turnover had been 95 per cent trading and 5 per cent manufacturing. By 1985 the mix was 50 per cent trading and 50 per cent manufacturing and services.

To give some idea of the level of activity during that period, the group started an 800,000 hectolitre brewery (1981) in partnership with Kronenberg; a company providing the major Nigerian banks with computer hardware and software systems (1981); a seafood processing factory with a fleet of fifteen newly commissioned coastal trawlers (1982); the manufacture of plastic and paper printed packaging material (1982); a cube sugar factory (1983); an oilfield services company providing engineering, equipment leasing and maintenance services to the multinational oil companies (1983); and a 30 million litre per annum dairy plant producing UHT milk in tetrapak cartons (1984).

The above expansion phase culminated in 1985 with the acquisition of Alcan's Nigerian businesses. It was the largest transaction of its kind in Nigeria at that time. It remains one of the few examples of the controlling interest of a large-scale industry in Nigeria changing hands smoothly and without disruption.

CRISIS

Around 1984, Azad began to be heavily involved in non-profit activities, to the point where he was spending only half his time working for the group. He didn't discuss it in detail with his colleagues, though they were aware of his new interests. 'In hindsight I ought to have told them I was only going to be around for half the time now.

It might have avoided some of the misunderstanding. But I was living in two worlds, trying to keep a foot in both.' What had been a human desire to help others and be involved in the area of environment and development was threatening to turn into a problem for the group.

Other problems began to appear. The previously strong naira was massively devalued. Inflation soared in Nigeria and imports became extremely expensive. Nigeria was one of the world's great markets, but now it crashed. Imports were irreversibly damaged. There was a shift back to local produce, which may have been very good for the country's future but was disaster to numerous businesses. Many that had been thriving now looked closure in the face.

Azad had to make difficult decisions, although the diversifications of the previous half decade began to bear fruit. As Azad had predicted, the trading side of the business had finally shifted from boom to bust, but half the group's activities were now in manufacturing.

The diversification decision had been Azad's, conceived by him and implemented by persuading the senior management of the group that Inlaks' historic focus should be changed. It was just ten years since Azad had sat at lunch with his father and decided to throw in his lot with the family business rather than go off on his own. What had equipped him with the ability to analyse trends and make long-range policy – policy that in effect saved the family business from collapse?

'I was more ambitious than strategic! I was young, I was aggressive, possessing the boldness of youth, bordering on folly. My nature was basically entrepreneurial. Whenever I saw an opening, I went for it. I inherited a flair from my father for seeking new opportunities and getting excited by ideas – that was very much a characteristic of him. I learned by total immersion. As a child I often heard him on the telephone discussing business problems; I saw him in meetings, in conversations, talking about business within the family. In the three years I worked with him I sometimes travelled with him and sat in on negotiations, and I absorbed some important lessons through this experience. Just as a youngster brought up in a family of musicians is likely to be proficient on an instrument at the age of six, so, unknown to my father and to myself, I was being trained as an entrepreneur.

'I probably wanted to differentiate myself from the past. I wanted to make my own mark. The past was all about trading. Going into manufacturing would be something new for the business. I suppose that there was an element of wanting to prove myself.'

ETHICAL DILEMMAS

Despite being rescued by the manufacturing side, the group's consolidated accounts showed a loss for 1987. This year was the low point in its history. But it was the only year that showed a loss, and by 1988 recovery had started.

It was a changing world, however. The crash of the late 1980s had been caused by the devaluation of the Nigerian currency and the collapse of the demand for imported goods. But another issue was emerging which plunged Azad into a serious predicament. For some time corruption had been present in Africa but it was possible to do business and keep away from the areas it affected. Now it was reaching into every area of life and threatening the national economy. For the first time Azad was faced with moral and ethical dilemmas that threatened the core of his business. He was being offered opportunities that required him to condone things he was not prepared to condone; but to reject the opportunities would mean the inevitable loss of the trading empire.

It was an agonising time for Azad. Decisions made on ethical grounds were leading to the closure of offices, competitors taking over contracts and a great deal of criticism from people who were unable to understand why Inlaks was losing business – business built on years of nurturing relationships with key trading houses, brokers and bankers in the City of London and shipping agents on the Baltic Exchange.

Azad is philosophical about the criticism at that time. 'The popular opinion was that I had lost my grip. It was said that when I was young I had been a very good trader with good instincts. But now I had lost my way, and other people had come in and pushed Inlaks out. We weren't competitive any more. We were no longer hungry, focused and lean. We'd made too much money. There were all sorts of theories.'

There might have been some truth in it, concedes Azad. After years of immensely successful trading, the old fire and drive were not quite so strong. But there was a much stronger process happening. Azad was realising that if he were to continue with large-scale commodity trading in Nigeria, it would mean doing things that would be very difficult to live with.

He came to accept the fact that Inlaks was going to have to get out of trading. At the same time he recognised that things move on. 'And who knows, my father in the same circumstances might have made exactly the same decision.'

Azad speaks in a more reflective mood about this period. 'I think it is important to define what you stand for as a business. You need to be specific, write it down, make it visible at least to yourself. This is hard work. You then need to try and stick to these values. This meant that Inlaks could not indulge in large-scale trading in Nigeria from the late 1980s.

Of course, life being as it is there is always some degree of compromise. But it is better to have values, I think, and strive for them than to be totally governed by expediency. What is interesting is that Inlaks today does stand for something in the Indian community far beyond what is warranted by the actual size of our operations. And many of those who criticised the withdrawal from trading, whilst employees, now proudly declare they used to work for Inlaks. The good reputation that we enjoy cost millions in opportunities avoided.'

Azad gesticulates, the old trader in him emerging. 'I hope it was worth it!'

CONSOLIDATION 1988-92

After the reduction in trading Inlaks concentrated on running its manufacturing and service business. The group prospered. Azad stood down from a number of charities, telling them that he had been neglecting his duties closer to home.

In 1992, however, he became aware that the winds of change had begun to blow once more. 'I was beginning to feel that some of our businesses no longer made sense in their respective environments. I felt we were becoming too centralised and bureaucratic and that I was getting out of touch with the market and the essentials of our businesses.'

The group was marketing a range of packaged seafood items through some of the major retail chains in the UK and these were not doing well. 'I spent a whole Saturday wandering around super-markets in London, and came to the conclusion that the marketing consultants who had put us into this concept had sold us a lemon. We were selling low-value items at a high price, in fancy packaging, with no added value. We did not stack up against the competing products on the shelves.'

'To confirm my view,' he adds, 'I showed our products to my wife – actually I should have done that before we launched the product! – and she said, "I won't buy these. They aren't good value – it's just a gimmick!" On Monday morning, we closed down that range.'

RE-ORGANISING 1993-95

Azad's emphasis became focus: Inlaks should have a few significant businesses in each territory and run them well, be close to them and understand them, invest in them and develop them. Everything else had to go.

The pace of the divestment was stunning. In the space of eigh-teen months the group sold five major concerns. Other operations were closed.

On the other hand there were substantial acquisitions. As American oil service companies pulled out of Nigeria, Inlaks bought up their assets, hired their personnel and took over their contracts. Its aluminium company expanded its product base through substantial capital expenditure. A venture in Ghana was started, producing collapsible toothpaste tubes for Lever brothers. 'We bought businesses in our key area of focus.'

Again there was criticism. The group was less wide ranging, its traditional interests were being abandoned. But the critics tended to forget that while assets were being sold off, others were being bought; and the overall turnover was the same. Also the necessary changes had been carried out with great concern that employees should be given appropriate redundancy payments and assistance in finding new jobs or in starting up on their own.

The real point of conflict is between the old South Asian model, which says that membership of the family entitles you to a job for life irrespective of your performance and that selling a business is an anathema regardless of the company's profitability; and the model of a constantly modernising organisation, continually re-inventing itself in order to stay afloat in the rocky seas of the modern business world.

SURVIVAL IN THE SECOND GENERATION

Ask Azad what qualities are most needed to run a multimillion-dollar group with international interests and he replies that there is no set formula; what matters is having clear goals and the focus to achieve them. 'Some bosses out there are very hands on, others are strategists. Some are forceful, extrovert personalities; others are shy and inward looking – yet they get results. At the end of the day I think what matters is: does the business survive? Does it provide a creative work environment, is there room for renewal and creativity? However, survival is key, because without it all the other good things can't happen.'

A high proportion of family businesses, 70 per cent or more, die in the second generation. Inlaks' continuing survival is therefore a major achievement: 'You have to be results orientated,' says Azad. 'And what is important is self-honesty, the ability to look at disasters and mistakes head on and say, "What have I learned from that?" You have to suspend the very human instinct to make excuses. We'd all like to be perfect and successful all the time. We've been programmed in our culture to worship success. It's humiliating to admit failure.'

On the other hand he warns against excessive introspection. There's a difference between learning from mistakes and wallowing in guilty post mortems. 'You mustn't overdo it. Otherwise you miss out on the great gift of the failure, which is the fact that you can learn from it.'

THE BIG ISSUE

What makes a successful company is the ability to consolidate success without losing the entrepreneurial genius that first launched the business.

Azad reflects: 'What made the organisation great can, in a different environment, cause it to founder. How do you build an organisation that can be creative, can entertain new ideas, can take risks, can reinvent itself periodically as the need arises? And at the same time has enough discipline and structure to channel that creativity successfully to the marketplace so that the whole thing doesn't disintegrate into an anarchy of bright ideas?'

For Azad, this is one of the imponderables. 'My big issue over the past ten or fifteen years has been, how do you create that balance? How do you become professional but not too professional, corporate without being too corporate?'

INLAKS TODAY

Inlaks has been tempered in the fires of change. It has come through several major business cycles as a strong, honed and committed organisation.

The span of its activities is still intriguing, given that its chairman professes focus. The current portfolio ranges from aluminium rolling and processing, oilfield equipment leasing and information technology in West Africa, through tea plantations in India, to gas turbine repair in the United States using patented technology to service customers such as Delta Airlines and General Electric. And that touches on just some of the group's activities.

There are always projects on the boil. Inlaks has just taken over the majority shareholding and management of Sonu Shivdasani's tourist air transfer company in the Maldives – Sonu being Azad's brother. The American concern is expanding its aerospace business through a vigorous acquisition strategy, the textile plant in Bangalore is doubling its capacity with machinery imported from Switzerland, a computer software company has just opened in Ghana, starting an oilfield services operation in Angola is being looked at. And so it goes on.

When confronted with all this, Azad exclaims: 'Where is the focus? Despite all my emphasis on focus, we are still mind-bogglingly diverse. Actually, it's not that bad, as we now have good businesses that make sense for where they are, run by good management. It's more the case that we are now a series of separate companies, each with a fair amount of autonomy with clear, focused management.

'To tell the truth, we never seem to have too much cash. Maybe because we keep on investing whatever we've got. Remember what it was like when we were children? Our pocket money was never quite enough!'

While Inlaks is not one of the biggest companies to come out of the Indian diaspora, it is certainly one of the most interesting and worth watching.

Kumar Datwani

'The best is yet to be! Today there are more opportunities for entrepreneurs than ever before.'

Kumar Datwani had worked late into the previous night. Still in dressing-gown and slippers, he made coffee before our interview in the kitchen of his spacious Lowndes Square flat, neighboured by embassies and overlooking the garden of the square. The flat is an attractive mixture of Indian and Western décor, with plentiful evidence of an enthusiastic love of art. It symbolises several aspects of Kumar's commitment to Britain. One is its location, a discreet reminder of the immense financial success of his family business, SKD Pacific. Another is the fact that he maintains a residence in the UK at all. Though he is away from London for a large part of the year, the flat has the atmosphere of a family home. Two of his children have been educated in Britain.

Kumar – an Indian businessman who at present is based in Hong Kong – represents both the past (in his strong entrepreneurial values) and the future (in his willingness to adapt the traditional family business structure to a new, global era). He is a good example of the effects of the Indian diaspora and the increasingly global thinking that successful South Asians are developing. He set up business in London, Paris and New York; then realised that New York was by far the most profitable, so made the New York office his major centre. He later set up his manufacturing plant in India; then realised that he could get better financial servicing from Hong Kong and moved there. He is a 'diaspora man', following the flow of business wherever it leads. Now he has come full circle, having decided to return to Britain in 1998.

It's not only his decision to return to the UK that justifies his inclusion in this book, however. Kumar Datwani has been investing in the British economy over the years in a number of ways. He also represents the future, both as a Hong Kong South Asian and as an international entrepreneur whose business, like an increasing number of UK businesses, can no longer be compartmentalised within national boundaries.

Men like Kumar Datwani are a stake in the future, the first wave of a type of entrepreneurial business person that we shall see increasingly as the map of the world economy alters in the coming decades.

Kumar first moved to the UK in 1978, fulfilling an ambition he had had from the early 1970s when clothing from India became extremely popular in Britain. By 1978 the trade had risen to dizzying heights. Kumar's new business imported goods from India and before long from Hong Kong as well. Though stretching over several continents, it was very much a family business, and after a few years the company had bought out its Hong Kong agents in order to keep control of that part of the business. Kumar moved to Hong Kong to take over the supply office there and became interested in the property market, which was to become the family's second major area of operation.

He was already a global businessman. He had set up the UK office from France, where he lived for four years; before that, he had spent seven years in the United States, working in New York for the family business. His experiences in different countries are a useful example of the various situations in which an entrepreneur might find himself. Throughout this book, one of the common factors in entrepreneurial success stories has been hard work, unsocial hours and a single-minded willingness to adapt – to establish oneself in a foreign country as thoroughly as possible, to acquire language fluency and skills as good as possible, even though the costs in terms of deferred satisfaction and 'normal life' have been horrendous.

The toughest country Kumar lived in, he considers, was France, and the greatest problem there was the language. Without a good grasp of a language it's impossible to do business in it. He studied at night school until he had mastered French. At the same time he began to set up business.

At that time, French bureaucracy was a nightmare. Freshly arrived from the entrepreneurial United States Kumar struggled with mountains of paperwork and obstructive officialdom. 'You couldn't register a company if you didn't have an office, and you couldn't get an office if you didn't have a company – it was a Catch 22. For six months I had to sit in Paris twiddling my thumbs.'

In Hong Kong things were easier. The company began to do very well from 1981 onwards, and Kumar turned his attention back to the US market, with its potential 250 million customers. Today he is interested in Europe again, attracted by the strength of the EU economy and the opportunities it offers. And of all the EU countries, he is most interested in the UK: 'the economy speaks for itself at the moment'.

RETURN TO BRITAIN

The decision to return to the UK involved entering a new line of business: property development. His decision to go into property was, again, entrepreneurial. In Hong Kong he had been increasingly involved in the property business, with a wealth of experience going back to 1978. He has always had confidence in Hong Kong, 'especially during the big property crash of 1984'. Many in the foreign business community watched the historic visit by Margaret Thatcher to sign the handover treaty and believed that Hong Kong was finished. There would be no revival, they were sure. 'But on the contrary; the biggest boom in the property business took place after the 1984 crash, and continued right through to the present boom.'

Kumar was able to profit from the boom because he had seen it coming. Foreign investors left it too late; the local Chinese read the signs better and made a big killing. Having been in Hong Kong for fifteen years, SKD Pacific had many local contacts who told them of imminent foreclosures, and gradually the property side of the business expanded during 1984–89. At that point the company launched into the European property market. All the time the mainstream business, garment manufacture, was continuing. The two divisions of the business were organisationally separate, but developed into an effective structure – the garment trade provided cash flow and the cash flow was directed into property.

His decision to invest in the British property market, and his preference for the residential sector over the commercial, are characteristic of Kumar's approach. When choosing a new area of business to develop he looks for one in which he has established a core competence, rather than one with which, although it may have a proven business plan, he is not familiar. 'I would rather do things I've already tried, and improve on them.' He puts his success largely down to this.

FAMILY BUSINESS

Kumar has escaped some of the classic problems that many South Asian businesses struggle with. For example, he finds few problems with involving outside professionals in the family business and attributes much of the company's success to them – though he insists that guidelines have to be established from the outset and must be thoroughly worked out.

His attitude to the succession problem that so many South Asians face is also flexible. His partners and colleagues know that it is not a foregone conclusion that his children will even work in the same business. He has set up a structure within his own family whereby his children will have the resources to start up in business on their own account in a field of their choosing. This is good for them, as it's the best way of learning; and his present employees don't feel threatened. Senior employees know that they will not be sidelined in favour of inexperienced family members, as has happened in many South Asian companies, sometimes with unhappy results for motivation and morale.

There are many examples of successful entrepreneurs who have begun their careers in this way, with seed capital from their fathers. It largely explains why so many South Asian entrepreneurs have achieved great prosperity at a very young age. The combination of the entrepreneurial heritage and example, and the finance to turn it into a thriving business, has enabled many to skip the further education process and go straight into business.

Kumar's workforce is several steps removed from that close-knit entrepreneurial succession pattern. 'I want the people who are working for me to feel that they themselves run that part of the business. My children aren't going to take over their jobs. And that is important, because in business you have to do two things. One, you have to retain the professional people in your company; and two, you have to diversify and let your company grow.'

As a result, his staff are committed to building on the success the company has already achieved and to taking it even further.

A Time for Entrepreneurs

Kumar Datwani found the Conservative years an excellent climate for entrepreneurism, but believes that New Labour inherited a solid economy and that Britain will continue to be a highly favourable environment for entrepreneurs. 'I feel that today there are more opportunities for entrepreneurs than ever before,' he says. 'The UK economy looks the best out of all the countries in the EU at the moment, and the next two or three years look very good for Britain. I've been aware of the indicators for several years. The signs were there in 1996: consumers spending more, the residential property market definitely turning. It had fully bottomed out, and now there's an upward movement.'

In Kumar's opinion there has been a new mood in Britain since the Thatcher years. People are much more entrepreneurial than before. He believes this mood will continue. 'In that respect the UK has acquired an American way of thinking. In America, opportunities come on a daily basis, and there's no end to them.'

He admires Kenneth Clarke, whom he regards as 'one of the finest Chancellors we've had'. He's a bit more cautious about Gordon Brown. Shortly before the 1997 General Election, he described New Labour as something of an unknown quantity but remained optimistic that a Labour victory would not change the commitment of South Asians to Britain; after all, there has been a long association between UK South Asians and the Labour Party. Perhaps there would be a slowdown in investment of future profits – 'people may not invest in the same manner that they've been doing under a Conservative government'. But certainly he didn't anticipate any significant reduction of international investment in Britain. After all, he was at that point planning to bring major inward investment into the UK in 1998. And though the pace of change has taken many by surprise, Kumar's broad analysis of predicted future trends still looks good.

STRENGTHS AND WEAKNESSES

South Asian businesses have usually started with limited capital, but their family manpower has been a valuable compensation. But that is a negative benefit, making the best of things because no other option exists. Over the years, Asian businesses have made a virtue out of necessity. They have created additional strengths out of the need to survive in a difficult environment. This is a remarkable achievement.

If there is a weakness, Kumar says, it is that too many Asian family businesses do not avail themselves of professional manpower and professional help. This is the biggest limit to growth and it condemns you to a self-imposed ceiling. If you want your business to grow to the highest levels, eventually you have to have professionals running it. Once established, it has to be taken to the next level and the professionals must come in, whether those professionals are from outside the family or members of the family who have been professionally trained. You must, after a certain point, be able to handle a boardroom or a bank manager, and you have to have familiarity with the legal side of the business.

Kumar believes that this actually places a higher responsibility on the family management than would be the case if they were let off the hook while the professionals managed.

'Take expertise. If you're in technology, you have to buy in skills and expertise. But then you have to understand those skills and share that expertise yourself, because if you are dealing with professionals you have to talk at their level. Otherwise you will be taken for a ride.'

Fund manager Jayesh Manek (p. 155) has suggested that some of the problems currently faced by Asian small businesses might have been avoided by converting the high cash valuations of their businesses at their peak into stock of some sort. Kumar agrees. Essentially, such businesses would have been converting their invisible goodwill into an asset on the balance sheet, and that would have protected their business values and interests. This was advice that would have been routine for most financial advisers, though an unfamiliar idea to many South Asian businessmen, who prefer to consult within the family. 'Only a minority have the far-sightedness to upgrade their business to include professional advice from outsiders. The majority generally don't, mainly because it's a private company and they don't want a third party looking in. Secrecy has been an invisible limit to the growth of many businesses.'

HONG KONG AND GLOBAL INTERESTS

Kumar's view on the future of Hong Kong is entirely optimistic – 'The best is yet to come!' His main business there, SKD Pacific, continues and the sixty Hong Kong employees remain.

SKD Pacific employs around 1,400 staff worldwide. Over 1,000 are based in Sri Lanka, 3–400 in Bangladesh and around 50 in New York and London. He foresees a huge expansion of the Pacific Rim in the next millennium; this is a bubble that won't burst. He looks for growth to Indonesia and Malaysia, and sees a great deal of growth potential for Vietnam once it has secured Most Favoured Nation status from the United States. Much of the growth in these countries, he believes, will be in infrastructure industries such as roads, tunnelling, airports and power generation.

For himself he remains true to his personal philosophy of entrepreneurial success: 'You have to have patience and go on working at it; you only fail the day you give up. So you never give up! Of course luck does count too. Just this afternoon I took a taxi and the driver said: 'It's funny, this trade; you never know who'll stop you. One day ten people hire you, and other days you don't get two.' So I would say luck does count. It's like being in the right place at the right time. But – if you keep working hard, it's often possible to make the right place happen at the right time. As long as you are focused, as long as you keep on working hard, the situation is bound to change or turn to your favour at some point.'

Bharat Desai

'Since day one, I've worked hard to keep the entrepreneurial culture alive so that our people out-think, out-perform, and out-service companies ten times our size. I want every one of our employees to think and act like an owner, because I believe that's when our customers get the best from all of us.'

You're the CEO of a public company, highly successful in its field, but the market has some doubts about your company's long-term future. Five years ago you invested heavily in new computer technology but you don't need consultants to tell you it's already beginning to be out of date. The software you commissioned at that time does what it's supposed to do, but it's not flexible enough to keep you at the cutting edge. Your internal IT department just doesn't have the expertise or the manpower to do anything more than maintain the existing system; and you can't afford the downtime, or the capital expense, to put new systems in place. And if you could, what's going to happen in another four or five years' time, when your systems are obsolete again and your competitors who bought later than you did are benefiting from their more up-to-date equipment? Where do you go for help?

You could do worse than knock on Bharat Desai's door.

THE SHRINKING VILLAGE

As we approach the millennium, planet Earth is shrinking fast. Journeys become shorter, networks become larger, television makes neighbours of us all and the Internet gives us access to most of the world for the price of a local telephone call.

Even young industries like computing and telecommunications have changed beyond recognition. The computer industry is still one in which entrepreneurs can make vast fortunes and be young enough to spend them, but companies such as Bharat Desai's Syntel owe their massive success to more than microchips.

What is sometimes called the 'third industrial revolution' is a marriage of affordable computer technology and global telecommunications. Only a few years ago businesses sent their data to be processed by computer bureaux, where white-coated technicians fed punched cards into machines the size of small houses, like priests of some obscure mystery religion waiting on a mysterious and unpredictable god. Today, PCs sit on most executive desks, laptop computers and mobile phones are common sights on commuter trains, and your child's Nintendo or Sega console has more computing power than some mainframe computers possessed not so very long ago. The PC you buy today will be out of date in about eighteen months' time, and computers with twice the power will be available for half the price. But the greatest change has been brought about through the interface between computers and telecommunications, which has made possible data links, e-mail and, largest and most celebrated of all, the Internet. 'Cyberspace', a term derived from science fiction, describes the new 'virtual' landscape of much modern business.

Cottage industry and home office (SOHO) offer new ways of working. Research and publishing will soon be transformed by the Internet, and it is predicted that banking, various advisory services, software marketing and even music purchasing will all be very different once access to the Net speeds up and governments put their countries on-line. Most significant, in business terms, is the rise of such developments as the 'Bangalore phenomenon', in which a gifted generation of Indian computer experts services clients all over the world through the new infrastructures of communications satellites and related technologies. A company in Brazil can have its computing handled in India by people who need never visit the client's site.

Bharat Desai – who chose not to locate in Bangalore, but decoded to open Syntel's first Indian offices and facilities in Mumbai (Bombay) because of its superior infrastructure and resources – aims to equip businesses to negotiate this explosion of technology.

Why Britain?

Bharat's company Syntel, which has sales of $100 million per annum, is based in Troy, Michigan, from where it markets system integration and application outsourcing to clients across the world.[1] His concept of 'intellisourcing' solves the problem most companies have of deciding how far to buy into a rapidly developing technology. He offers clients the pick of global computing talent delivered to the client using on-site, off-site and off-shore teams. Even if your office is in Iceland, Syntel can be your computer partner. Where it is necessary to install a project team on site for a client, that team works with Syntel's Global Development Centres in the United States and India to bring the best talent together by means of high-speed data and voice communication links.[2]

So what was Bharat Desai, Syntel's President and CEO, doing in London in the spring of 1997 with an open chequebook, looking to hire staff and buy office accommodation for a UK operation? Why didn't he do the whole thing by telephone from the United States? Having established a truly entrepreneurial empire in Troy that could reach and service every part of the globe, why put down roots in England? Why not do as they do in Bangalore and run it all from their desks at home?

'I'm hoping to tap into the multicultural talent that's available in the UK and to deploy it throughout Europe,' Bharat explains.

'And it's very important for us to be close to our markets. We need two kinds of proximity. A proximity of interface, which we have through our technological links. But also we need a proximity of communicating with our clients and understanding their business needs.' That, he believes, is the first and vital step. Afterwards the details can be worked out in whatever location the competence to do so exists. But first comes that initial interface with the client, the 'management engagement model'.

Bharat intends his company to become a 'virtual organisation' whose structure is in cyberspace and into which clients hook by means of telecommunications. Paradoxically, developing a virtual organisation means that a great many local cultural barriers have to be grappled with. To serve the organisation that will transcend boundaries, Syntel needs people who understand those barriers and how best to bridge them. The management engagement has to take place at local level if it is adequately to address the nature of the client's needs and the kind of delivery that will be of maximum help to that organisation.

Bharat Desai had come to London to set up a local base for his virtual organisation.

Syntel: an Entrepreneurial Empire

Travel and a global perspective are second nature to Bharat. His father was an accountant in East Africa. When Bharat was eleven years old, his father put the family on a ship bound for Ahmedabad in India. Bharat later graduated from the Indian Institute of Technology in Bombay. Already familiar with two continents, he settled in a third when his employer, Tata Consultancy Services, sent him to Detroit to work on a project for Burroughs. One of his tasks was the design of banking software.

He was one of the first Indian software engineers to go to the United States. Immediately attracted by the country, he liked the open highways and the entrepreneurial climate. He decided that this was a country of boundless opportunities for anybody willing to work hard. In 1978 he left Tata and studied in the evenings to gain an

MBA from the University of Michigan. He paid his bills by working in the daytime as a systems analyst.

In 1980, while still studying, he and his computer engineer wife Neerja – a colleague at Tata who was studying at night for her Master's degree in Computer Science – set up Syntel. For a student operation it didn't do badly; some work came its way and sales for the first year were $30,000. But Bharat now had a dream, of a global network that would link factories and software experts. 'The velocity of technological change has gotten to a point where most organisations not primarily dealing with technology find it almost impossible to keep up. They're asking, "Are we in the food business, the retail business, the finance business ... or are we in the technology business?" Increasingly they're deciding, "We are going to concentrate on our core competence, and find some information technology partner to help with the technology and, most important of all, help us to implement a technology strategy."'

The idea of a global solution did not take shape immediately. By 1988 the vision was well defined: General Motors had become the company's first major client in 1982 and Blue Cross/Blue Shield of Michigan had followed; in 1984 annual sales reached $1 million. But the company was still too small, turning over around $7 million. There were other problems, too; a company such as the one Bharat and Neerja had in mind needed a whole infrastructure to support it. Before this further stepping-stone could be achieved, the company had to position itself in an industry where other companies were moving in conflicting directions.

Defining the vision and setting up the brand was the easy part. The challenge now was making it happen, creating an enabling organisational infrastructure of people and processes and placement – all needing to be constantly modified, refined and re-thought as new technologies appeared and competitors entered the market.

Until the late 1980s, Syntel could be described as a classic entrepreneurial venture, as typical of South Asian flair as all the other entrepreneurial ventures that I mention in this book. Some key features were:

❏ **Substantial return on capital.** Bharat's starting capital was $2,000. By October 1997 the market capitalisation of the company had reached $375 million.

❏ **Hard work.** Like Gulam Noon's accountancy lessons and Judge Mota Singh's legal studies (p. 130), Bharat's studies in the United States were undertaken outside working hours in addition to a normal working day. In Bharat's case, he studied at college in the evenings.

❏ **Aggressive marketing of the product/service.** It took five years of constant telephoning before Chrysler Corporation decided to become a client.

❏ **Initiative in approaching obstacles.** At school in Mombasa, where there was considerable social and racial discrimination between African, European and Asian schools, he organised a cricket match between his school and the local European school (a piece of entrepreneurial bridge-building I can personally vouch for; I attended the same school as Bharat – our school scored a stunning victory, I might add).

❏ **A creative attitude to disappointment.** 'When you're faced with adversity there are two possible reactions. You can look for people to carry you because adversity has weakened you. Or you can actually draw a lot of motivation out of adversity – a very South Asian trait.' A major tenet of Bharat's entrepreneurial creed is to look at the advantages in a situation rather than the disadvantages.

'I'll give you an example. I was probably the first person of Indian origin to get into the American software service industry. I think most people thought I was cheeky even to try: I should have been an ordinary programmer, or gone off to work somewhere else. I don't think it's a national prejudice, America's very open to all cultures. But there are biases in some people's minds who can't step outside their accustomed paradigm. I'd ring up and say, "This is Bharat Desai. Ringing from Syntel." They'd say, "This is *who?*" There I was, out to make a sales pitch, and I was stuck on my opening line. For the first month or so it was incredibly aggravating because I never got farther than that. But after a while I decided to turn it into an advantage. I started to ring companies and just leave my name. As I told them what my name was, I said to myself, "You'll remember me when I call again. Because nobody else has got a name like mine!"'

❑ **Quality**. The struggle to be remembered, to persuade the right people to pick up their telephones and answer his calls, was only part of the battle. Once gained, business had to be secured. 'I decided that if I ever landed a customer I was going to make sure we serviced them so well they never needed to go elsewhere. I created a culture for the organisation that I called "customer focused". In the same way, we aimed for strong delivery. If we promised to deliver something, we made sure we delivered more and better than we promised. It was an attitude that got us through those early, difficult days; another example of creating positive advantage out of a hopeless situation.'

There were times when the outlook seemed hopeless. In the first five years business was often difficult. Though sales were rising, cash flow was a constant problem. 'We never went out for funds or established any major lines of credit,' says Bharat, who believes that was one source of the company's strength.

The fact that the company was headed by two immigrants made matters even tougher. Persuading the large automobile companies like Ford and Chrysler was Bharat's greatest challenge and his most daunting task. Looking back, he is tolerant of those who rejected him then. 'It's understandable that people may want to do business with someone with whom they went to school, rather than someone whose name they cannot pronounce.'

One executive of a large company told him: 'Listen – I don't want you or your salespeople to ever set foot in this company again.' The executive later resigned. The company is now Syntel's second biggest customer.

SYNTEL GOES GLOBAL

The early, classically entrepreneurial phase of Syntel's success lasted until the early 1990s. There were two reasons for the massive leap in the company's revenues in the early 1990s. First, the professional services industry only then began to grow. Secondly, Syntel itself at that time expanded nationally and globally, placing itself in the optimum position to take advantage of the potential of the new worldwide technology.

Growth came as the United States slowly emerged from recession. 'Downsizing' was the buzzword of the dawning of the new decade, and it was clear that employment was not going to return to previous levels. The recession, in fact, had actually helped to force a process of change that was already happening but now occurred much more rapidly. *Time* magazine saw the way things were going:

> As the U.S. shifts from manufacturing to service industries and the so-called knowledge economy, locations near waterways, railheads and raw materials – traditional spots for great cities – have become less important. Computers, fax machines and improved telecommunications have enabled large corporations to shift back-office operations out of expensive downtowns and into small towns and suburbs ... [quoting David Heenan's *The New Corporate Frontier*] 'Downsizing led to outsourcing of suppliers, and has now led to a movement to ship out the whole company. After all, with new technologies, you can run even a global business out of a small town.' He's right. Just ask IBM (Armonk, N.Y.) or General Electric (Fairfield, Conn.).[3]

By 1993 *Time* was reporting continued downsizing, crippling loan conditions for business start-ups – and a rapid rise in outsourcing and consultancies. 'Even as IBM executes plans to lay off 25,000 employees in 1993, it maintains contracts with 300 outside firms to handle tasks ranging from running the computer giant's payrolls to designing software programs.' The magazine had a word of warning for the President: 'If Bill Clinton hopes to solve all these problems in the long run, he will have to deliver on promises to improve the education and skills of the work force and the strength of the nation's infrastructure. Only that will restore U.S. competitiveness and create new jobs in a global setting in which people and their skills are the resources that really count.'[4]

The new employment situation forced Syntel's hand. By 1987 Bharat was finding it difficult to compete for the few good, trained computer professionals. As *Time* pointed out, training had been neglected. Advertising, headhunting and other conventional methods were of very limited use. The whole industry was facing a major shortage of competent professionals.

In 1988 Bharat decided to look outside the United States to the fast-developing computer industries of Europe and Asia. He began bringing staff in from abroad on temporary visas: mostly they came from India, but there were also Chinese, Britons, Australians and New Zealanders. By 1995, around 800 of Syntel's 1,200 US employees were immigrants. Armed with new staff resources, the company rapidly acquired new clients. The American Insurance Group, which has been with them since 1990, was typical: '[AIG] did not want to spend its time doing system development or programming, so it decided to go to a company specializing in these fields to get such work done.'[5]

GROWTH GOES ON

Bharat is still an entrepreneur, though he now heads a global company from a gleaming edifice in Troy, where his roots are. His company has grown phenomenally. In 1994, revenues had risen to $67 million; by 1995 they had increased by almost a third to $90 million. Clients included Ford, Chrysler, K-Mart and state and local government, the company had 1,500 employees and offices in Michigan, California, Illinois, North Carolina and New Jersey – and an office had been opened in Bombay. In New Mexico, Bharat won a $25 million contract, against strong competition, to renovate the state's revenue-collection systems. In 1996 the company received the Q1 Preferred Quality First award from the Ford Motor Company, and Bharat Desai received the 1996 Michigan Entrepreneur of the Year award.

His entrepreneurism shows in the niche opportunities he sees and exploits, like the Method2000 solution he launched in 1996 to help companies prepare for the widely publicised problems that much commercial software will cause in the year 2000. But it shows also (and even more clearly) in his attitude to Syntel itself.

COMING TO BRITAIN

Bharat is choosing his British staff carefully. 'I look for people who are risk takers. Ours is a company culture that encourages risk-taking, it allows for mistakes – and you will make a lot of mistakes. We believe in allowing our people the freedom to fail … And though you do need processes to manage an enterprise, I am very conscious of the necessity of keeping the right blend of loose structure and very guided process. Entrepreneurs aren't very structured! So one has to get the balance right.'

The first UK appointment was Ricky Shankar, who had previously run Syntel's Mid-West region from Chicago. As somebody who knew the Syntel model intimately at all levels and could present it, he was given the job of opening the company's new London premises in Piccadilly. One further appointment from the United States joined him later. His strategy was then to hire staff from among UK computer professionals, the first wave being 'engagement' staff to manage customer relationships once the first contracts had been signed. They would serve as interfaces with the delivery organisation and the customers' user organisations.

Bharat and Neerja are in an unusual situation as regards family background. Unlike Shami Ahmed, for example (p. 145), who took over his father's business as a going concern and whose large family all had a shared financial interest in the company, Bharat Desai and

Neerja Sethi started up Syntel on their own. They have two children, both born in the United States. Bharat's mother and Neerja's parents are regular visitors from India, and the family frequently goes back to the subcontinent. 'I keep in touch with my extended family in Gujarat, of course. And I have some very close friends in India – people I went to high school and college with during those very precious, special years of one's life. I try to keep in touch with them.'

But there is no extended family in the United States with expectations of being given jobs as of right and financially supported. In fact, it is the other way round. 'I take it to an extreme,' Bharat acknowledges. 'I don't appoint any of my relatives. In fact some members of my family applied to work in Syntel and concealed the fact that they were related to me, because it gave them a better chance of getting in! My sister, for example, came to the United States and got a Master's degree in business and computer auditing from Illinois. I went out of my way *not* to give her a job. I didn't want to give the impression that this was a company that relatives could get into easily.'

Quality of staff is supremely important, in Bharat's view. You have to keep ahead. If Syntel comes up with an innovative and effective software solution, this is sure to be scrutinised by the company's competitors as soon as it gets on to the market. By mimicking the best points of the product and integrating them into their own new releases, competitors can leap-frog into the lead – a process in which Syntel is also actively involved! So attributes like staff quality become crucially important in keeping market position.

On 12 August 1997, Syntel launched an initial public offering to sell three million shares of common stock in the company. Apart from the obvious advantages, Bharat sees it as an opportunity to build up the sustainable advantage of having highly motivated, highly qualified staff. 'I want every single Syntel employee, at whatever level, to have an opportunity to buy stock in the company. So they'll be coming to work in a company that they own. And my job will be to train them to think like owners.'

6

Against the Odds:
Berjis Daver

'Bookmakers have always been entrepreneurs on-course. They determined the prices, they were betting with their own money, their own opinions, their own knowledge. They put their money where their mouth was; and if they got it wrong, the only way to get it back was to keep betting and have confidence in their judgement.'

You don't have to read this book to discover that there are a great many South Asians in the professions. You will not travel far in the business world without meeting key people whose origins are in the subcontinent. And anyone who cares to turn on the television can watch South Asians delivering news reports, acting in soap operas, or starring in major feature films. Have your appendix out or your teeth looked at and the face behind the surgical mask might very well be South Asian; attend a parents' evening at the local school and, in many parts of Britain, you'll almost certainly see a strong South Asian representation among the pupils. These are commonplaces in British society today.

It may have come as a bit of a shock, on the other hand, to open a copy of *Sporting Life* and find that the hotly tipped favourite for

Chief Executive of the National Association of Bookmakers was a South Asian.

Berjis Jal Daver denied the report the next day, but the idea was not a bizarre one. Mr Daver held the key position in British gambling. He was, until he retired in June 1997, Chairman of Ladbroke Racing Europe, the company that boasts it will take a bet on almost anything. Under him, Ladbrokes has been established as the world leader in betting, with a turnover of around £1.5 billion from 1,900 high street outlets; 12,500 staff in total are employed to run the shops and telephone betting service. Market share in the UK is 25 per cent and profit increases are well ahead of inflation, not to mention those of competitors.

Origins of an Entrepreneur

Gambling is not a business in which Asians are often seen, let alone one in which they dominate. Berjis Daver is one of very few in the industry.

Like the Tatas and the Godrejs, he is from the Parsi community and his family originally came from Bombay (Mumbai). The Parsis follow the teachings of Zoroaster, a great Persian prophet. Islamic persecution from the eighth century onwards led to most Parsis leaving Iran and settling in India and beyond. Today, small groups of Parsis live in the western Iranian desert, in and around Mumbai, in East Africa and in many major cities of the world:

> They are renowned for their intelligence, integrity, industriousness, and philanthropy, and their contributions to commerce, industry, education and social work.[1]

In 1980 there were around 120,000 Parsis worldwide. There is a small Parsi population in Britain (the first Asian MP was a Parsi). The numbers are not likely to expand greatly, as Parsiism is a non-proselytising religion. It teaches that everybody ought to follow the faith into which they were born.

Berjis's family came to Britain in 1954. They had been living in Karachi, separated from the rest of the family by the Partition of India in 1947. It was easier to go to the UK than to get back to Mumbai. 'My late mother had always had a dream of Europe, probably fostered through the days of the Raj. She came to England on her own, an unaccompanied woman wearing a sari. She reconnoitred the situation, and cabled for her three children to join her. I was fourteen. Dad was going to stay in Karachi and work and send money and we would have a wonderful British education. My story says something about what women were like in those days. Mum came from a little mountain village at the base of the Himalayas and she actually had the courage to come here on her own with three teenagers – a journey many would not contemplate, let alone achieve.'

But finances were suddenly frozen at home and the family's situation changed drastically. The plans for an expensive school and a middle-class home had to be dropped. The problems of those early days meant that the family never integrated fully into the London Asian community; the struggle to survive meant there was little time for community events or even socialising.

The family, with typical Asian determination and inspired by Berjis's remarkable mother, clawed its way back to a good standard of living. Much was expected of Berjis. 'It's typically Parsi, probably typically Asian – if you haven't got two degrees, you're a failure!' His sister and her husband had both studied psychology at Birkbeck College, London. Berjis thought it sounded interesting and followed in their footsteps, though he didn't want to enter the profession after graduating. Indeed, he wasn't very interested in the usual South Asian career path at all. Long years of training for a profession with low pay didn't seem an attractive option.

It was 1960. Betting shops were being legalised. A company called City Tote in Avery Row, off Bond Street in the heart of London, had a chain of nine shops. Berjis had always been interested in racing – 'Don't ask me why, there are no family connections with racing at all; but I used to go to the races.' He went to see the general manager at the City Tote shop in Westbourne Grove.

'I've been to college,' he said. 'Have you got any jobs?'

The manager was extremely suspicious. Betting shops didn't see many job applicants fresh from college.

'What are you really after?'

'A job,' said Berjis.

There was a short and heated discussion, as the manager tried to find out what ulterior motive was driving this persistent young man.

'Well,' demanded Berjis finally, 'are you going to give me a chance or not?'

The manager decided. 'You can have a day's trial.'

At closing time Berjis was put on the payroll.

The newly appointed psychology student was put to work in the shop chalking up race results on a blackboard. It was a business in which most people had to handle most duties at some time. He learned how to settle the books at the end of the day, how to work the cashier's desk and much more. It was a useful apprenticeship.

In 1962 he took a break from betting shops, returning in 1970. At that time Ladbrokes was creating a new management structure, under which Berjis was made a shop manager. It was a visionary scheme that was initially more in the minds of the directors than the staff; at the beginning the job involved little more than looking after the shop. 'The scheme wasn't really in place,' says Berjis. 'But it grew very fast. And I grew with it.'

However, although most successful South Asian entrepreneurism succeeds largely because of the Asian cultural background, Berjis was swimming against his community's cultural tide. Most UK Asian culture is opposed to gambling. Asians – a major group in personal savings statistics – have a strong concept of stewardship of money. As Berjis points out, their commitment to educating themselves, getting steady work, saving and being respectable citizens makes it unlikely that you'll find Asians as large bettors in betting shops. Neither will you find many betting shops in areas with large Asian populations (apart from some in areas where the Asian population growth has been relatively recent). Betting shop proprietors don't regard such sites as desirable; they prefer areas with Italian or Chinese populations – both nationalities are keen gamblers. Another cultural factor is the reluctance of Asian women to enter betting shops; quite a few nevertheless bet by telephone, some heavily. What puts them off going into betting shops is the predominantly male environment, although recently more women have been using betting shops because they can bet on the results of foreign lotteries and play the betting shops' own numbers game, a recent and popular innovation.

There is also a spiritual reason for Asians to be the minority ethnic community least represented in gambling circles. Islam forbids betting, so the whole Moslem community is excluded (though some individuals like the Aga Khan and some Lottery winners have contravened this ban). For Hindus and Sikhs gambling is also taboo. So there is a large ethnic community opposed to gambling. Beside the religious dimension is the ethical: one is supposed to earn one's living, so gambling is usually disapproved of. Even in today's Asian society, upbringing and national and religious affiliations have meant for many young Asians that horse racing and other gambling opportunities just do not exist in their lives.

In the subcontinent, it's a different culture. Gambling occupies the aristocracy. Places like Bombay (Mumbai), Bangalore, Calcutta and Madras and the Indian Derby have attracted major names in international racing. But there is a 30 per cent betting duty, which keeps most of the population away from betting, though as a tax it's a very well-administered one. The strange anomaly of the different betting habits of Asians in India and in Britain is probably explained by the fact that British Indians tend to be middle class. In Britain it's the poorer social groups who are attracted to betting shops, or the wealthy who buy into the whole culture of racing – a culture which in Britain is very colourful (there are two racing newspapers) and very well informed.

RISING THROUGH THE RANKS

The last bastion of British formality to fall – if it ever does – may well be Royal Ascot. Working at the heart of the class-conscious, supremely English institution of racing betting, rising through the Ladbroke ranks, Berjis had plenty of opportunity to use his native entrepreneurial skills. 'Every manager was responsible for training. Today we talk about "life-long training" as if it's some new thing, but we've had it in Ladbroke from the beginning. We used to go off and set up shops. I'd train the staff. Then it was on to the next one. Everybody was part of a very dynamic, growing young business, and that's how it grew. And I grew with it. I wanted to do development work; I had a spell as Area Development Manager. We set up a National Audit Centre, and I was made its manager. So it progressed.'

Unlike many South Asians working outside their ethnic culture, Berjis was never aware of a 'glass ceiling' as he progressed up the company establishment. The somewhat autocratic Chairman, Cyril Stein, was an entrepreneur of the old school. An Armenian Jew, he had suffered discrimination and bigotry himself. Today Ladbroke is still a company with virtually no Asians. The only raised eyebrows Berjis encounters, however, are those of other Asians. 'I'm probably considered the black sheep of the family! They don't really like it. People cover up their surprise by being wonderfully amazed – "What a novelty! An Asian in professional gambling!" Then they usually ask me if I've got a hot tip… But it would be much more acceptable to them if I were importing rice.'

In his daily work Berjis has experienced very little discrimination, even when working away from the office. There were isolated incidents, such as when he had to go to Scotland as part of a team negotiating with strikers – an unpleasant experience, 'very racist indeed'. But in general there has been little resentment.

Stein's chairmanship created a company atmosphere not unlike that of an Indian extended family environment. He ruled with an iron hand and wasn't slow to bellow at his employees. 'Eventually he wouldn't bow even to the City. He became the sacrificial goat and left the company a few years ago.' Stein's management philosophy was a seedbed for entrepreneurs. 'He was very clear in his objectives. What more do you need to run a company? Get some good people; once you know what you want out of them, let them loose to develop their initiative. And that's what he did.'

One skill Berjis brought to Ladbrokes was an interest in management, the result of his level of education and knowledge of psychology. It gave him an edge over the shop managers, for Ladbrokes needed to change from the old ways when senior staff rushed from shop to shop with large quantities of money running the business out of petty cash. In its way that was very entrepreneurial too, and it's surprising that it worked so well for as long as it did. But Ladbroke, like many entrepreneurial companies mentioned in this book, reached a point where professionalising was unavoidable. In the early days, if a shop had a good trading period, the manager would be instructed to pay a generous staff bonus straight from the till. But now the tax authorities wanted better organisation. 'But you see, betting shops were still new. We were leading the charge; we were inventing the business day by day.'

Helping a Damaged Generation

In 1985 Berjis was appointed Managing Director of Ladbroke Racing, a position he held until 1995. The training methods of Ladbroke were well known and admired. In 1991 he was invited to join the Board of the newly established North West London Training and Enterprise Council. He agreed. It was the Ladbroke way. If there was a challenge you went for it. It was the beginning of a relationship that has continued until today: Berjis is still a Director of North West London TEC and has been Chair since March 1996; he is on the Board of London First; and he is a Board member of the London TEC Council.

The North West TEC has a large take-up both in Harrow (with around 40 per cent ethnic minorities) and Brent (54 per cent). He sees the role of the TECs as proactive, seeking out people and matching their skills to jobs. 'A lot of British companies are very stuffy. I've even felt obliged to dress up for evening committee meetings at which I was a volunteer, doing it in my spare time. A lot of that has to be broken down. On the other hand, there is quite a reserve in Asian businesses – I'd like to see more of them employing non-Asians. It's absolutely right that so much is being done for ethnic minorities – but I think there's got to be reciprocity.' You can't, he says, just build a little Asian or Caribbean enclave. There are still too many cultural barriers, and Asians are sometimes guilty of some of the things they criticise when they experience them from other people.

He would like to see Asian family businesses more open to outside expertise, for he feels that the family is not necessarily the best tool of management. But he also considers that the City is too often wedded to short-termism, rewarding management for simply achieving staff reductions without any strategy for the human resource skills needed for growth in the medium and long term.

New Labour, New Opportunities

Berjis has good working links with the government. Invited in 1996 on to the Labour Party National Lottery Advisory Group chaired by Jack Cunningham MP, he was a strong lobbyer. The arrival of the Lottery had meant immediate losses for betting shops, which now faced falling profits and fixed overheads. The loss of profit was around 35 per cent, but overheads were still the same – nobody reduced the price of heating for betting shops because the Lottery was now in business, for example. Berjis, together with Tom Kelly of the Trade Association and others, fought for government concessions and eventually gained a 1 per cent reduction in betting duty (a larger benefit than it might seem) and the introduction of slot machines into betting shops. In that campaign Berjis got to know several leading Labour figures, such as John Prescott and Robin Cook, now Foreign Secretary and a great racing enthusiast.

A New Way of Thinking

There is much still for the TECs to do in working with the ethnic minorities. Participation in programmes and creation of jobs are still weak; there's a tendency for old-guard thinking and a desire to set up specialist commissions, which would actually marginalise the ethnic minorities by defining them as problems. 'There's a lot of rhetoric and conferences,' Berjis admits, conceding that bodies like TECs are plagued by consultants. There has been progress on the ethnic issues, but many government and other agencies continue to treat ethnic issues as fringe issues. This is not to say that ethnic issues should be highlighted. They should be covered by the sort of all-inclusive approach that any good manager would incorporate within their general techniques and management practice, he says, adding ruefully, 'Of course it doesn't happen. Everyone has a group and the ethnic minorities are represented on all those the groups but it still doesn't add up to enough. It will be interesting to see the results of the government's insistence that socially excluded people should be helped.'

Ethnic Issues In North London

In North London unemployment is not a major South Asian problem, as it is for Somalis and Vietnamese, for example. In Harrow, with the largest Asian population in North London, Asians have a high staying-on rate at college, determined by cultural necessity: education is vital. Asians also get more support from their communities, and their poor are better looked after, than is the case for many of the other ethnic minorities; that is certainly so for Parsis and Indians. There are some major philanthropists, such as the Tata Foundation, and a caring approach to the people.

In the North London TEC area there is an unusually large ethnic minority mix. Their interests are part of the lobbying the TEC undertakes. London's unique problems need determined solutions: these include disability, gender and race, and equal opportunities.

OPPORTUNITY

'I had a magnificent equal opportunities programme in my company – and the result was zilch. You won't get a better framework than mine, it's absolutely brilliant, it's monitored, it's set out, it's gone over, it's refreshed. And the net result is almost nothing. That's what we've got to crack. The structures are in place but the results aren't showing in terms of jobs. That's what we're finding in North West London TEC.'

The problem exists throughout the UK. There has been improvement – but nowhere near enough. Often the main problem is sheer prejudice, for example companies discriminating against applicants because their address is in a known ethnic community. 'We can't do it on our own,' says Berjis.

7

Law and Law-givers

Although the UK South Asians who appear in the news head-lines tend to be the industrialists and entrepreneurs, there are many who have achieved great success and influence in a wide range of other walks of life. Often they have done so against the tide, as can be seen when Britain is compared to the United States.

'As well as black faces in the Clinton cabinet, America has black judges in the Supreme Court, blacks at the top of the civil service and big companies, and scores of black mayors and police chiefs. In Britain, black or brown faces are rare or unknown at the top of most firms or professions.'[1] *The Economist* went on to judge that in many ways Britain's ethnic minority population was actually better inte-grated than that of the United States, but it acknowledged that pro-motion and appointment to higher levels of office in the UK are very difficult for ethnic minorities to attain.

Yet the barriers are gradually being breached. In this chapter I want to look at several UK South Asians who have made inroads into two of the most closed of shops: English law and government. Some, indeed, like Dina Dattani, have breached several barriers at once. Nazreen Pearce became in 1994 the first Asian woman to be appointed a circuit judge, having sat in crown and county courts for ten years. Another woman pioneer is Ayesha Hasan, a solicitor with a large practice specialising in Islamic law, who was the first ethnic member to join chambers and the first Asian on the committee of the Family Law Barristers Association. A fourth is Usha Prashar, who in 1997 was appointed the Chair of the Parole Board. Ms Prasher came to Britain on her own as a schoolgirl from Nairobi. Her career, which included joining the Race Relations Board in 1971, brought her into membership of bodies such as the Lord Chancellor's Advisory Committee on Legal Education and the Royal Commission on Criminal Justice.

There are others, too, who have achieved high office and seniority among the lawyers and among the law-givers – in Parliament. But it is still a hard mountain to climb, as the story of Judge Mota Singh shows.

His Honour Judge Mota Singh, QC

'I burned a lot of midnight oil. I had to work very, very hard, and I had to be twice as good as my white opponents.'

The journey from the offices of the Kenya National Railways to Southwark Crown Court, where Judge Mota Singh sits, was a long and arduous one. In a profession in which few Asians have risen to the highest ranks, Judge Mota Singh is a very well-known establishment figure.

His rooms at Southwark are lined with reference books and have all the trappings of any working legal office. It's a scene indistinguishable from thousands of similar offices throughout the UK (though few have such a stunning view as this one, overlooking the Thames near Tower Bridge). The similarities end, however, as the judge enters: instead of the conventional wig, he wears, in keeping with his Sikh faith, a gleaming and immaculate white turban. It would be difficult to find a more immediate visual symbol of the achievement of Mota Singh in breaking into the inner circles of the English judiciary.

Judge Mota Singh's links with Britain go back a very long way. Born in Nairobi, he came to the UK in 1954 to study law. He was called to the Bar in 1956 at Lincoln's Inn and returned to Kenya to practise as a barrister. In 1964 he came back to the UK, intending to continue at the Bar.

It has always been particularly difficult to become a barrister. Getting work depends on being a member of a recognised set of chambers and on knowing solicitors who will give you briefs. Mota Singh soon found that if you were not regularly in court so that solicitors could see you at work, you didn't get many. Most entrants to the Bar had private means. Mota Singh, who had a young family to support, had not. The Secretary of the Bar Council advised him that he faced an uphill task. He had not practised in Britain, he needed a regular income, he had no place in chambers. And, Mota Singh adds, he had 'a suntanned face' to add to his problems.

Somewhat disheartened, he began to look for other work. He toyed with the idea of becoming a solicitor, and narrowly missed a job in the legal department of the Confederation of British Industry. Eventually he was appointed to a post with a large property group, despite the fact that the company was looking for a solicitor rather than a barrister. He spent fifteen enjoyable months with them, then approached the managing director with the proposal that some of the briefs being sent to counsel from his department could be handled by himself. The director agreed and Mota Singh found himself practising at the Bar with a solid income.

A complicated case in the Court of Appeal, lost in the lower court and predicted to lose on appeal, gave him the chance to break through. Arguing a complex case for a day and a half, he was successful; his career at the Bar was launched.

BIRTH OF A BARRISTER

Judge Mota Singh's career is unusual in the South Asian community in that there was almost no legal background in his family. His route to the Bar is a story of astonishing single-mindedness. His father was in the garage business. Mota Singh's first ambition was to become a doctor, but this was not possible. He was offered a scholarship by one of the Nairobi Sikh Institutions, but for family reasons could not take it up. He left school with A-levels and worked first in the police force, then in the accounts department of the railways, and finally in the office of a firm of advocates.

While there he began reading for an external BSc, and then discovered that it was possible to read for Part I of the Bar examinations as an external student. He organised two friends to join him, became a member of Lincoln's Inn and began to study for the Bar. When he went to the UK to complete his studies he was married with a child; all three went to London together. He worked to support them during the day, read for three hours at the Westminster Library on the way home, and went on studying at home, often into the early hours of the morning.

Judge Mota Singh's is a classic story of dedication, hard work and family commitment. The commitment was two way; his wife went out to work to help support them. They were able to live without asking for help from his two brothers in Nairobi, who were supporting the rest of the family. The brothers were also remarkable people; one has followed Mota Singh into the legal profession and is now a solicitor.

Mota Singh left Kenya because he could see the way things were going in East Africa. He had been Secretary of the Law Society of Kenya, an alderman and for nine months a Member of Parliament. He knew that things were likely to be very different in the UK.

HURDLES AND OBSTACLES

A solicitor can simply put up a brass plate and wait for people to come and employ him or her. But at the Bar a growing number of bright law students or recent law graduates are finding it almost impossible to get established because of the numbers applying. They have passed all the necessary examinations, they have paid all the appropriate membership fees, but they can't get a seat in chambers. It has been known for 1,200 to apply for fifty or sixty places.

There are almost 400 circuit judges; only about four are Asian. Statistically, there should be between fifteen and thirty. But numbers are not the only factor. Another is experience. Talent and qualifications are not enough; to be a judge one has to have ten years' experience at the Bar. Judge Mota Singh is optimistic that the number of potential judges will be much greater in around five years' time, as the pool of experienced lawyers grows from which the Lord Chancellor can select.

The need for candidates to have personal wealth or private means may be disappearing. Just as in other walks of life, South Asian lawyers have often arrived in the UK with very few resources and have sometimes become very successful. Asian barristers frequently appear before Judge Mota Singh and he is often impressed by their quality. While he doesn't believe in handing out favours, he does make a point of encouraging and giving what help he can – for example, passing on word of chambers becoming available, or of chambers and solicitors looking for recruits seeking articles. Twenty-five years ago, no such help was available for Judge Mota Singh: 'I burned a lot of midnight oil. I had to work very, very hard, and I had to be twice as good as my white opponents. But I was lucky. When I came to the Bar here there were only two or three other Asian barristers, and they weren't very well known. But because I was getting enough work from the property company I didn't have to look for work from solicitors – in fact I had so much I was able to "feed" members of my chambers.'

He was also fortunate in the courtesy and respect that judges showed towards him. The judges greeted him kindly in court and occasionally sent compliments through Mota Singh's clerk – 'who could then let solicitors know that Mr Singh was well thought of by the judge!'

Mota Singh expanded his own clientele from the property company that had given him his first briefs, until he was the barrister of choice for many of the large insurance and property companies. His clients included John Lewis, Redland Properties, Norwich Union Property and many more.

ASIAN REPRESENTATION IN THE LAW

The ghettoising tendencies of thirty years ago when Asians would mainly represent Asians are waning, in Mota Singh's view, despite the presence of discrimination in the legal profession. Asian solicitors' firms are branching out and representing a wider range of interests. Asian counsel appear on behalf of major British clients, and many no longer have a client base drawn mainly from the Asian community, though that early tendency does persist in some quarters today. You still find chambers that only represent Asian, West Indian or African clients. Paradoxically, what began as a survival strategy has turned into a liability; such chambers are struggling today. By contrast, chambers and solicitors' firms that have reached the wider market have been forced constantly to raise their professional skills and standards, with the result they are becoming ever more competitive. Many Asian solicitors are equity and salaried partners in British firms.

Ethnic integration is very much part of Judge Mota Singh's philosophy, as the millennium approaches:

We should be loyal to this country. The main allegation against the Asians has been that whether you are in East Africa, or in some other part of the world, you are not loyal to the country to which you come – or rather, that your loyalty is divided. Asians have always looked over their shoulder to India or Bangladesh or Pakistan or wherever they come from. And I want to say this: you're citizens of this country now, be loyal to this country. You can do so and still preserve all those good things. Of course India will always be there and you will always have an emotional identification with India. India is India: that's where your family is, and India will always be there to welcome you. But the holding of a British passport imposes certain obligations too. As I see it, there's far too much emphasis on rights and far too little on obligations. If obligations were fulfilled, rights would flow automatically.

Dina Dattani

'Forget it, Dina. You're female and you're brown. Choose something else!'

Dina Dattani is a quiet, softly spoken woman whose words carry strong conviction and who has a reputation for working long and unsocial hours to win a case. Her single-minded determination goes back a long way. From a very early age – she arrived in Britain from Uganda as a child in the immigration influx of 1972 – she wanted to be a lawyer, even though it was not a profession with which South Asians had very much involvement. Her family advised against the idea. Nobody else in the family had been a lawyer and the legal world was an unfamiliar one. There were very few Asians in the profession and fewer still achieving much success in it. And they felt there was less money to be made in the law than in the professions that South Asians traditionally preferred. Her advisers at school and university were particularly blunt. 'Forget it, Dina. You're female and you're brown. Choose something else!'

Dina was persistent. She qualified in 1984 and spent the next two years articled to a firm in Northampton, staying on for a further year after articles. She was adamant from the first that she did not want to be labelled as an 'ethnic lawyer' dealing only with clients from the ethnic minorities, but the fact that she had Asian language skills meant that she was increasingly categorised. Local legal firms ignored the fact that an employee with Dina's background might have opened up international opportunities or been useful in other pioneering ways. She found herself dealing almost entirely with Asian clients in criminal, legal aid, matrimonial and other similar cases.

At that time it was extremely difficult for young Asian solicitors to convince legal firms that they had the skills to progress. It was as if speaking an Asian language and coming from an Asian back-ground were the only worthwhile skills one had; as if one were an Asian first and a lawyer second. Partnership prospects were bleak too; even today, Asians have to try harder. In the majority popula-tion a solicitor can expect to be offered a partnership three to five years after qualification. His or her Asian counterpart will have to wait from eight to ten years, and will usually have to bring into the firm a client portfolio of their own before being offered a partnership – a requirement not demanded of non-Asians.

BUCKING THE SYSTEM

There were two ways forward. One was to remain within the estab-lishment and to fight to change it. That would have meant years of frustrating toil. The other was to set up in practice on her own account – a risky step in many ways, but one that meant she could do high-quality work from the outset without the distraction of hav-ing to fight the system as well.

For reasons of centrality and access to a high quality of corporate work with a cosmopolitan, 'colour-blind' client base, London was the obvious place to set up. In 1987/8 Dina made the move.

In some ways the change was not as radical as might have been expected. Many of her clients were still Asian, because that was the community in which Dina lived and where she had the best contacts. The major difference was that she had a choice about the kind of work she did for them, and the freedom to seek corporate clients. There was some resistance to the new firm from other lawyers and other institutions; Dina knew that some banks were advising corporate clients not to use her but to go to larger firms, and sometimes banks would not recognise her firm.

BARRIERS TO GROWTH

Dina's story illustrates one of the central problems that UK South Asian professionals often encounter when they move away from family businesses and try to enter mainstream professions. The rate of education and qualification is high, but in some professions opportunity does not match it. Many legal firms state that they are equal opportunities employers but have few Asian names on their letterheads. The picture painted by BBC television's series *This Life* is a fiction. Its Asian characters – members of a group of attractive young lawyers with the world at their feet and money in their pockets – are not typical. The Asian female lawyer around whom many of the plots revolve is from a privileged background. Dina's careers officer at school would have counted her as the exception that proves the rule.

The Law Society, Dina believes, could do more to improve the lot of Asian lawyers. 'Recruitment policies need to be monitored to ensure that equal opportunities practice is being maintained. Positive steps need to be taken to encourage ethnic minority intake within firms. Although there are now Asians in the lower levels of the legal profession, there are very few at partner level in the major firms.'

Nevertheless, as perceptions change the situation is beginning to alter. Until recently it was much more difficult for Asians to enter the legal profession than to become accountants. Lawyers are conservative by nature; accountants have a more global approach to business. American lawyers recognised it first, but the British legal profession is beginning to catch up and realise the worth of Asian lawyers in a global marketplace:

> The value of people like myself is only now increasing within the legal profession because Asians have done so well here, and India is an emerging market into which British and European firms want to enter. The prosperity of Asia means that we all benefit: firms that want to get work from Asian businesses have had to take positive steps to recruit Asian solicitors who can readily identify with this client base.

CURRENT CONCERNS

During 1996 Dina began to consider joining a firm with a presence in India or a policy of extending links with the subcontinent. In January 1997 she became a partner with City firm Lawrence Jones, 'one of the most global-thinking firms I've come across'. She is one of three women out of fourteen partners and the only partner from the ethnic minorities.

In the present situation of the UK South Asian community she believes that change should be managed positively and the opportunity taken to deal with some of the problems that have been encountered in the past. For example, the traditional system by which sons inherit their parents' wealth and the daughters do not, but are looked after by the sons, is beginning to change. She frequently advises clients that a fairer division between family members would be a very positive step forward. This is particularly significant advice in view of the marked lack of motivation to succeed that she sees in the younger generation – 'perhaps because they have not had to face the same difficulties'. This contrasts with earlier generations' 'sheer hard work and unquestioning determination no matter how challenging the task'.

Nevertheless, her overall predictions are positive. Asians are expanding far beyond the retail businesses that were once their typical occupation. They are willing to experiment, to go into other fields, to get first-hand professional help and apply it. As a lawyer handling patent applications, Dina is aware of Asian game designers, software, engineering inventions and much more: there is currently a flowering of South Asian creativity. Add to this the fact that British Asians are investing in India, and so sharing in the economic revival taking place in the subcontinent and the emerging tiger economies of the Far East, and it's not surprising that Dina Dattani – who sees more closely than most the problems of the British South Asian community – is also optimistic about the future of Britain's South Asians.

Law and Politics

South Asians, like many other minority groups in Britain (such as women and Liberal Democrats), are not proportionally represented in Parliament in a way that reflects their numbers in the country. The huge changes brought about by the 1997 General Election resulted in many more women in the House of Commons, but there are only five Asian MPs.

Keith Vaz retained his seat as Member for Leicester East, which he first won in 1987. Born in Aden of Indian parents, he came to Britain in 1965 and took a first-class honours degree in law at Cambridge. He has had a varied parliamentary career, serving as might be expected on a number of race-related committees, but also, from 1987–92, on the Home Affairs Select Committee of the House of Commons. He was the 1988 Asian of the Year. A frequent spokesman on Asian matters, in 1997 Vaz published a significant report pointing out the 'glass ceilings' that still prevail in British society, limiting promotion opportunities for ethnic minorities.

Piara Khabra was elected MP for Ealing Southall in 1992, having worked as a teacher since his arrival in Britain from the Punjab in 1959. He has been very active in Southall community affairs and has a strong interest in education.

Ashok Kumar also entered Parliament in 1992 as MP for East Cleveland and Middlesborough South. An Indian, Kumar is a scientist by training. Before becoming an MP he was the first Asian to be elected a councillor in the North East (Middlesbrough Borough Council).

Marsha Singh, Member for Bradford West, was one of the large influx of new Labour MPs brought into the House of Commons in the 1997 landslide Labour victory; as was Mohammad Sarwar, the Pakistani cash-and-carry tycoon, who won the safe Labour seat of Glasgow Govan.

1997 was a good year for South Asians in the House of Lords, too. Lord Navnit Dholakia became the first Asian to be elevated to the House of Lords under the new administration. Born in Tanzania, he arrived in Britain in 1946 and had a distinguished career in local politics as a Liberal Democrat. Now a LibDem working peer, he also serves on the Police Complaints Authority.

He joined a small group of Asian peers, among them Lord Raj Bagri, a leading industrialist, the first person of non-British origin to chair the London Metal Exchange; his peerage was awarded for service to industry. Lord Swarj Paul, an Indian, has been described as 'the most notable Asian in the City'. He is the founder of the Caparo Group, a steel stockholding business. Now retired from business, he is an active member of the House of Lords, a leading philanthropist and a staunch Labour supporter.

Inside and outside Westminster, South Asians can often be found in positions of political and legal influence. Lord Meghnand Desai, for example, is Professor of Economics at the London School of Economics. He was born in Baroda and came to the UK in 1965, having studied at Bombay and Pennsylvania Universities. He was adviser to the Labour Party on economic policies until 1993 and became a peer in 1991. On the other side of the House Baroness Shreela Flather, the first Asian woman to become a peer, was born in Pakistan but came to the UK from India to study law at University College, London. She began as a teacher but moved into politics in the 1970s, breaking down several barriers on the way. Before becoming a Conservative peer she was the first Asian woman mayor in Britain.

The first Asian woman to be appointed a circuit judge was Nazreen Pearce. Born in Aden and educated in Pakistan, she came to London in 1959 to study law and passed her Bar examinations at the unusually young age of twenty. Having two years to kill before she could be called to the Bar, she studied for an external degree at London University.

A lawyer with a strong influence on political events is Andrew Surendra Popat, who studied law both in Britain and the United States. An East African Asian, Popat was Campaign Director for John Patten in the 1987 election and his legal adviser on law and order, and was prospective Parliamentary candidate for Bradford South in 1990.

Many leading South Asian lawyers, as might be expected, are involved in race relations, disadvantage and other ethnic-related issues. But many also have reputations and influence extending into a much wider field. Pranlal Sheth, for example, is admired for his business success as much as for his considerable political reputation; he is very involved in human rights. Likewise Rabinder Singh, a British-born South Asian, is a recognised authority on human rights law in the European context and has written some influential books.

THE ASIAN IN THE STREET

Besides political leaders, representatives and spokespersons, UK South Asians themselves have a powerful voice and influence in British politics.

The 1997 election, which overturned so much of British politics, also marked the recognition by the main political parties that the Asian communities held the key to success or failure in a surprisingly large number of constituencies. The 'Asian factor' was crucial in thirty-six constituencies where the number of Asian voters was larger than the winning margin in the previous general election. So the party that successfully wooed the Asians could be reasonably sure of victory in those constituencies.[2]

The wooing was passionate and intense. Zee TV (an Asian satellite and cable television station received in one in three British Asian homes) ran a series of party political broadcasts aimed specifically at Asian homes. The Labour Party's highly polished production featured Lord Paul and fashionable restaurateur Ali Amin. Its English script was adorned with Labour slogans in Hindi, Urdu, Gujerati, Punjabi and Bengali.

The Conservatives featured Lord Bagri sitting in front of a portrait of John Major and speaking in aristocratic Hindi. It was a significant choice of spokesman, for he is one of the pioneering South Asians who have broken out of the ethnic business world and achieved distinction in traditionally white-dominated structures.

The Liberal Democrats used publishing and property tycoon Ramesh Dewan, who like Gulam Noon is a personal friend of Paddy Ashdown's. And the Scottish National Party, making a play for the Asian vote in Glasgow, scripted its broadcast in Urdu and adopted an up-beat, pop video style.

The two main parties each fielded ten Asian candidates and the Liberal Democrats thirteen. However, many young Asians were politically disillusioned and said they would not vote. And a Mr Peter Patel of Birmingham set up the Fourth Party, proposing to field up to four candidates in the Midlands campaigning for better representation of Asians in Parliament.

Of course, there was great disappointment that so much effort yielded so few South Asian MPs. However, it is quite certain that political activists in all parties are now convinced of the importance of wooing the Asian vote in any UK general election.

8

The Next Generation

Almost everybody interviewed for this book had something to say about the next generation. This is not just the usual concern of one generation for the next. The over-riding question asked of the new generation is, can the entrepreneurial success and effort of the first generation of immigrants be repeated, or has the process of acclimatisation and assimilation gone so far that the cutting edge of entrepreneurial flair has been blunted?

In this chapter I want to consider three Maharajahs whom I have called 'second generation', because all were educated in Britain. Strictly speaking the term ought to include people actually born in Britain (though Shami Ahmed was a very young baby when he arrived). However, the first immigrants arrived in the late 1960s and early 1970s, and I want to look at careers that have developed over some time (though of course there are a number of entrepreneurs such as Reuben Singh, who in his early twenties runs a fashion accessories business worth millions).

Generally speaking, the second generation has moved on from its predecessors in so many ways that it amounts to a clash of cultures. Sometimes it's simply a case of wanting to strike out independently and build a business similar to the family business, but without the need to do things the way one's parents did them. The story of Shami Ahmed is a good example of a peaceful leaving-of-the-nest with the support and encouragement of parents. Sometimes the clash is painful, as when the young entrepreneur wants to take a much more professional approach to business, and wants to bring into the family firm outsiders whose suggestions involve radical changes in hallowed procedures. In Part Three of this book we shall be looking at some of those issues. And sometimes the new generation has its own entrepreneurial vision so far removed from parental models that all the older generation can do is sit back, marvel and cross its fingers. Sonu Shivdasani, whose older brother Azad appeared in Chapter 5, is an example of this.

Sonu Shivdasani shares Azad's gift for interacting with different people from different walks of life. He decided not to join the family business but to branch out on his own. He has created an exclusive up-market island resort in the Maldives in the Indian Ocean. Soneva Fishu (the resort is named after Sonu and his wife Eva) has been featured along with its founders in the *Tatler*, the *Financial Times* and leading fashion magazines.

The resort is consistently praised for its remarkable combination of natural paradise and understated luxury, and great hospitality and comfort.

Sonu's creative flair is demonstrated by his more ambitious strategy, which is to manage a chain of up-market, exclusive resorts across the span of South East Asia. His resort-management company based in Bangkok, Soneva Pavilions, has highly qualified management and already manages several third-party resorts. The larger strategy is in the process of being developed.

'Sonu,' observes Azad, 'is a fine example of the emerging generation of Maharajahs, and his progress from such an original and brilliant first venture should be most interesting.'

Second-generation entrepreneurial success stories are often in the UK news. An example is Rumi Verjee, a forty year old who arrived in Britain from East Africa in his early teens. Verjee's path to wealth began with acquiring the UK franchise of Domino's Pizza; his business interests now include ownership of Thomas Goode in London's Mayfair (purveyor of fine china and glass to the crowned heads and aristocracy of Europe) and a large stake in Watford Football

Club, which came about through his friendship with the singer Elton John. Goode, the jewel in Verjee's portfolio, was a typically entrepreneurial gamble. Like many of the aristocracy it served, it had fallen on hard times; its customers spend less freely than they used to. Not the first immigrant to take on the task of restoring a great British institution, Verjee – a lawyer by training, called to the Bar at Temple Inn – set about turning the company round, a task he sees as not unlike managing Watford.

Typical of a much younger generation is Ajaz Ahmed, who at 24 is one of the many making fortunes out of CD-Roms, virtual reality and the Internet. His company, New Media, has sales exceeding £4 million and he is comfortably assured of a growing stake in the new and expanding computer and cyberspace industry. Like many who reach millionaire status very young, Ahmed now faces many of the problems we have already discussed regarding the management of expansion and change.[1]

Such problems have been spectacularly surmounted by his namesake Shami Ahmed, whose hugely profitable fashion empire has made his brand a household name and to whom we now turn.

Shami Ahmed

Dosh (Channel 4) is presented by Shami Ahmed. No, I hadn't heard of him either, but I had heard of Joe Bloggs, the jeans company he founded and very modestly mentioned last night. This man is seriously rich but, despite that, his links into lessons about haggling and making money at car boot sales never sounded patronising: 'You don't get what you deserve, but what you negotiate.'[2]

Shami Ahmed is a charming, courteous and articulate young man, whose body language lets you know that time is limited, there's lots to do and lots of opportunities to be snatched before the moment passes. He has his finger on many pulses. He's aware of factors like design, technology, marketing and many more that are no longer optional extras in business but essential matters to understand if success is to be achieved. Shami is one of those second-generation Maharajahs who have understood that these factors need to be mastered and used. It's an understanding on which his success is clearly built.

His Legendary Joe Bloggs fashion empire is a prominent player in the world of wealth and high finance; his personal wealth is at least £50 million, putting Ahmed somewhere in the top twenty richest UK Asians. It is also a major force in the world of high fashion; he hit the headlines when he made the most expensive – and probably most uncomfortable – pair of jeans in the world, encrusted with diamonds and costing more than £100,000. These were for The Artist Formerly Known as Prince, who had joined a growing list of Ahmed's showbiz clients. While Shami's jetsetting and nightclubbing have taken a back seat since his marriage in early 1997, his lifestyle is still opulent; he owns a Rolls-Royce and a Bentley, and has homes in London and Manchester.

Shami is a second-generation South Asian whose life has been almost wholly lived in Britain. His family came to the UK from Karachi, Pakistan, in 1964 when he was two years old and settled in Manchester. He left school (where he had a reputation as a very sharp dresser) at 16 to join the family wholesale clothing business, Pennywise. Manchester in 1980 had already taken over from Liverpool as the musical and style capital of the North, and was becoming a centre for youth, fashion and street culture. The 1980s were more materialistic than the 1960s and 1970s, and there was money to be made out of garments. In the eight years that Shami worked for his parents he had plenty of opportunities to get to know the market and identify a number of profitable unexplored niches in the rag trade.

His first step to fame and riches came when he realised that for customers wanting to buy jeans, the only choice was between expensive designer-label products and cheap mass-produced ones that had no pretensions to fashion. He hit on a way of giving mass-produced jeans individual distinction: pre-washing. At the age of 24 he went into business on his own account, and The Legendary Joe Bloggs, selling a range of garments, was born.

He thought of the name on impulse and kept it because everybody laughed when he told them. Most South Asian firms have only recently moved from calling themselves by ethnic names – so that 'Patel's' might become 'BriteWare'. The name 'Joe Bloggs', which Shami chose because it was 'British and common-sounding', sums up the gap between Shami the second-generation flamboyant clothing icon with a flair for publicity, and his parents running Pennywise or his property-dealing grandparents. Shami talks about 'psychological marketing'. It's one of the ways in which he's discarded many of the tenets of his parents.

Another is his attitude to banking.

SECOND-GENERATION BANKING

As I have shown, Asians prefer to go first to their own networks for funding, secondly to Asian banks and only as a third choice to British banks. Nevertheless, Shami is sceptical about the quality of banking that the first-generation immigrants received from Asian banks. He argues that it wasn't quality service, efficiency and specialist expertise that made them use Asian banks. It was because the bank manager spoke the same language. As we have seen throughout this book, the discovery that somebody comes from the same region, city or even village as you do immediately establishes a bond of trust. It is, Shami agrees, an important matter when a business is starting up and its proprietors have difficulty in communicating and are unfamiliar with the way things are done. 'I don't criticise my parents for banking with Asian banks. But when you begin to be established in your business, they can't help you much more. All they can say is, "We're from the same village." That's not enough.'

His frustrations began while he was working for his father. Asian banks were undoubtedly filling a need, but more was needed. In Shami's opinion the banks were unable even to understand expansion proposals, or to help their Asian clients to grow in the UK marketplace. 'They themselves never really understood the UK marketplace – they were from the same countries as us and they had limited knowledge.' For Shami it almost amounted to a betrayal. 'They let us down.' The banks were so inadequate at meeting the needs of South Asian businesses that they prevented them from growing at the rate that they could and should have grown.

Shami now gives his business to banks like the Hong Kong and Shanghai Bank (and to the Midland, which it owns) and thinks that 'English banks like NatWest are very good clearing banks when working within the UK market'. His enthusiasm for dealing with the Hong Kong and Shanghai Bank comes because it is flexible enough to run with his ideas. 'When you've got a business idea and you want somebody to support it, if you don't get the right support at the right time you miss the opportunity. Missed opportunities very rarely come back. If you're deep in takeover talks and your bank doesn't understand what you're doing and why, it's gone. You don't get lots of time, and opportunities don't come along every day.'

Nevertheless, he still believes that the old Asian values of trust and integrity are essential. He has been able to finance his business using British banks and financial institutions, but he still feels that lenders in the UK could be more flexible. 'International banks understand you better because they are used to dealing with communities where trust and track record matters more than the specific figures on your bank balance.'[3]

SECOND-GENERATION MANAGEMENT STYLE

It's not just in his choice of bank that Shami Ahmed shows the generation gap between him and his forebears. It's true that he does not face the same problem that many Asian companies do, that of conflict between generations as the family boardroom becomes the arena of struggle between one generation's entrepreneurial instinct and a new generation's paper qualifications in management. The Legendary Joe Bloggs is Shami's own brainchild, a second-generation product from the start. But there is a great deal of difference between the business styles of previous generations of Ahmeds and Shami, still in his mid-thirties.

His father ran Pennywise with typical Asian reserve, playing his cards close to his chest, revealing as little as possible of his plans, his business decisions, even his assets. It was partly modesty, and partly because like many Asians he came from a country where corruption in business was common and it was good commercial sense to cover your tracks. In Shami's opinion, that approach would be commercial suicide. He has taken Joe Bloggs to an 86 per cent brand awareness, a front-runner among the ten most successful jeans manufacturers in the UK. It's a British brand manufactured in Britain (though legislation on the minimum wage may well force a move to manufacturers in Europe or the Far East). His whole business depends on the name Joe Bloggs being shouted from the rooftops and maximum exposure in advertising, the media and entertainment.

Top sportspeople wear his clothes. A major sponsorship deal with cricketer Brian Lara led to the Legendary Brian Lara range – and a pitched battle with Levi's, who forced Shami to abandon his plans for a '501' line in celebration of Lara's (now legendary) 501 runs for Warwickshire. Shami agreed to spell the number out in words, which still cheekily flirted with the magic number made famous by Levi's. And Joe Bloggs is now associated with major names in rock music, including Take That, Stone Roses and Apache Indian. A sponsorship deal that got Joe Bloggs in front of the 1991 Cup Final crowds only became more of a news story when Paul Gascoigne objected. It all gets Joe Bloggs talked about.

'Branding, brand names – branding is communication. It's telling people about your product and it's telling people what you do. The biggest failure in Asian businesses is not knowing how to market themselves.'

The Joe Bloggs philosophy revolves around letting the world

know what Joe Bloggs is doing; not only by high-profile advertising, but in the constant information flow between the in-house export department and the overseas distributors. It's an open style of management, reflected in the young, dynamic staff he employs. All departments take part in regular briefing and progress meetings, and channels of communications within the company are designed to be as open as possible. He is open about his future plans, too. He was happy to talk about a proposed takeover that would hopefully make Joe Bloggs the largest Asian fashion group in the UK – it turned out to be his acquisition of Elizabeth Emanuel, a name most people in the UK remember to a greater or lesser extent since the Emanuels made Princess Diana's wedding dress.

Of course, any expansion of Shami's business interests is good news for the UK jobs market. He is a striking example of the benefits that South Asians create in employment. Even if they only employ Asian staff, those workers will thereby be removed from the unemployment register; you could argue that Asian entrepreneurs are in such cases funding the cost to the state of their own immigration. As has happened in Germany, Britain is acquiring labour capital at no cost. But Shami Ahmed is one of many South Asian entrepreneurs who employ large numbers of people from outside their minority ethnic community. That's why he featured in the launch advertising for the Commission for Racial Equality's 1997 initiative 'Roots of the Future' (opposite).

SECOND-GENERATION TECHNOLOGY

There's a legend, probably apocryphal, told in Alan Sugar's Amstrad computer company. It tells of an occasion when Sugar is said to have summoned his designers to watch a computer being assembled in the Amstrad factory. Pointing to a microchip on the main circuitboard, he demanded, 'What is that?'

'It's a 386,' somebody volunteered.

'Wrong,' snapped Sugar.

Another designer tried. 'It's the main CPU processor,' he said.

> **'Get back to where I came from? Could you just run that by the 2,000 people I employ?'**
>
> With the success of the Joe Bloggs label, Shami diversified and now presides over a company that is worth millions. Of course he knows that some people, because of their bigotry, will put his success down to pure luck. But rather philosophically he says, 'Just think, if it wasn't for that word luck, people who hate you wouldn't have any way to explain your success.' The reality is that Shami Ahmed has got where he is today by persistent hard work, determination and by having an eye for the main chance. However, he's quick to point out that he's not the only one to benefit from all this success. With hundreds of suppliers it means jobs are being created all the time (which in a small way improves the employment figures of the country). These employees will all have an income, which means spending power, which ultimately means a small boost to the economy of the nation.
>
> Of course Shami Ahmed alone doesn't make that much difference to the economy, but the fact is there are thousands like him throughout Britain.[4]

'Wrong,' Sugar retorted.

A third hapless designer had a go. 'It's a 16-bit processor with a built-in cache, rated at 25 MHz, surface mounted.'

'Wrong.'

There was a lengthy pause as the designers looked at each other and remained silent. Sugar jabbed a triumphant finger at the scrap of silicon.

'That,' he observed impressively, 'is £18.30, quantity rate.'

Like several other entrepreneurs in this book, Shami Ahmed has used new technology to secure his position in the market. New technology enabled him to provide customers with a varied range of washed jeans. Today new technology keeps him ahead of the field. It's an industry he prefers to use rather than diversify into, however.

'High technology and all that is a massive growth area, no doubt about it. Unfortunately for me, I don't understand it.'

Like Alan Sugar (whose Amstrads dominated the PC industry for several years), Shami Ahmed cheerfully admits his lack of technical expertise, explaining that he is a businessman not an electronics engineer or computer programmer. 'People like me have never been to any business school. We just left school and went straight into business. I hire experts. Who needs brains when you can buy them?'

Joe Bloggs's manufacturing process is intensely streamlined. The quality of the products is maintained by a system of controls to check that the design specifications are being maintained. Computerisation of order control, warehousing, stock control, accounting and other processes is comprehensive. Researching the market and keeping ahead of it is a major priority, and a team of in-house designers works with freelancers throughout the UK to supply the company's design needs. Joe Bloggs has an unusually complex corporate structure, and technology plays a very large part in maintaining it at full efficiency.

SECOND-GENERATION EXPANSION

One obvious question to ask a 34-year-old Maharajah who has risen to the top of an entire industry is: 'What do you intend to do with the rest of your life?'

There's a sense in which Shami's future plans come full circle back to the family environment in which he started out. His father, Nizan Ahmed, started out with a market stall which he and his wife Saeeda ran. Next he opened a shop. Then he opened more shops. In 1976 Pennywise was started as a wholesale clothing company, carrying a range of well-known labels such as Levi's. Joe Bloggs was the first Ahmed own-brand label. It was an interesting expansion philosophy, however. Rather than merely joining the family business, the five Ahmed children had their own ideas about new directions and opportunities, and Nizan Ahmed, with a degree of imagination unusual in a first-generation owner-manager, agreed. So Shami began his new venture with the support and participation of his father, rather than being cast in the role of the son who had turned his back on all that his family had achieved.[5]

Now Shami views future expansion with the same openness that his father did back in 1986. The company has long since expanded from its seed product, jeans. The main products today are jeans and denim jackets, shirts and T-shirts. The company also sells toiletries, shoes and music. Shami is expanding his own interests beyond the garment industry; like his grandfather before him, he has successfully set up in property.

'In the past two or three years we've begun to diversify into property. Property and fashion, that's the future. Maybe hotels ... I don't know. I'm too ambitious to have an ambition! I don't care to do things by a particular time. Ambitious people are usually dangerous people, because they've set themselves a time limit and they will stop at nothing to achieve it. I wouldn't operate that way. Unless I could keep our good name, our dignity and our respect intact, I wouldn't.'

His laid-back air is deceptive – 'There's no guarantee as to what I'll do. I may do less; I may do more. Who knows?' – for he is an inveterate entrepreneur, always on the lookout for new business opportunities and retaining the flair and imagination that made Joe Bloggs legendary.

Like his father, he recognises where his gifts are concentrated. All business, he considers, is about common sense and should be directed by the same ethical standards. Success in business is to do with the people involved, he maintains. 'If you get into a business you don't understand it's usually because you've forgotten the principles that you operate on in the business you do understand. Often you're backing the wrong people, who don't have as much knowledge of the business as you thought they had. But get the right people, and you find that people make the business, whether it's computers or running a hotel. If the person's right you're backing him or her, not the business.'

Shami is open about his limitations. 'I understand garments. I don't understand high technology ... I have a number of good people working for me who have grown up with the company and have been promoted to more and more senior positions – and that's good, because your staff need to know that you've only got two hands and you can only be in one place at one time.'

The phenomenal growth of Joe Bloggs and the radically different management style of Shami Ahmed will force some difficult decisions – will the company ever be floated on the stock market and, if so, when? And how will the presence of shareholders and a new kind of accountability affect the business that has so far been run by Shami, his brother and his three sisters? This second-generation company looks likely to avoid many of the problems that earlier generations faced: succession, professionalising, generational conflict and much more.

SECOND-GENERATION PHILOSOPHY

❏ **On motivation**: 'The fight is not with others. The fight is within yourself. The fight is to make yourself better, to look at your strengths and weaknesses and to ask, every day, "Why did I do that? What should I have done? How could I have done that deal better? Even if it was a success, how could it have been made a bigger success?"'

❏ **On corporate philanthropy**: 'I think giving to charity and other good causes is a very important matter. But a lot of people seem to do it for publicity and what they get out of it. We do a fair amount of charitable work, but it's done in a private way and we don't try to get publicity out of it. We don't give sponsorship in exchange for promoting our logo, for example. I wouldn't rule out the possibility of a Joe Bloggs Charitable Trust some day … But we'd want to be sure we weren't doing it for our own benefit.'

❏ **On qualifications**: 'The real test isn't whether you pass or fail inside the examination room, but whether you pass or fail in the outside world, when you've left the examination room behind.'

❏ **On talent**: 'Whether you're living in Manchester, London or Paris doesn't matter. Talent has no limit. Talent has no colour. Talent has no location.'

Jayesh Manek

'Everybody looks at the same information. It's how you interpret and use that information that matters.'

Not many wealthy and influential South Asians have had the opportunity of a dry run at empire building. Jayesh Manek, courtesy of a leading national newspaper, has. His quiet life as a pharmacist in Ruislip was turned dramatically round in 1994 when he won the *Sunday Times* 'Fantasy Fund Manager' competition. The competition, borrowing an idea from TV light entertainment, asked players to put together a theoretical share portfolio and submit it to the newspaper, the progress of the chosen stocks increasing or decreasing the imaginary capital with which they began, and the winner being the person who had prospered most at the end. The television programme on which the competition was based worked in a similar way but with imaginary football teams drawn from real-life players.

The competition was the kind of game that City commuters played on the 8.15 a.m. to Waterloo. Manek, an enthusiastic amateur, beat them all; his 41,000 rivals (many of them professional fund managers) included the vice-president of the prestigious J. P. Morgan. He turned his imaginary £10 million into an astonishing £502 million and, having amazed everybody and collected £100,000 prize money, he went on to beat all the odds by collecting a second £100,000 when he again won the following year.

Manek, a Ugandan Asian whose family came to the UK in 1972 when he was sixteen, instantly became the darling of the City, a ready-made guru on the financial scene. In May 1997, for example, his photograph appeared in the *Sunday Times* alongside a feature on the directory *Company Refs* and other 'form guides' for stock market investors.[6] In a panel alongside, subheaded 'Manek backs Refs', soundbites from Jayesh Manek on general investment principles and *Refs* in particular were printed. '*Refs* saves me time because it has all the relevant statistics in one place,' he said, though he went on to point out that fortunes are not made from *Refs* alone. Nevertheless, the publishers of *Company Refs* must have been delighted: such a warm endorsement from one of the City names of the moment would have been expensive if they'd had to pay for it.

The City queued up to offer Manek employment. He won't say who approached him, which led to some speculation in the financial press as to who the interested parties might have been. 'Most of the papers got the identities of the parties wrong. But I did have a few approaches and I looked seriously at a couple of them.'

He turned them all down. 'We had some good meetings but that was all. We didn't get to the stage of talking fees and salaries, because the initial interest was from them, not me. I think the main stumbling block so far as I was concerned was that I'd have been expected to fit in to an institutional set-up and work within a structured framework. I'm not blaming them. Large institutions need to have bureaucratic procedures in place and so on to standardise structures and investments and all the rest. But I didn't want to be confined in that way.' Instead, he chose to launch his own fund with partners in Bombay, exercising his proven flair and talent for hair-raising investment by choosing the volatile small Indian business market.[7]

Ask him the secret of his investing success and he points out that, though he looks at the same facts and figures that everybody else does, it's how you interpret and use them that matters. For example, he quotes American findings that 98 per cent of investors never invest in shares at all-time high prices – reasoning that they cannot rise higher – but points out that he has done very well out of just such investments. It's not a matter of playing mysterious hunches, either: he argues that after a recession it takes two or three years for share prices to rise again. During that period, people are reluctant to sell and take a loss. Once they reach their break-even level, more people are willing to sell, glad to break even. Past the previous all-time high, when nobody is losing money any more, there are relatively fewer sales. So, given the right shares and all other things being equal, there is a momentum developing and a likelihood that the momentum will increase, which an astute investor can identify or even predict. Because of the widespread mistrust of high-priced shares, few investors deliberately ride on that momentum. Jayesh often does.

This very entrepreneurial approach to shares is characteristic of Jayesh's approach to life in general. His business career is typical, in its exploitation of niche opportunities, efficient use of low capital and determination to expand, of the UK South Asian entrepreneurial community.

ORIGINS OF AN ENTREPRENEUR

In 1977, as a twenty-year-old pharmacy student at Brighton Polytechnic, fascinated with figures, Jayesh was influenced by a Kenyan Asian uncle who enjoyed discussing the market with his nephew at every opportunity. Their mutual interest was not so much actual investment as 'speculating about speculating', a theoretical interest that Jayesh followed up with a good deal of reading up on economics.

His first investments were in 1982–83. He began with a small sum of around £1,000, chose his brokers through friends' recommendations, picked a few stocks and broke even. The next step was participation in privatisations, beginning with BT – 'which obviously did quite well' – and including most of the privatisation issues. 'Apart from a couple of disasters, most of them have done quite well,' he says.

It was a spare-time activity, for he had completed his pharmacy studies in 1977 and in 1980 with his two brothers opened their first pharmacy near Harrow. Interest rates were at a peak, it was a bad time to buy a business, and they were starting with nothing except 2,000 square feet of premises that had stood empty for two years – so there was no goodwill to capitalise on from previous owners (or indeed to pay for). It was a high-risk venture, starting from scratch in an new area; even the professional press took notice of the ambitious project. The business took a year to establish and was funded entirely from cash flow. In 1982 and 1985 they went on to open further pharmacies.

The family business seemed set to flourish and expand further, but a setback came in 1987 with the introduction of regulations that strictly controlled dispensing pharmacies. Suddenly it was no longer possible to open pharmacies as one might open a shop.

Unless, reasoned the Maneks, you actually were a shop. Take away the dispensing element, sell off-the-shelf, non-prescribed medicine and increase other stock such as cosmetics, and you had a shop that was unaffected by the new regulations and was a new, marketable concept in its own right. Within a year they opened their first 'non-dispensing pharmacy', followed by three more in rapid succession, all located in railway stations.

FUND MANAGEMENT

In the early 1990s an operations manager was employed to look after the day-to-day operations and Jayesh concentrated on the overall strategy. As a result, he also found time to return to his hobby of investing in the markets.

His approach to personal investment was to concentrate on a few stocks rather than a wide portfolio. It was a high-risk strategy and he was investing larger sums. 'You become very attached to the stock you've invested in, almost emotionally so,' he says, recalling a pharmaceutical stock he had backed in the expectation that the company's performance, growth potential and acquisitions policy would make it very profitable. But the company ran into serious problems in the United States and the price dropped from around £5 to £3. Believing recovery to be just a matter of time, he doubled his investment despite profit warnings. A further drop to £2 and a second profit warning followed, but Jayesh kept on buying and did so until the stock bottomed out at just over £1. 'You become attached to it, because it's one of your chosen stocks. I could have sold out and taken a loss, but I kept hoping the fall would reverse. You feel as if the stock owes you money.' In the end his faith was rewarded; a change of management and a new CEO so revitalised the company that within eighteen months it became the target of a successful hostile takeover. Jayesh's stock, much of it bought during the depressed period, rose sharply in value and he made a handsome profit. As he tells the story, it's reminiscent of Kumar Datwani's account of property purchasing in Hong Kong during the slump there. For him too, it was just a matter of time.

When the Fantasy Fund competition was launched in 1994, Jayesh was competing with the professionals at their own level. He knew that the prize money would attract top financial investors, and he devised an aggressive style of play against them. The rules allowed players to hold from three to ten stocks; he adopted a high-risk strategy of staying with very few stocks. He disliked the loss of focus that comes with spreading the risk over a large portfolio, often as many as 150 stocks. After all, for several years he had been investing with his own money.

He took the top position in the first week and immediately bent all his efforts to keeping it. He chose small capital stocks, keeping them for between one and three weeks as the rules demanded. In that timescale the only factor that mattered was short-term gain. There was a wide choice of small capital stocks available that measured well against Jayesh's criterion of relative strength in the immediate few weeks. He won the first competition by a comfortable margin.

The rules changed in the second competition and only around five small capital stocks were available. Jayesh was forced to change his strategy. 'One looks for special situations where results are due this week or next, and if you suspect they will exceed expectation then you go for it.' He began to familiarise himself with every financial publication and statement that might give hints – 'almost like real trading!'

Forced into large stocks with smaller movements, Jayesh's margin of victory was smaller the second time round. Nevertheless, he won, this time against 15,000 people, virtually all City professionals.

ENTREPRENEURISM AT THE MILLENNIUM

Today Jayesh manages his own investment fund (with real money). He chose Indian stocks partly because his family originates from India, partly because he has followed the markets there for some time, but mainly because he sees the long-term importance of India in the global economy. 'India has been independent for fifty years; but India plc has only been floated on the world market since 1991. So it's still small a capital stock as far as I'm concerned, from the world market point of view, and so like any small cap stock it's bound to be volatile. But if you take the medium-to-long-term view the prospects are good. I'm attracted to India because over the next quarter century it's going to be a force to be reckoned with.'

The Jayesh Manek of real-life investment is a more conservative operator than he was in the Fantasy Fund competition. Today he spreads his investments more widely and does not look for immediate gains. His performance has been 'satisfactory, above markets'. He plays the percentages: 'My expectation is to outperform the market. If it's rising at, say, 10 per cent annually, then over any long-term period the stock market itself will always outperform any other kind of investment. So if I'm managing a portfolio I'm happy just to consistently outperform by a reasonable margin. That way one doesn't have to take risks.'

Consistency, of course, is everything. 'It's got to be a strategy of stock selection. It's very easy to come up with a very high-risk strategy, do well one year and then not do at all well for the next three years.' Very different to the competition environment, where one can go for spectacular coups and high risks.

As a professional financial investor, Jayesh looks back with mixed feelings on his years as a retail entrepreneur. Start-up finance was not easy to find. His family helped, but the main problem was acquiring the large funds needed. For various reasons he did not approach Asian banks. The major high street banks were not too keen to help, but eventually a bank was found ('It wasn't one of the big four. It was a bank willing to take risks with new ventures') that was willing to help without any strings.

The reason for the banks' reluctance was that the Maneks had no track record. Also the banks had little experience of dealing with small Asian businesses. 'They've learned since,' says Jayesh. 'There's been a transition.' Now, eighteen years later, the Maneks' shops are flourishing. The chain was slimmed down when some of the shops were sold to other groups, but the family still owns four outlets. Having created a unique concept in pharmacies, Jayesh feels that it can be developed further to open more shops, with the right management structure in place.

Fund management remains his main interest, though both his own approach and the financial world itself have changed greatly since he first became interested in investment in his twenties.

'Technology has made a lot of difference, and you can't ignore it. There was the agricultural revolution, then the industrial revolution, and now we're living through the technological revolution. You've got to use technology, because it can help you make decisions faster. And it can be a useful element in selecting the right stocks – in other words, you don't necessarily use technology to choose them but you do look for companies that are going to benefit from technology.' He quotes the situation five or six years ago when the major banks were making several thousand staff redundant. It wasn't because the banks were performing badly but because technology was taking over. 'Now of course, there was a cost to the redundancies. But three or four years on, that's worked through and the banks' shares have gone up three- or fourfold in the past four or five years. So you look for companies that would benefit from the new technology, companies that are already taking it on board.'

So Jayesh keeps abreast of technology, both in his office and in looking at the business world. However, he does not consider that any piece of software comes near to duplicating human judgement in making investment decisions. 'Computers provide accuracy, but they don't help you make the choice. The human touch is still the key. You can't replace the individual with a machine.'

He smiles. 'So we come back to where we started. Everybody looks at the same information. It's how you interpret and use that information that matters.'

Chai Patel

'We live in a society where old age is neither respected nor valued. Age becomes a problem, in our materialistic, health-and-fitness-centred society ... I decided to develop a quality-driven, customer-centred commercial approach to the provision of nursing and residential care.'

I have talked a great deal so far about the typical South Asian family, in which the young are nurtured and the elderly valued, widows and widowers are looked after by their sons, and members of the family who have long since retired from active daily involvement in the family business are regarded as having wisdom and experience that earn a respected place in the family council.

Of all the symptoms of the gradual erosion of family values in many parts of the South Asian community today, one of the most telling is the weakening of commitment to the older generation. Some elderly Asians are virtually abandoned by their families, living in inconvenient flats and rarely visited by their busy offspring. It's not surprising that a fast-growing business in the South Asian community is the provision of sheltered housing and retirement homes.

In this new industry, the largest 'continuing care' company is Care First. It runs over 12,000 nursing and residential beds, several day centres and a range of outreach services. Formed in 1996 by the merger of two leading continuing care companies, Court Cavendish and Takare, its Chief Executive was a man still in his early forties, Dr Chai Patel.

There can't be many entrepreneurs who have had such a clear

vision of their aim in life from such an early age as Chai Patel had. His CV looks as if it was plotted with a straight edge. Born in Uganda of an Indian railway worker's family on his mother's side, he was brought with his family to Britain in 1970. He was fifteen years old and started working for his O-level examinations immediately at a comprehensive school in Putney. His father chose Putney deliberately; he wanted to be part of the community and to integrate with the country to which he had come, and one of the reasons he came to the UK was his admiration for British values.

Putney was skinhead territory, and as a newly arrived immigrant Chai would have had a tough time were it not for a lucky incident in his first few days at school. He was placed next to the leading school skinhead, but managed to stave off the inevitable harassment by helping him with a maths problem. This bought him insurance against attack for the rest of his schooldays and was a good early lesson in negotiating skills and interdependence.

It was medicine that dominated Chai's mind, even then. His father, who bought a confectionery shop and sub-post office and became a sub-postmaster, told him later that at the age of five Chai had announced his intention to become a doctor. A good crop of O-levels was a first step on the way to Southampton University and membership of the Royal College of Physicians, even though he had to go home at lunchtime during his O-levels to help in the shop because of unexpected staff shortages. A distinguished academic career took him into medical posts in the Wessex Region and eventually to a coveted MRC Fellowship at Pembroke College, Oxford.

He'd grown increasingly concerned about the National Health Service. 'I felt that the NHS was evolving into something that was not what I had wanted to enter. So rather than complain and become cynical, I decided to get out.' He was anxious to make a contribution, and he could see that the NHS could not cope adequately at every life stage. A professional background in geriatrics and other age-related areas focused his ambition to set up a commercial caring company. There was certainly a huge need. It was being realised that at the beginning of the twenty-first century, half the electorate would be elderly; by 2001, three in twenty people would be over sixty-five. There had to be a better way, he felt, of caring for the elderly than the unsatisfactory methods he had observed in the NHS in his work in Southampton and Bournemouth.

Having decided to go into the commercial sector Chai set about training himself, which he did by a major career change: in May 1985 he joined Merrill Lynch in the City and was headhunted by Lehman Brothers Kuhn Loeb the next year, where he rose to become vice-president, managing funds worth £250 million. 'It was my apprenticeship,' he says modestly, disarming suggestions that moving from medicine to the world of City finance was a rather peculiar move.

'Merrill Lynch taught me early on the importance of communications, the importance of analysis and the importance of setting very focused goals,' he says, adding that he got into investment banking by being introduced to one of the directors of Merrill Lynch by a mutual friend. They sent him to New York for three months' training – 'I remember feeling that the cleaning ladies knew more about investment banking than I did!'

He was still on course to realise his life-long plan. By 1988 he had amassed enough capital and judged the time was right to set up Court Cavendish. Within three months the company had established two homes. Within nine months Chai had bought out his partners and acquired Ladbroke's Care Homes division. It was one of the largest buyouts at that time; the company moved from capitalisation of half a million pounds to total capitalisation, debt and equity of £32 million. The number of beds increased from 100 to 700, and the staff of three to several hundred. Chai was drawing heavily on his City experience as he raised capital and dealt with the many aspects of forming a coherent group, particularly as it was a period of steep recession and high interest rates – 'it was quite an interesting discipline of managing debt and cash flows'. In 1993 the group was floated on the stock exchange with a capitalisation of £50 million.

In 1996 Chai merged Court Cavendish with Takare, to form Care First. Now the number of beds was 12,000 and the company's 135 homes were to be found all over the country. He was Chief Executive of the new company until he resigned in August 1997 over differences in the boardroom. The shareholders were solidly behind Chai, but he was already looking to the future.

Chai's press-cuttings album has a rather repetitious feel to it; subeditors have enjoyed devising variations of the 'Man with a Plan', 'Medic with a Mission' style of caption. But his single-mindedness is remarkable. He readily admits that running the whole show throughout made him a wealthy man, but quotes one of Charles Handy's dictums that very few people work to make money; most people work to do something which makes money.

In his plans for the future, he has a very clear idea what he wants to spend his money on. 'My goal is that when I'm fifty I shall stop working for money, and work because I want to, at what I want to do. So my economic target is to create a financial self-sufficiency by the time I'm fifty.' Chai's interests are broad and his charities numerous, and there is little doubt that he will be in a position to give them full attention when he reaches the age he has set for his 'retirement'.

Talking to Chai Patel, it's obvious that his father and mother have been very major influences in his life. He speaks with admiration of the courage it took to move to a foreign country and deliberately choose to live outside the areas where the majority of Asians lived. 'At my father's funeral, people were crying as they remembered how deeply he wanted to integrate. He was a brown Englishman. He'd integrated, but he hadn't abandoned his intrinsic Hindu nature.' However, Chai feels that he inherited his single-mindedness from his mother, who is a strong and determined woman.

It is his sense of reverence and obligation towards his family that lies behind certain key policies of the care homes he has established over the years. There is no 'ghettoisation'. The homes are open to all and are open communities – often in the past, care homes have had the atmosphere of closed communities, institutions of dread.

His respect for his family also strengthens his commitment to, and respect for, old people. 'Your connection with history is through your elders. Through them you understand from whence you have come. And just because you are old, and perhaps ill or disabled or frail, you can still have quality of life if people are prepared to give respect and dignity to elderly people, and see them for who they are, not what they have become.'

He believes passionately in these values. His message to Court Cavendish focused on an image which he often uses: 'I told them that I lit a candle; that they are turning it into a torch; and that one day, through the energy and vision of many people, it will turn into an inferno.'

Strong beliefs are very much a part of Chai Patel's outlook. A convert from Hinduism to Christianity, he has retained his links and respect for his family's faith; and the very cross-cultural values his father bequeathed to his family reflect his father's commitment to integration. 'Even now people say how brave my parents were to allow their children to marry across cultural, ethical and religious borders.'

The religious dimension is very much part of Chai's thinking: he is suspicious of rational choices made outside spiritual contexts. So although he rationally regards wealth creation as legitimate and not his primary purpose anyway, he finds it impossible to be a successful entrepreneur without also acknowledging the need to make a contribution back to society.

'I'm driven by several things,' he says. 'Poverty is one of the great social evils. I've seen the horror of it in India. Nothing erodes values and morality faster than economic poverty, because it reduces everything down to the basic instincts of survival. So if you want a civilised society that cares for its old and disabled people, you need economic stability and security.'

That firm belief explains why the years dealing in millions in the City were not a diversion from Chai's purpose, but an essential part of it. 'I am enjoying commerce, and being a doctor was also very fulfilling and satisfying. The balance of the two is critical, but both are needed. With the blend of experience and training I have had I feel I can make a difference on a wider scale than otherwise. And that's important.'

Part Three

Challenges
For the Future

9

Identity and Self-Expression

'This generation is crossing into the mainstream. We're going to explode ... These second generation guys have attitude and don't give a damn.'

Imran Khan, Editor, 2nd Generation[1]

The first generation of South Asian immigrants did not have a problem of identity; their identity was defined for them. They were outsiders, usually displaced people, sometimes bringing with them British passports and always a foreign culture. They were clearly Asians even if a piece of paper conferred British identity on them. Though many of them had lived and worked in outposts of the British Empire, had seen the British at their most British and had even taken on some of the characteristics of British culture, in Britain they were marginalised, partly because of the colour of their skin but most of all because they had arrived from outside. Their culture in the UK was usually an attempt to recreate India, or East Africa, or Pakistan – whatever part of the subcontinent they came from. They were strangers in a strange land.

UK second-generation South Asians, who have either been born in Britain or have lived in Britain for so long that they can hardly remember their country of origin, are in a quite different situation. They have a foot in each of two worlds. They have been brought up in South Asian families, and have inherited all that I described in Part One of this book. But they are also British, as entitled to be called British as anyone whose family has been established in the country for generations.

For many young South Asians the result is social dislocation and identity confusion. Integration is only superficial and at the key moments in life, such as relationships – boy/girl relationships, dating, sexual activity, marriage and so on – the ethnic and cultural differences between the two worlds cause problems. 'It's similar in a small way to the problems that British Jewish youngsters experience,' says Berjis Daver. 'I remember that when my daughter was twelve, only eight years ago, she was invited by her best friend – a Jew – to a New Year's party. But before the day of the party she was told that only Jews were allowed to go. It was a kind of ethno-sectarianism, and it is common in all second-generation ethnic minority communities. Where do the new generation fit in? I see so many people who don't know what their role is. They feel themselves to be neither one thing nor another.'

Another problem for some South Asians is the developing gap between those whose parents entered into retailing or other business when they came to Britain, and those who went into jobs that did not offer large financial rewards. I know of one businessman, for example, who is struggling because there is no reserve of family money on which he can draw. His father was a civil servant who was respected, got his pension and his OBE, but was not able to give his son the capital or the entrepreneurial example which would have given him a kick-start into business. Such situations may perhaps be made worse by the fact that the UK South Asian community often defines itself by its wealthy achievers; understandably, much is made of the fact that some Asians are among the richest people in Britain, and *Asian Who's Who* and similar publications are catalogues of success.

Manubhai Madhvani regards advertising success as a characteristic trait of the South Asian community, and regrets how in Uganda in days gone by he used to flaunt his own wealth. 'I was queuing up to pay my bill in the petrol station and the attendant said, "A

Mercedes-Benz! A great man is coming!"' Ambition is, he agrees, indispensable to success. But he is concerned about the number of young Asians whose ambitions are a big house and a Rolls-Royce. He prefers the attitude of his Jewish friends: 'The more they earn, the lower the profile they keep.' Much preferable, in his view, to the quest for making money for its own sake. As he points out, a tree overburdened with fruit will never grow high.

Nevertheless, many young Asians feel a deep sense of obligation to be successful, and it is a complex matter:

> Young Asians appear to be far more likely to be influenced in their choice of career by their families than are their contemporaries from the majority white group. Indeed, many feel that thay have not just to achieve in a career, but to achieve in a career that is both recognisable and socially acceptable from their family's point of view.[2]

ROLE MODELS

However, UK South Asians with a high profile have an important function in helping their community towards identity and integration. They serve as role models. For example university cricketers Mark Wagh and Anurag Singh, whom I mentioned in Chapter 2 (p. 45), certainly see this as an important consequence of their success. Singh acknowledges that Asian role models have great value for young Asian boys whose parents, with an eye to a successful career for them in the professions, sometimes tend not to motivate them to take cricket and other sports seriously. Even so, cricket may not have such a beneficial effect in some state schools with poor facilities and fixture lists, where players are forced to join Asian leagues or venture into club cricket. 'In some senses it might come down to cultural background. Little things might make them feel uncomfortable. In some cases, it's not a question of losing Asian cricketers to Asian leagues. We are losing them full stop,' says Singh.[3]

It's fortunate that there are a number of South Asian cricketing role models to encourage young Asians by example. Probably the best known of all is Imran Khan, educated at Keble College, Oxford, record-breaking captain of Pakistan, and the first Asian to be awarded the title of Asian of the Year. A later holder of that title, food tycoon Gulam Noon whose story is told in Chapter 3, is a revered figure in the London South Asian community and a keen cricketer.

Sometimes it is figures in the business world that young Asians want to imitate. If I may give another example from my own experience: when I meet another South Asian who is from Trinidad, a name that sometimes crops up in conversation is Kirpalani's Store. It's the largest department store in Trinidad, known all over the Caribbean. Everybody shops at Kirpalani's. I know the Kirpalanis well because they are relatives of mine. I first met them when they visited us in Kenya. We hadn't been in touch with them since the Partition, but now that both families were prospering we had started to make contact with each other again. When I heard them talking about their success and what they had achieved, it made me feel very proud of my family and of being a South Asian. The Kirpalanis were more than relatives. They were role models.

AN ASIAN BOOM?

Today's generation of young UK South Asians is beginning to capitalise on both its Asian and its British roots. They have many of the same characteristics that their parents display, but now these have developed in lives lived entirely, or almost entirely, in Britain. Links with the subcontinent may weaken and their sense of a cultural inheritance diminish as time goes by and the third generation grows up. But though it is more desirable to retain that heritage than lose it completely, in Manchester, Birmingham and other centres of South Asian population you will find South Asians who have succeeded in mixing their Asian background with a prosperous business, even in the changed and often difficult world of the approaching millennium. It is this making of a new identity composed of elements of both Asian and British culture that encourages Manubhai Madhvani to hope that ground will be won in politics too. 'I think Asians have done wonderfully well,' he says, and points to the fact that neither Asians nor white politicians ever realised that the Asians would be so influential.

One of the most explosive areas of British life in which UK South Asians have succeeded in establishing a new identity of their own is the media. In theatre and film, Asians have moved on from art as propaganda, using the rhetoric of the drama to argue the rights of ethnic minorities, to a theatre that uses the South Asian culture as a landscape in which to set powerful and compelling dramas that may reflect Asian issues but also transcend them. Playwrights like Hanif Koureshi use the UK Asian situation as a powerful metaphor; and unlike some Asian drama of the past, the audience is much greater than the Asian population itself. Actors, too, cross ethnic boundaries, so that somebody like Art Malik is equally likely to be seen playing a part in which the actor's ethnicity is irrelevant as one which calls for an Asian.

That doesn't mean that today's UK South Asians in the arts want to play down their Asian heritage. Far from it. Even in modern multi-cultural, multi-faith Britain, it is surprising how few British people respect or even recognise the immense wealth of South Asian arts and culture. Yet it has been well documented on television and radio and in books such as Prabhu Guptara's *Black British Literature*,[4] and an exhibition on the printed book throughout India's history drew large crowds at the Frankfurt International Book Fair a few years ago.

Such a rich diversity of ethnic culture is one reason that so many people found it difficult to accept Lord Tebbit's comments on multi-racialism made during the 1997 Conservative Party conference.

How many Britons know that India's film industry today is larger than Hollywood's – or that Indian literature was rich and plentiful when Britain's was passing through the Dark Ages – or that Sanskrit predates Greek and Latin? South Asian culture contributes to British life in many ways. In literature, novelists such as Salman

Rushdie achieve recognition and win major prizes. In dance, ethnic companies attract audiences from far beyond the ethnic communities, and dance fashions like Bhangra have nationwide popular influence. In mainstream music there is a recurring influence of South Asian culture. In the heady days of the 1960s the Beatles made sitar music popular, in the 1970s Ravi Shankar and Ustad Ali Akhbar Khan could fill a concert hall with white as well as Asian audiences, and the South Indian Kathakali dancers and musicians could generate enough ticket sales to justify bringing them lock, stock and barrel for a tour of the UK; and today South Asian musicians have a strong presence in the popular charts in groups and performers such as Echobelly and White Town. New ethnic and fusion repertoire prospers and the current interest in world music has put money in quite a few record companies' pockets. This musical explosion often contains a political and social agenda. 'Popular music is not simply a reflection of socio-political situations, but is involved in a series of dynamic interactions – sometimes reflecting, constituting, or subverting, at other times tangential, reactionary, and, occasionally, anarchic,' write Raminder Kaur and Virinder S. Kalra in a study that explores this subject to a depth beyond the scope of this book.[5]

There are other cultural contributions: the *Melas*, for example, a festival of Asian culture which like the Notting Hill Carnival plays a part in the local economy; and the Asian contribution to arts management, entertainment, TV, local radio and so on, both mainstream and ethnic. Sikh musician Jas Mann, a.k.a. Babylon Zoo, sent one demo of his single *Spaceman* to Parlophone. It was picked up by the radio stations and went on to become the fastest-selling debut single of all time (according to *Q Magazine*). Jyoti Mishra (White Town) did even better. His record *Abort Retry Fail?* was a huge success on radio; its 'A side', *Your Woman*, went to No. 1. *Abort Retry Fail?* was a back-bedroom production, composed, performed and produced entirely by Mishra using amateur equipment.

10

And Now For the Bad News

We have seen many positive achievements in this book so far. Everybody in the UK should be proud of them as British achievements. But we must now consider what has been a background theme in this book so far, and something which is obvious to anyone who reads a newspaper, watches TV or walks around British urban centres.

UK South Asians are at a point of change – but change brings mixed blessings. Not all South Asians have succeeded. There is a great deal of social disadvantage, much racial discrimination and hatred, and a loss of traditional values and certainties. The old family structures are under threat almost everywhere, and some of the qualities that made successful entrepreneurs out of many first-generation immigrants are not working to quite the same effect in the world that the second generation is facing. In mainstream Britain there are glass ceilings limiting how high members of the ethnic communities can rise, and in the ethnic sectors new limits to growth are imposed by a changing political and social environment.

The UK South Asian community is still a successful, entrepreneurial community that produces more than its share of gross product and features to a disproportionate degree in British education, British industry and British wealth. But there are questions that must be asked. How far is Asian success threatened in modern Britain? To what extent have South Asians contributed to their own problems? If nothing is done, is there catastrophe ahead – and if, as I have argued, South Asians are making a large contribution to UK plc, what would be the implications for Britain as a whole?

Nobody looking at UK society can be misled by the illusion that the South Asian community is uniformly prosperous. Generalisations about South Asian family structures and cultural background have some value and of course I have made much use of them in this book. But generalisations about prosperity are dangerous. For example, the Indian community has fared much better than the Bangladeshi and Pakistani communities. Indians from East Africa have tended to prosper more than Indians from the subcontinent. The UK North–South divide affects the South Asian community as much as it does the majority population.

For many South Asians, too, the price of business independence has been high. There has been deferred satisfaction, long hours, low pay in the early years, often racial unpopularity, and social disadvantage for large sectors of the South Asian community that will never be cited in proofs of South Asian business success.

The problems faced by the South Asian community in Britain are, however, more than the predictable side effects of intense entrepreneurial activity in an economy that has been through difficult times. There are pressures on the South Asians that are unique to their community, and I want to argue that unless we understand them we will not understand the very real possibility that this wealth-creating, disproportionately successful community might be under terminal threat.

THE ROLE OF THE MEDIA

A major agent of change is the world's mass media. South Asians, both in the UK and in the subcontinent, are looking at the world in a very different way to that of previous generations. The media, with their characteristic focus on the centre of culture rather than the fringe, record – and in some respects contribute to – the changing of established traditions and the weakening of established values. Take soap opera, which has a truly global audience: Indian villages can now watch the infidelities and glamorous business swindles of oil-rich Texan barons and the pre-marital experimentation of Australian teenagers.

It would be naïve to say that soap opera is a wholly destructive agent of social change or that the media are not capable of social critique and moral exhortation. The subcontinent has good cause to be grateful for movements like Band Aid and Comic Relief; my own organisation, Christmas Cracker, has raised millions of pounds for projects such as helping street children and AIDS victims, none of which could have happened without the help of the media. Yet although the media may not always change society, they always reflect it; not always prescriptive, they are by nature descriptive. A window has been opened not only on to another world but on to a different set of values. Ironically, the television set – the single most powerful media vehicle in British homes – was one of the first things that most first-generation immigrants purchased as they began to achieve a good standard of living. It is an investment that for some families has badly backfired.

The traditional authority system in the Asian family has often been gradually weakened as models of weak families and corrupted family relationships are beamed into British homes. Soap operas like *EastEnders and Brookside* (some watched regularly by around a third of the UK population) present views of relationships that conflict with the Asian (and traditional Western) traditions of faithfulness within marriage, respect for parents, business integrity and so on. They are also damaging to concepts of the nuclear family and the responsibility of the young towards the old. *The Cosby Show* (in its time one of the most popular TV sitcoms in the United States and very popular in the UK) is an isolated example of family comedy that respects the elderly, emphasises the value of family relationships, and doesn't try to argue that the most successful children are those who are sharpest at outwitting and outsmarting their parents. But it's one of very few programmes that do.

British South Asians receive these messages from two directions: from the television in their own home, and through the extended family network and business connections in the subcontinent. In India (a country with a long history of cinema and visual arts) the middle classes number about four times the population of the UK, and they can afford terrestrial television and also satellite and cable TV. A constant tide of Western materialism and Western values arrives in the subcontinent daily, and is exported back to the British Asian community as people talk by telephone, visit each other and do business together.

KEEPING IT WITHIN THE FAMILY

A second agent of change is the cultural factor, the weakening of the key structures of Asian society that I described in Part One of this book.

The family, as we have already seen, is the core of South Asian business life. For example, many Asian entrepreneurs consider that borrowing from people and organisations outside the extended family is something to be ashamed of. This is an attitude I have often encountered. For example, an Asian refused to allow me to visit him at his own address but insisted on coming to my office for our meeting. He didn't want those close to him to know he was talking to a representative of an official agency (it happened to be the Prince's Youth Business Trust).

The Asian preference to go to their nuclear and extended families, from which an entrepreneur will expect to gain loans and receive business advice and to which he will expect to be accountable, is a positive aspect of the Asian community. It's quite unlike that of some other minority communities, who simply do not trust outside agencies and moneylenders. The Asian family business circle and its family councils, as I have already discussed, are tied up with filial respect, with social standards and even with a religious world view.

The family business structure is tellingly portrayed in Hanif Kureishi's Oscar-nominated film My Beautiful Laundrette (1985), set in the South London Asian community. The wealthy uncle funds his nephew's entrepreneurial venture into laundrettes, characteristically involving turning a rundown and semi-derelict premises into a spanking new, gleaming success. The family is involved in the decision making, the planning, the advising; while the young man is encouraged to stretch his entrepreneurial wings, the family is in the background, equipped with a wealth of experience and business expertise – and cash. My *Beautiful Laundrette* well illustrates the nature of the system at its best: the family council with its complex network of respect, dependency, affection and incentive.

Identity crises
The film also illustrates the old structures in the process of breaking down. The young entrepreneur is torn between his homosexual relationship with a white boy and the demands of his own close and supportive family. Two worlds are in conflict: that of the older generation, with values, standards and an ethos of its own, and the world of the young man – an Asian, one generation removed from his cultural and ethnic heritage.

It's a generation gap with cultural consequences. He is caught in the dilemma of being a second- or third-generation Britisher – yet not a Britisher. The culture from which he is becoming distant, paradoxically, is often more British than modern Britain; the journalist Malcolm Muggeridge once observed that you only find real British life in old India nowadays. Kureishi portrays his London Asians in well-heeled surroundings, relishing the Thatcherite revolution: typical British middle-class suburbanites.

GENERATIONS IN CONFLICT

Yet it's also a gap with business consequences. Those young Asians who go to university or business school often return to find the family business distinctly unsympathetic to new and modern ideas, even though a failure to take such ideas seriously may well marginalise it to the point of extinction.

Integrating each new generation into the family business is often difficult. Most South Asian businesses were founded to escape the nightmare of unemployment and so that the founder could be his own boss. Arriving in an alien culture, the jobs and status they could expect were lowly, so the first generation of immigrants worked long hours to create security for themselves. Many had been prosperous in their home countries, and intended to give their children the kind of opportunities they would have had at home. They sent them to good schools, they financed their further education and they gave them all the advantages they could.

Two things followed from this. One, very few second-generation South Asians, now well educated and often professionally qualified, wanted to come back home and run the corner shop. Not only in retail business but in all business, the question of succession became very important. The family business is a key part of the extended family concept. What happens when the line of succession fails because a new generation wants to look elsewhere? And how do you sell a family business when that business no longer has its major asset – the intangible family commitment that made it prosper?

The second problem is that a whole generation of South Asians is coming through the education process and many of them are being disappointed. Possession of a good degree, or membership of one's professional organisation, isn't enough to guarantee you a job – especially if you are from an ethnic minority, and particularly a black ethnic minority. It is not a level playing field, and the only way to level it is to be better qualified, better motivated, more single-minded than the majority population's graduates. Thus many youngsters are entering the marketplace and finding that corporate Britain has very little to offer them. Jobs are not easy to find.

Characteristically, some have created their own jobs. In my own organisation our printing is done by a firm whose owner, Vinod Gohil, graduated from university. He found it impossible to get a job, so he set up as a printer. He's doing well, though he often works eighteen hours a day; his work is of very good quality and he has created his own 'bubble of success' in a generally hostile marketplace.

Not all graduating Asians, and even fewer school leavers, have the inclination or the opportunity to set up in business. One option is to go abroad, to places like Canada and Australia where there are Asian communities. The extended family reaches there, easing entry into the job market and sometimes offering better prospects than existed in Britain. The consequence, of course, is a loss of skilled workers who would otherwise have contributed to the professional skills pool in the UK.

For those who stay, there is a real danger that unemployment will lead to social problems. In the months while this book was being written, Asian youths were involved in riots in Bradford. Less recently, in riots in Birmingham and Toxteth, Asian youths were burning shops and looting. In Bradford, the controversial film *Border* aggravated inter-ethnic friction and a shop was burned down by a gang of youths. It could be argued that one reason for these acts of violence was social frustration aggravated by unemployment.

Judge Mota Singh has seen the beginnings of Asians in trouble with the law. 'So far we don't see many Asians in the courts, by and large. But it's no longer the case that Asians are a solid, law-abiding community that never offends the law. So far as the criminal courts are concerned, there's probably only an occasional fraud here and there, but those few will be on a massive scale – VAT frauds of two or three million, that kind of thing. And there are organisations in London for Asian Battered Women ... previously Asians rarely appeared in court. The crime may have been happening but the community was self-policing. Now they're in court in greater numbers, which implies some sort of social breaking down.'

People in positions of authority have not always caught up with these worrying trends. I was recently at a meeting where I was in conversation with a town councillor. 'Of course,' he said, 'the image of the Asian is a very positive one. High standards of behaviour, and we all know that Asians are strongly influenced by parental role models.'

When I gave him chapter and verse for some of the more serious incidents in which young South Asians were involved, he was crestfallen. 'I'm very disappointed to learn this,' he said. 'I'm very disappointed indeed.'

Here was a key decision maker, who had not noticed what was happening and was assessing a situation using out-of-date stereotypes. Yet social breakdown is a simmering problem that may one day come to the boil if steps are not taken to deal with it.

CHANGING PATTERNS IN THE UK

Many of the changes that are beginning to affect the UK South Asian community are not unique; they are shared by the whole population.

For example, the honouring of elderly relatives and the respecting of mature wisdom are key Asian values, as I have already shown. But the devaluing of age and experience that has marked much of modern British life is beginning to affect the South Asian community. In some families, the elderly have become a burden; hence the recent rise in popularity of Asian retirement homes and sheltered housing. This is a new and profitable business. Residential homes are already a profitable market, and Asian establishments can reasonably charge a premium because they can undertake to locate in an Asian district, to hire staff who understand Asian ways, to observe Asian festivals and religious calendars and much more. Many establishments of this kind are pleasant places, run with characteristic enterprise and efficiency. Yet there's a sense in which the fact that a demand exists for such places at all is an indicator of social disintegration; in previous generations people in old age were looked after by their children, and there would have been too few unsupported elderly South Asians to justify whole buildings devoted to housing them. Dr Chai Patel, whose story is told in Chapter 8 (p. 162), speaks powerfully of the implications of the growth of his industry (though it should be noted that only a small part of his business caters for Asians).

As the distinctives of UK South Asian society become vulnerable – both those distinctives worth preserving and those that are rightly discarded – UK South Asians become more vulnerable to the social pressures that the West as a whole is facing.

Motivation

Another shared social change is the vulnerability of many established value systems as society becomes more liberally inclined and materialistic. Whatever John Major's ill-fated 'Back to Basics' campaign really meant to achieve, it certainly highlighted the fact that in many crucial areas the UK was close to moral bankruptcy. In such a climate, the nuclear family – let alone the extended family – is vulnerable; filial respect and attachment to the family business are often early casualties, and so is motivation.

Long years of high unemployment in Britain have left a legacy of long-term unemployed. The longer a person is unemployed, the more difficult it is for him or her to re-acquire work skills and motivation. In the days when most Asians worked in local family businesses, or were part of a workforce that considered itself a kind of extension of the employer's own extended family, there was a great deal of motivation. I have already quoted Kumar Datwani, who has said that Asians are not clock-watchers and that they take it for granted that they won't leave work until the task they are working on is complete. This is still a characteristic of large parts of the South Asian community. But in some areas and in some local communities, the motivation of new generations is not as strong as it was in the old.

Alienation

Perhaps that is only to be expected. The new generations are one step further removed from the country of their family origin. Much of what my generation did when we arrived in the UK was intended to create a little India or a little Kenya within our new country. We ate Indian food, we dressed in Indian clothes, we did many things just as we did them in Kenya. For us, our Indian lifestyle was a living memory that we wanted to cherish. For the second generation, it's a story their parents have told them, but many of them have never been to their ancestral country and probably never will. They think of themselves as British first and South Asian second. Often they have no interest in Asian customs such as arranged marriages, and today, although a large number of marriages are arranged ones, many are not.

Of course, sometimes progress is not negative. My wife and I do not intend to arrange marriages for our children. This does not mean that we believe arranged marriages are an evil institution; as a rule they survive rather better than most Western marriages, and I have nephews and nieces whose arranged marriages will probably be very happy. As a follower of Christ I very much hope that my children will marry people who share their faith, and I must admit to 'arranged meetings' – in that we do encourage them to play an active part in the church youth club! On the other hand, a tradition that I do think should be ended (or drastically rethought) is the ancient one of bride's dowry, which can leave a poor family paying off the cost of the daughters' marriages for the rest of their lives. In some parts of the South Asian community it is already dying out for various reasons, and I think that is a good thing.

But bad traditions should die because the community recognises they are bad, not because its young people reject them simply because they *are* traditions. There is a very serious dimension to social change: the family and the business are inextricably intertwined. In most South Asian communities you cannot have one without the other. In many and subtle ways, any disintegration of the family opens the way to economic and business disintegration, with potentially disastrous consequences. It's like bringing down a house of cards. Business and economic success are interlinked with the survival of family structures, social structures and values, and if one is threatened the other is at risk.

The long-term scenario could be very problematic. There is already a fear of the unknown as many South Asian families contemplate change. They have some crucial questions: 'How will this affect my extended family? Will my son accept the arranged marriage I plan for him? Surely a girl from India is a safer prospect than a

British Asian girl?' (It tends to be the case that an Indian bride is seen as the best choice for a boy, whereas for a girl a boy from the UK South Asian population is sought.)

The aim is preservation. Change is destabilising, it threatens the status quo. One of the most disturbing developments of which I am aware at present is the beginning of arranged marriages between cousins and second cousins. This is not common and it is considered as undesirable in the South Asian community as in the majority community – but it's happening in a few cases as a bulwark against change. One possible scenario is that a reaction against change will be to make most South Asians marry within the extended family. Thus the network and family relationships which I have already described as one of the great strengths of South Asian society could turn in on itself; where the well-being of the business depends on the well-being of the family, this may introduce new and serious problems.

It may seem extreme even to envisage such huge social problems. But there are already major problems on a scale and of a type that were uncommon in first-generation immigrants. For example that single-minded willingness to work unsocial hours – originally so necessary to ensure the family's security – can, when security has been gained, all too easily turn into a workaholic obsession that keeps husbands (or, increasingly, wives) at the workplace for unnecessarily long hours, with serious consequences for the family. A rise in the suicide rate among young Asian women is just one indication that increasing wealth doesn't automatically lead to a higher level of contentment.

The Family Firm In Trouble

Some of the crises faced by the South Asian community, however, are not the result of inevitable change, but the consequence of families and companies struggling to come to terms with a new business world. Time moves on, and what was appropriate three decades ago is often inadequate for a business in the modern world.

In the majority of UK South Asian businesses, the owners are reluctant to approach government and other public sources of funding and business advice. As a result, though the South Asian community, and in particular the Indian community, is extremely successful (notably as entrepreneurs), there is very little take-up of Training Enterprise Council and other government help. The danger is of a potential marginalisation of the South Asian community at the very point where it is strongest: the economic life of Britain.

Why are South Asian businesses so reluctant to look outside their own community?

Discrimination

One reason is discrimination (and the perception of discrimination, even where no discrimination is intended). The London TECs' report *London: Open City* found that discrimination against ethnic minorities is still widespread.

Discrimination happens on the personal level – as, for example, in vandalism and local antagonism towards ethnic minorities in inner-city and other urban situations, and in the more organised antagonism of movements like the British National Party. It can be seen in the disturbing reports of disaffected white youths who are forming gangs: often antagonism erupts into serious violence, and it is a two-way process. There has been at least one case of a gang of Bangladeshi youths killing a white boy.

There is also residual structural discrimination. Judge Mota Singh acknowledges that this is so even in the legal profession:

I think it would be foolish to deny that discrimination exists. It is in every walk of life, in every strata. And neither the Bar nor solicitors, indeed the legal system in general, is immune to it. It may not be obvious, it may not be overt, but it is there. I accept that the Bar Council and the Law Society have introduced policies that are against discrimination of any kind, on grounds of race, colour or sex. Whether those policies are working is another matter ... Nevertheless, there is strong anti-discrimination direction from the leadership of those bodies, and where there are complaints they are looked into.

Another contributing factor to the reluctance of South Asians to approach funding agencies is, of course, the common failing of those agencies to locate and communicate with their prospective clients.

External trading patterns
Having looked at social change within the UK South Asian community, and the changes in the Asian business community, I now want to look at the changes that are happening in the larger marketplace, both in the UK and worldwide.

My cousin was a pioneer of mass-produced Tandoori food in the UK, one of the first to develop a range of flavours and a Tandoori brand product. In the mid-1980s he told me about a machine he had seen in California that could take chicken drumsticks, breasts and thighs, marinate them and ensure a uniform taste. It was revolutionary for the 1980s. It could produce huge quantities at a consistent quality and at a very competitive price. The companies marketing such machines are like many UK South Asian businesses: niche enterprises, entrepreneurially brilliant, with enough of an innovative edge to tie up major contracts with the large retailers. It's a characteristically South Asian story, of which Noon Products plc, whose story we have already considered, is only one of many examples.

The problem is that a huge threat hangs over all such businesses: the threat that some large multinational will step in and take over the market that has been so painstakingly developed by the small entrepreneurs. Such companies are less interested in initial profits than in market share. With millions of pounds available, and the ability to subsidise manufacturing at a loss for several years in order to beat the competition and secure market dominance, they would be almost invincible.

It's already happening.

I am aware of at least one international company, a household name, that is planning to bring skilled Indian chefs from the sub-continent and set up Asian food-manufacturing plants in the UK. Such developments are unlikely to affect the main contracts of Noon Products plc, where relationships between clients and suppliers have been established over many years and rivals offering to undercut Noon's prices have been turned away. But many smaller companies will be faced with the threat of extinction, and many promising entrepreneurs will not be able to gain a footing at all.

A similar threat (or, looked at another way, a similar spur to competitiveness) is the way in which the larger companies are exploring the possibilities of the free market and of multiple focus in their retailing. For example, a proposal was put forward by a major supermarket chain to build medical units on its sites. The proposal has been turned down, but the thinking behind it is very significant. It's a bold concept, innovative and creative; and South Asian businesses need to take a hard look at it. A start has been made in that direction, as I have already pointed out, by some South Asian retailers who have brought medical attendants into retail premises. But the supermarket project envisaged doctors' surgeries, so that if you have a sick relative you can combine medical attendance with shopping. A brilliant idea – and one to which Asians running high street pharmacies need to pay heed.

We may be looking at the break-up of the old high street shopping concept itself and the creation of new 'high streets', in out-of-town, industrial estate and hypermarket sites. Such sites have had an immense impact on neighbouring towns and high street retailers, who are often already struggling with 'red routes' and parking schemes that make it much easier for shoppers to go to the large out-of-town stores than to try to find somewhere to park near the high street.

In 1997, the Asian newsletter *BreakOut* announced a programme of research and seminars confronting the problems of the 'London corner shops'. A survey conducted by the London Chamber of Commerce Asian Business Association had found that seven out of ten corner shop owners did not expect to be trading in ten years' time. Reasons given included rising crime, restrictive parking controls, punitive business rates and competition from the major supermarkets. 'But it is not commercial pressures alone which threaten the future of local corner shops. A significant number of retailers expect their business to close after their retirement as no-one in the family wishes to continue running it.'[1]

In such a state of change, the problem for the South Asian community is knowing where to invest, and whether to invest in the long term or the short term.

They have many examples to consider. In Tenerife in the Canary Islands, there has been a great deal of development in the south of the island. The northern region was well established and prosperous, and investing there meant an immediate return on one's investment and a thriving economy. Investing in the south was a risk, but offered a much higher potential return. Today, southern investors are enjoying a very good return on their money, while the north has all but closed down. What has happened is a recycling of wealth from north to south; and similar shifts are happening in British business today.

In the past South Asians have been good at anticipating trends, and their cash mobility has enabled them to move quickly to exploit the possibilities. But there are new factors today. The immense buying power of the large supermarkets is one. For example, own-brand retailing has brought prices down drastically. Peeled tomatoes, a basic ingredient of South Asian cooking, used to be 24 pence a tin. Now the major supermarket chains are selling them at 10 or even 9 pence a tin. Of course there is almost no profit, but it gets the customers in – just as in our family shops we stocked milk, a messy and inconvenient product but essential if we were to appeal to casual, last-minute shoppers.

In that kind of market you cannot speak of competition any longer, in the sense of a 'fair fight' on the grounds of selling a superior product or service. The prices and blanket media advertising are far beyond what the local retailer can achieve. As shopping patterns change, many families (including Asian families) stock up in bulk at the supermarket with items that they would in the past have bought from their local stores.

Global factors

Apart from the threat of losing their innovations to richer competitors with more buying power than they themselves possess, yet more threats lie ahead for many South Asian businesses. For example, there is a growth of 'import substitution'. It is possible to manufacture a product in one country and bring it very quickly to the other side of the globe for selling. So the process of importing skilled staff from a distant country can be taken even further: the technology is already in place to have food manufactured in the best-quality plants on the subcontinent, making use of local technology and expertise, local software, local labour, local subsidies. It can then be brought to Britain and, because of the low manufacturing costs, will have a competitive edge in the marketplace.

BUBBLES OF SUCCESS

In this broad overview of problems facing the South Asian community, it is hard to escape the conclusion that many of the problems have been created, or at least aggravated, by the very success story with which I began this book.

That story can be described as a series of 'bubbles of success', like the domes that science-fiction writers sometimes imagine scattered on the surface of an alien planet, protecting the aliens from the dangerous atmosphere and inhospitable climate. The UK South Asian community likewise is often regarded as a subeconomy that has successfully insulated itself from recession. But, as we have seen, the bubbles are beginning to be buffeted by chill winds.

What should government and official agencies do about these bubbles that lately have begun to look so vulnerable?

A model economy

One temptation might be to leave things as they are. That would have some benefits: it would give the majority population the opportunity to look closely at this subeconomy and use it as a model from which to learn, and whose strengths it can seek to harness. To take just one example: the informal links and extensive global business connections that I have described at length could be immensely useful to British trade if properly harnessed. On a business trip to the Middle East I once sat in a Kuwaiti market, drinking tea and chatting to other businessmen about business networks we all knew intimately: Geneva, Kuwait, Lagos, even Peru! We discovered we had friends and colleagues in common. Our associates owned neighbouring plantations in South America. So we made a deal. We were in business. Those global links and networks confer a keen competitive edge, and the international contacts on which they function can result in lucrative contracts for UK plc.

The values of the South Asian family and community are still highly visible and demonstrable despite the problems, threats and vulnerability that we have discussed in this chapter. That could prompt a question for the majority business community: might such values usefully be inculcated to help UK success in the global economy? They have certainly helped the Asian community's success in the wider arena. But the question that is becoming urgent is this: are the bubbles of success able to go on protecting, or are the forces of change within and without liable to burst them? Already, as we have seen, there is dangerous vulnerability. The corner-shop success of the 1970s and 1980s is now facing stiff competition, niche markets are under threat, social problems are rising.

In the next chapter, I want to look closely at ways in which the UK South Asian community, this valuable resource, can be helped to continue to succeed. The dynamic of immigrant survival and immigrant genius that produced the first generation of UK Maharajahs has given way to a more complex economy, and if the same level of success and the same contribution to British prosperity are to be sustained, we need to act quickly.

11

A Helping Hand

Stories such as Shami Ahmed's (p. 145) are encouraging. They show that the second generation of South Asians can build on the successes of the first generation and explore new avenues of enterprise of which their parents and grandparents never dreamed. The other side of the coin, however, is that success of this kind is counterbalanced by the number of South Asian businesses that are struggling in the late 1990s. Often the problems of inter-generational conflict and other issues such as those we have already discussed are simply too large to be overcome by flair, native genius, good networks and hard work.

In this chapter I want to look at some of the positive things that are being done in terms of helping the running of family businesses: changes in accountant–client relationships, the targeting of financial advice and guidance to the South Asian business community, and ways in which the family business itself can be helped to begin to reflect the changing business world and today's economic climate.

If you walk from London's gleaming futuristic Barbican Centre into Old Street, you might think you were stepping back some decades. This end of Old Street belongs to an area that suffered ter-ribly in the war and has not always fared much better at the hands of the planners. Once the great highway out of London to the north east, the street begins today with buildings that are nondescript and unimpressive. Thus the façade of 26–34 Old Street belies its modernised interior that houses the Blackstone Franks Group of financial advisory services.

The partners include well-known authorities like Robert Maas, the taxation expert who heads the Tax Consultancy Division. The firm is a member of Integrated Advisory Group International, a creative linking of multi-disciplined professional firms whose members offer legal, tax and advisory services in over twenty-five countries.

Blackstone Franks is one example of City firms that have recognised both the importance, and the specialised needs, of the South Asian community. It specialises in advising foreign investors, immigrant businesses and ethnic minority businesses. One of the partners, Subhash Thakrar, is a specialist in immigration; inward investment into the UK and South Asian businesses represent at least a quarter of his clients.

On the other side of town, in a huge glass and masonry palace off Ealing Broadway, are the West London offices of Grant Thornton International, financial and business advisers with a special interest in owner-managed businesses. The West London office has a large South Asian catchment. In the early 1990s the company launched a special initiative aimed at Asians throughout London and the South East, under the direction of one of the Partners, Anuj Chande. 'We identified the Asian business community as very much an integral part of the owner-managed, closely managed business sector, and one that desperately needed good business advisers, good lawyers, good accountants and good bankers.'

Much of what follows in this chapter draws on the experience of these two firms – one, a medium-sized City firm, the other, one of the top international firms – through Mr Thakrar and Mr Chande. To this I have added my own observations from many years of working with South Asian companies.

CHARACTERISTICS OF THE RELATIONSHIP

In many respects, of course, South Asian businesses are no different to businesses in any community. Grant Thornton's 'Prima' advisory programme for owner-managed businesses is not aimed specifically at South Asians, but many of the issues it identifies are very relevant to South Asian businesses. They include: tension between family leadership and professional viability; the need for succession planning, as a business built on the entrepreneurial skills of one generation lives on into future generations; bringing professionals from outside the family into the family business; financial planning; and much more. In 1996, in a survey conducted by Grant Thornton and Business Strategies Ltd, the priorities of UK small to medium-sized enterprises (SMEs) were listed (in order of importance) as:

❑ Growth and control
❑ Income and investment
❑ Size
❑ Family succession
❑ Partners

These are issues that will not be unfamiliar to those who have read this far!

It is a deceptive similarity. A solution based on British SMEs in general can provide only limited help in analysing specifically South Asian concerns. There are certain areas in which Asians uniquely need help from their financial advisers. We've seen them repeatedly in this book.

Asians live and breathe business twenty-four hours a day, seven days a week
They want to have access to their business advisers at any time. They want to be able to pick up the telephone and talk to their accountant at night, at weekends, or whenever they need to. They tend not to abuse that access, but it's very different to the way that

most business is run in the majority population, where the weekend tends to be sacrosanct. In the South Asian companies with which I have had personal involvement, the evenings and weekends are the obvious times to visit the accountant, outside office hours. This is partly because the daytime is the time to make money; and partly because the distinction between work time and family time is much less rigid in South Asian homes.

Asians need advisers who have cultural sensitivity

Earlier I told the (true) story of the accountant who put up with a lengthy wait to have a meeting with his clients. He understood that the important religious festival at that point in the calendar would naturally take priority over a business meeting. There are many more examples of the kind of cultural awareness that is essential if a good relationship is to be built between client and adviser. For example, think about the MD who disappeared during a day of crucial negotiations. It turned out that his oldest daughter was getting married in a few days' time and he had to go personally to the airport to collect family members flying in from the subcontinent. An unwary adviser might have suggested that the MD send somebody else so that the negotiations could continue. It would have been a serious error of tact. In Asian families it is essential that proper respect be paid to older relatives (who might, moreover, be totally non-executive but highly influential members of the family council).

Asians demand confidentiality

Client confidentiality is of even greater importance to Asians than to most clients. One reason is the close inter-connectedness of the Asian community. It would be easy for an unwary accountant to reveal the identity of a client without even mentioning the name; friends and colleagues would be able to recognise them from details the accountant had thought insignificant. Asians are generally reserved about their business affairs, which is not to say that there are not those who enjoy publicity and use it to their business advantage. In fact this has even led a significant number of South Asian businesses to switch their financial affairs to accountants from the majority population, after their South Asian accountants talked too freely about their affairs to others.

Asians want value for money
The days are long gone when Asian businesses looked for the cheapest stock or services available. Nowadays the emphasis is on value for money. This is a positive development for South Asian businesses. It means that although a financial service might be more expensive than others, if it saves more money than it costs it's clearly worth it.

Asians want credibility
There are other, intangible benefits for which South Asians are willing to pay more if doing so brings intangible, but definite, advantages. A prestigious accountant's name on the balance sheet can improve credibility and have other benefits too. There is still a great deal of suspicion of the Asian business community in the UK – they're seen as sharp operators, who have their own way of going about things and like to play their cards close to their chests. A reputable accountant on one's financial statements can pay dividends. For example, bank managers have sometimes decided to fund projects because the name of a high-profile company is involved in the proposal.

Asians have broad horizons
The global South Asian diaspora has created an internationally minded community with strong business links with the subcontinent. They need advisers who understand international business and can advise on expansion, new markets, imports and exports and much more.

Asians also are keen on expanding their business by acquisition, both of businesses and of premises. Some stories have become legendary, like the one about the Patel family in East London, who in the early 1980s bought a shop every year in Green Street, Forest Gate, until they owned an entire terrace; they only stopped because the next house in line belonged to the Metropolitan Police, who weren't inclined to sell.[1]

An adviser who can specialise in different areas is a definite plus for Asians looking to expand by acquisition.

INCREASE AWARENESS

Significantly, points like these are much the same as those that Western businesses must also bear in mind when they are dealing with overseas Asian businesses. For example, an article in *Long Range Planning* discusses the role of the family in Asian business:

> The family-controlled firm and the state-owned enterprise are the most common ownership structures in Asia. Foreign firms seeking local joint venture partners in Asia will, of necessity, face the prospect of allying with family-controlled firms. Family control in firms creates special concerns that alliance partners should anticipate. Signs of family stability, well-laid succession plans and clearly demarcated professional decision-making represent attractive characteristics for foreign partners.[2]

The authors urge readers to approach such relationships bearing in mind issues like succession, familial relations over-riding competence, and mismatching of authority and position – issues as relevant to the small South Asian retail outlet in a British town as to the huge Tata Group in India.

I want to suggest that a first step in helping the South Asian community to manage change and survive the various threats it is currently facing is to increase the awareness of South Asian concerns among financial advisory services, accountants and other institutions. That means recruiting more South Asians at every level, it means creating South Asian service units in areas with large South Asian populations, and it means training all partners and senior staff in understanding the specific issues. You don't have to be an Asian to advise Asians, but you do often need the right training to do so. Winning Communications Partnership ran a basic training course for clients like the Cabinet Office and the Inland Revenue, attended by equal opportunities directors and executives dealing with members of the Asian community. Some of the questions raised by the non-Asian attendees were as simple as, 'Why did a particular Asian client not want his books examined on such-and-such a day?' It was explained that the day in question was the Festival of Diwali, when firms would ask the priest to bless their books and pray for a prosperous year's trading – a very private and important occasion.

Armed with such understanding, firms will be better placed to help South Asians tackle the key problem areas.

SUCCESSION

Entrepreneurs in the South Asian business community share a problem that all owner-managed businesses are liable to encounter: the matter of succession. Having built up the business by the commitment and hard work of the whole family, so that it has become strong and prosperous – what happens next? Who is going to take over the family business when the founder retires?

It's by no means a wholly gloomy picture. Although we have already seen several signs that a significant number of South Asians are choosing not to work in the family business, others are. Subhash Thakrar, for example, has an upbeat view of the future, based on first-hand professional experience. He can point to a good number of young Asian graduates who have gained their degrees and returned to the family business. 'I see the entrepreneurial spirit, the entrepreneurial blood that exists in the South Asian community, that's driving them towards business – and so I suspect that there's going to be much more qualitative growth in the Asian business than we've seen in the past.'

PROFESSIONALISING

If there is going to be an entrepreneurial second generation, it raises another issue. Is it still possible to do what these young Asians' parents did: to set up a business without going to college, to pick up necessary skills at night school or by paying for private lessons; and not to only to learn on the job, but also take the business into the big league purely by means of flair and energy?

Professionalising is a big issue now. Families are having to come to terms with the growth of the family business beyond its available skills. Many are recognising that the time has come to recruit outsiders. What kind of qualifications should be looked for? What role and status should the new recruits have? If the business and the family are inextricably intertwined, as we saw earlier, how can staff from outside be integrated into the circle of the family? Can they be integrated, and is it desirable that they should be? There are many problems of this kind. We will be looking at them in more detail in the next chapter.

In the South Asian community there is a history of notable business successes achieved despite the fact that the community has not had a strong educational background. But that generation was the one that sent its children to good schools; the stakes have been raised. Formal business qualifications are going to become essential in the future. Perhaps the word 'professionalising' has a misleading implication that South Asian graduates are all going to have to become accountants, lawyers, doctors or architects – but qualifications in business studies, and degrees in economics and similar subjects, are an essential preliminary to going into business if Asian businesses are to grow. The good news is that with increasing academic success in recent years among the South Asian community, it is a very achievable scenario.

Professionalising has to start with the basics, which is true of all small businesses. The 1996 White Paper on Competitiveness points out, 'Small firms have many strengths. Often they have exceptional drive and determination to succeed. They can innovate quickly and respond flexibly to customer needs. They offer choice in goods and services, often in niche markets and in local areas. But small firms are also vulnerable, more so than large firms, in a number of ways.

- ❑ Day-to-day pressures may lead them to plan only for the short term and to under-invest in skills and management training.
- ❑ They may be over-reliant on a small number of customers.
- ❑ They are more likely than large firms to have problems in managing cash flow and in raising money at acceptable terms for expansion.
- ❑ The burden of complying with regulation and of dealing with tax-administration and paperwork also weighs disproportionately heavily on smaller firms.[3]

Many South Asian businesses start small and grow. Capital purchase decisions, even the initial purchase of the business itself, are often made by gut instinct rather than on the advice of professional advisers, who could for example suggest ways of reducing tax burdens and improving the cash flow. In the early days the accounts are done in the evenings at the kitchen table (which is one reason that an accountant with a South Asian clientele must get used to the occasional evening call from his clients!). But as turnover, staff, profits, premises and everything else increase, the decision is usually made to call in outside professional advisers. Unfortunately, by that stage the business may have already begun to reap the consequences of the early days, when important decisions and long-term plans were neglected. One accountant describes the problems that result:

The entrepreneurial spirit often means starting up in business without taking professional advice. Most Asian business in the early years began like that and I can't see it stopping. So professionals like myself often have to unravel the problems. It's still the case in many South Asian businesses that they seek advice when they have a problem, rather than seeking it in advance so that later problems are forestalled.

Accountants dealing with the South Asian community are likely to have two main types of client:

❏ There are those who come for help with problems caused by decisions taken earlier without professional advice. Hopefully, the accountant can help such clients to understand why it is so important to make long-term decisions, so their businesses will perform even better; and, hopefully, they will pass on the message to their colleagues and friends.

❏ There is the 'younger blood' – those who have qualifications and a good grasp of business affairs. They are aware of the need to anticipate potential problems and to set up procedures for avoiding them. Working with them calls for being proactive, for creatively planning business strategies and solutions for the future, rather than reactively sorting out problems caused in the past.

FINANCIAL EXPERTISE AND CULTURAL IDENTIFICATION

Despite the expertise that Blackstone Franks has in advising on inward investment from the subcontinent, it is not a South Asian firm; and although among its publications are some dealing with matters that concern South Asian businesses particularly, you wouldn't say that its chief speciality is dealing with Asian firms. Yet it has a considerable number of Asian clients.

Does that mean that the South Asian business community is beginning to overcome its traditional reluctance to go outside for advice to the general professional market? Or do the firm's Asian clients choose that firm because it has a South Asian partner who is expert in and familiar with Asian culture, language, beliefs and business practice?

It's a little of both. Over the years the firm has built up an Asian constituency because Asians were understandably glad to know that they would find at least one senior member of staff who understood their culture and could sympathetically discuss specifically South Asian matters. Today, as firms' accounts become more complicated and financial processes are more and more difficult for lay people to understand, clients often prefer to go where the best expertise is to be found, regardless of the background of the expert. The trend may continue, as the new generation of South Asian business people takes on increasing responsibility within their family businesses, and begins to make decisions about the direction that the business will go in the future.

That's certainly so, for example, in the case of Shami Ahmed, whose business empire was built on the successful family business; in building his own company he not only moved on from his parents' company, but also from the banks his parents had used.

ADVICE AND TRUST

For every South Asian business looking out from the traditional South Asian business community, there is another one very cautious indeed about changing from the known and the familiar.

I've already mentioned the fact, recorded for example in Tradeways International's Croydon research, that many Asian businesses are wary of moving outside the Asian community for funding or advice, are reluctant to approach a high street bank for funding, and are unwilling even to have a representative of one of the government statutory agencies or bodies like Business Link visit their premises. But often the fault is in the banks and other institutions themselves. Here a leading Asian criticises British banks:

> Tony Deep Wouhra, chairman of the National Organisation of Asian Business, says that, in contrast to the people-oriented approach, banks focus too much on the figures. 'They don't understand the importance of the work ethic in Asian culture,' he says.
>
> Mr Deep Wouhra says that while the first generation of Asian immigrants to Britain had to rely on borrowing from family and friends, even the latest generation of Asian entrepreneurs, with established businesses, is still reluctant to go to

conventional British financial institutions.

An Asian bank might provide a solution to the cultural gap. But Mr Amin (Vijay Amin of Asian Business Initiative) is wary: 'There is a danger it may just be for the elite of the Asian business community.' He thinks the solution is for UK banks to rethink their approach.[4]

Seen from that perspective, the reluctance of the South Asian community begins to look understandable. Many organisations which claim that their brief is to help small businesses or ethnic minorities actually find it difficult to persuade some of the people who might most benefit from approaching them. There are few Asians in most Chambers of Commerce, few who will attend Business Link presentations, few who will go to such agencies for advice. The reason is usually a conviction that any government-funded organisation is unlikely to be committed and professional, and that if Asians do approach them they will end up wasting a good deal of time.

An example often quoted is applying for government grants – a process that many South Asians find, from experience, to be long-winded and frustrating. They conclude that by the time they've finished they might as well have gone to a relative or friend and borrowed some money.

THE FINANCING GAP

Entrepreneurs can rarely afford the luxury of long reflection about financial opportunities. Usually there is a need for a quick decision, or speedily arranged filling of an immediate financing gap.

When the need is for fast action and advice, language and cultural background become important. For example, anybody advising an Asian family business needs to be aware that in some cases, wealth is considered to be equally owned by all family members – which makes it difficult to apply conventional funding schemes, legacies, succession and other matters. There are complex issues to be resolved where a family member not directly involved in the business is expected to share in the profits. Specialists hired from outside the family may contribute far more in expertise and hours worked than several members of the family – yet the latter have equity where the outsider does not. It's certainly the case that Western values and practices are beginning to infiltrate many of the old South Asian family businesses, where the family wealth is formally divided between family members rather than being regarded as held in common; but the other approach, where family wealth is not the property of any one individual, is still frequently found. Obviously to give financial advice to such families demands somebody familiar with South Asian culture and aware of the different and often complicated attitudes to capital that such families work by.

That still requires a specialist adviser, rather than an adviser whose experience is in the main business community.

ASIANS IN ACCOUNTANCY

An obvious way of increasing the help available to businesses in the South Asian community is to increase the number of South Asian professionals, especially at senior level. This doesn't necessarily mean tokenism. Subhash Thakrar is not Blackstone Franks's token Asian partner (only around 30 per cent of his clients are Asian). He holds that position because of his professional abilities. This is not to say that the choice may not have been influenced by the desirability of having an Asian partner in place to service the increasingly prosperous Asian clientele. That would be a profitable development for the company and would raise the profile of mainstream accountancy in the Asian communities.

Apart from that, South Asians bring their own qualities and characteristics to the professions. Good at negotiation, effective at cost-cutting and with the ability to look inventively and creatively at problems, they are much in demand even by business people in the majority population. In London and Britain as a whole, many highly competent Asian accountants work in mainstream firms – for example Arun Shankardass, Group Treasury Manager at Commercial

Union's corporate headquarters in the City of London; and Pesh Framjee, who has been a leading light in the world of charity finance, accounting and legislation in the UK. Working in the international arena is Jim Wadia of Arthur Andersen, one of the largest and most prestigious international companies.

In the major international firms there has until recently been a shortage of Asian senior partners, even though at lower levels of the profession there are good numbers of accountants. This 'glass ceiling' is slowly disappearing, though in the largest firms South Asians reaching partnership usually do so as salaried rather than equity partners. That too is changing. Grant Thornton has 220 UK partners; three are Asians. One of the three, Anuj Chande, has recently been promoted to equity partnership. As in middle-sized firms like Blackstone Franks, there is no tokenism; in fact, as in so many walks of life, Asians have to work harder to succeed because they have to overcome the stereotyping and residual discrimination that are endemic in British society. But Anuj (who was one of the youngest partners when appointed) is the only one of the three actually working mainly with Asian clients, and that was not the reason for his being made a partner.

Even in the biggest firms the glass ceiling is shifting, but it's a very slow process. It is inconceivable that Grant Thornton will have an Asian as National Managing Partner within the next fifteen years or so. When the company's Asian initiative was being planned in 1991, 17 per cent of the professional staff in London were of Asian origin. However, very few of those were managers or senior managers.

Three caveats, before we go on. First, 'glass ceiling' is a term to be used with some care. It would be unwise, for example, to treat South Asians as a unique issue unconnected to other factors; representation of women in the ranks of senior management in the profession is also quite out of line with their numbers.

Second, the number of South Asians declines the higher one looks in the company because many use it as a training ground. They qualify in accountancy or some other branch of the profession, then return to the family business to use those skills. So there are fewer

South Asians at higher levels of the profession.

Third, there is some loss of South Asians from professional accountancy because the inherent inflexibility and bureaucracy that are found in many large firms eventually prove too frustrating. Some go to other professions, others set up as accountants or advisers in their own right. In such cases it is incorrect to talk of a glass ceiling.

Finance – and the Future

In this chapter I have looked at a number of areas in which, for the price of relatively small changes in practice and mindset, the South Asian community could be helped to solve many of its problems and to deal with many of the frustrations with which it is currently faced.

I want to end by pulling some of these threads together, looking at two specific areas which between them encompass most of the problems and most of the areas where change would be most beneficial. I am talking here about South Asian firms and their immediate local context; we will look at the wider issues of the UK economy as a whole in the next chapter. Let us first consider South Asians and banking, and then the question of the future of the family firm. We have touched on both already.

Banks and the South Asian business community

Despite encouraging developments, some of which I have referred to in Chapter 2, the issue of banking remains a vexed one in the South Asian community. So much so that early in 1997 a group of Asian businessmen considered setting up an Asian bank specifically targeted to the needs of the South Asian community. The problem, according to Vijay Amin of Asian Business Initiative, is not racism but a simple failure of British banks to understand Asian business. 'They still have a picture of the typical Asian business as the corner shop.'[5] The result is that sometimes South Asians like Paresh Kotecha, whose Aston Hotel chain turns over £7.5 million annually, will look abroad: he got backing for a major refurbishing project from Singapore and British banks lost £25 million worth of business.

Shami Ahmed's views on British banks are echoed by many in the financial world; having moved away from the Asian banks that his parents used, he feels that British banks are weak when it comes to providing venture capital, start-up advice and investment advice. Michael Syrett comments, 'You've got to have people used to dealing with Asian business people. They should be focusing on the person, their track record and their contacts, not their figures.'[6] Ronnie Foley, who is Head of Private Banking at the Bank of Ireland, believes that the Asian community presents a significant opportunity which needs to be met by banks that are relationship-based, offering 'integrity, continuity, and confidentiality' – the last a very important point, in a closed community where news travels quickly.

A number of bank initiatives are aiming to do just that. In February 1997 Barclays published a review entitled *Cultural Change and the Small Firm*. This was commissioned from Critical Research in October 1996 and surveyed a nationally representative sample of 400 small businesses with turnovers of less than £1 million. Barclays recognised the 'important role' of ethnic minority businesses within the small business sector, and pointed out that ethnic minorities form 5 per cent of the UK population but are responsible for around 9 per cent of new business start-ups, representing around 7 per cent of the total small business stock in the UK.

Barclays intended its review to 'help to promote better cross-cultural understanding and … assist the providers of business support such as Business Links, TECs and Enterprise Agencies, as well as the Government and banks, in supplying appropriately targeted support and guidance.'[7] The review found, in respect of the Asian community (of which in this context the South Asians are the substantial majority), that:

❑ Asian small businesses continue to dominate the retail industry
❑ Asians work the longest hours
❑ Discrimination is a major concern
❑ Asian businesses are family based
❑ Ethnic minority small businesses tend not to seek outside help

None of these findings will come as a surprise to anyone who has read this far. But it's encouraging that one of the UK's largest banks has considered it necessary to invest in a better understanding of minority ethnic businesses, including those of South Asians.

The future of the South Asian family firm
So let's finish where we began, with another view of the South Asian family firm caught at this critical point of change.

'Fine Fashions' is an imaginary UK South Asian family firm. It is a retail chain of four shops. A few years ago it had a mostly Asian clientele but now it mainly serves customers from the majority community. In 1989 it changed its name from R. Patel & Sons to reflect this. It sells a range of goods, from children's playtime clothes to formal wear. Fine Fashions shops carry no designer labels and none of its stock is very expensive; however, a reputation for well-made, hard-wearing garments with a touch of Indian style has brought it a good trade. There are a few major stores locally that are probably snapping up some of the business that would otherwise have come to the Patel family stores, but on the whole Fine Fashions is doing very comfortably, thank you.

So how do the Patels view the future? What as yet unsuspected problems may lie in wait for them?

One thing with which Fine Fashions is going to have to come to terms sooner rather than later is the family structure itself. Though much strength has been derived from it in the past, it is likely to be one of the biggest limits to growth in the future. It's taken for granted that a number of elderly members of the family, who haven't taken an active part in the business for years, should have an on-going financial interest in the business, rather than a pension. After all, those who have made way for the younger members of the family ought not to suffer financial loss. In some circumstances a lump sum might be paid to an older relative as 'compensation for loss of office' – but the Patels wouldn't do that. Such devices are for tax benefits, not for terminating a family member's involvement in the business.

But the problems are beginning to appear. Ravi Patel, who

founded the business, has handed over to his sons. None of them has the intuitive understanding of stock control that Ravi had. He was able to plan six months' purchases knowing that his shelves would be empty just as the stock went out of season. He was hardly ever left with outdated or out-of-fashion stock. His sons just don't have the same skills and quantities of garments have had to be sold off cheap. And there are other areas of business in which the gap left by those older relatives are sorely felt. They represent a financial obligation with no return, an experience and skills gap that must be filled. The Patels are already talking about hiring some expert staff from outside the family.

And now the arguments have started. How should the family accommodate new management personnel? What level of integration is desirable?

One of the big questions is whether or not to offer equity to the company's new management. Some family members are adamant that ownership should remain exclusively with the family for ever. Others argue that what is needed is not an employee but a partner – somebody who can bring into the business the competences and skills that have been lost through retirement. To get the right quality of help, shouldn't a share of the equity be offered?

The arguments have raged long and hard in family meetings. One or two family members are even beginning to mention the unthinkable: that the business should be sold rather than changed drastically by bringing in outsiders. That's not an unusual suggestion. Some South Asian companies have sold up for that very reason, even where some had young people who could have taken over; they recognised that the younger generation lacked the necessary skills.

Let's move on several years in the fictitious history of Fine Fashions. The new partner has done very well; a pleasant middle-aged man from the majority community, he has revolutionised the firm. Fine Fashions is now a name known all over the Midlands, and the new factory (established with a large loan from a wealthy relative in Dubai) is turning out own-brand garments as fast as the machines can operate. The next expansion is the expensive one. The company is facing a new crisis: re-capitalisation.

The obvious option, stock market flotation, is not so obvious to the family. Few traditional South Asian businesses go this route. A crowded shareholders' meeting with 49 per cent of those present demanding that the family change policy or diversify isn't something that sits easily with Asian business concepts.

Another option, that of selling the company, is much more attractive these days. Many South Asian businesses are sold as going concerns, leaving the family to enjoy a comfortable retirement or, if they wish, to start up all over again. There was much detailed discussion before the family decided against that idea and voted for the third option.

It is at this stage in the history of Fine Fashions that the family is likely to be most helped by the kind of assistance I have talked about in this chapter – or most hindered by its absence. The third option is to find fresh capital from other sources. To do that, the Patels will have to call in outside expertise, and they will not be looking only within the South Asian community. For example, venture funding might be sought from a high street bank.

There are many instances where financial advisers such as we have mentioned – companies like Blackstone Franks and Grant Thornton – would often become involved in South Asian business expansion. One common situation is the firm that has been founded by successful entrepreneurism but has no seed capital set aside. Perhaps the family had a small business in India and has come to Britain, where it has found a niche market that has kept the business afloat but has not grown and made the family wealthy. Companies in that situation often need help to move to the next step – establishing a manufacturing department, opening a few branches, taking on specialist technicians, investing in plant and equipment and so on. When there's no great wealth in the family, where do they go for the extra £50,000 or £100,000 they need?

The Patels, like many other South Asian businesses in similar growth situations, went to the professionals. The professionals analysed the company, talked at length to all the key people and prepared suitable business plans. They then introduced the company to potential investors, both to bankers of venture capital funds and to private capital. In either case, involvement would be on the basis of pure investment, rather than with the aim of securing participation in the business. A satisfactory partner was found, and the company was able to move on to the next stage of its expansion.

I have invented Fine Fashions, but similar stories are developing all over the South Asian community. I have told this one for two reasons. First, to show the practical problems that result from some of the distinctives of South Asian family life as South Asian business attempts to manage change. (This doesn't, of course, mean that those distinctives are bad in themselves: only that they can have unexpected consequences in running a business.) And secondly, to show that at crucial stages of growth, the firm's continuing prosperity depended on the quality of help it received from professionals in the majority community.

I know a number of (real) companies each founded by a single investor that now, after their growth and profitability have become clear, face a dilemma: whether to take more funds from the extended family, allowing relatively informal control of the business, but placing limits on growth – or to seek public funds through the alternative investment market, with its own accountability structures.

12

Building Success on Success

In the last chapter I looked at a range of ways in which the South Asian community can be helped if individual advisers, firms and professionals seize the opportunities that this remarkable enterprise economy within the UK presents.

Now I want to look at the larger dimension of British business as a whole. Much South Asian business is peripheral to the main UK economy. It is run and staffed by British South Asian residents, it pays taxes and follows UK legislation, but its point of reference is either the small UK ethnic minority population, or a country far away where the real benefits are often enjoyed. So my question in this chapter is this: how can we as a nation ensure that the UK South Asian business community is given the resources, and the incentive, to play its full part in the British economy; to benefit from government investment in the national economy; to share its considerable strengths with the majority business community and in turn receive the support and backing to which any segment of British business is entitled? And how can we make sure that the significant problems that some sectors of the UK South Asian community are facing are dealt with, and do not threaten the 'bubbles of success' that we have been considering?

How, indeed, can we build success on success?

PROFESSIONALISE — OR DIE!

I want to begin with an example from my own experience. I was working with the Inlaks Group during the period of acquisition that Azad Shivdasani discusses in Chapter 5 (p. 86).

The Inlaks Group was a family firm employing sons, in-laws, nephews and other extended family members. It became clear that if we were going to get high-quality professional management we needed to bring in outside professional help. Of course that raised many of the problems we've discussed in previous chapters: who would we recruit, what would their expectations be, how much control would inevitably pass to them, what status would they have within this family company and so on.

There was a shortage of qualified MBAs in the family. Our turnover had grown from a few hundred thousand dollars to a few hundred million, in over a dozen countries. We had a sprawling, huge empire. How were we best to manage it? We needed technology, advanced specialist business expertise and much more, and we could source none of it, in the quantities we urgently needed, from within the extended family. In the long run we knew we had only one option for the future: to professionalise. A transition was necessary – in fact, essential – if we were to survive.

As a family business we had developed our own ways of doing things and they had worked for us so far. Our problems lay in the fact that they weren't going to work for us very much longer; but we didn't know how to do things any differently. So we began to take steps to remedy our limitations.

We weren't familiar with board structures and committee structures. Now we had to get used to them. One of our tactics was to acquire companies that would help us with this transition. I began this book with an account of my arrival in Scotland, to head up an Inlaks acquisition. The uneasy reception I received when I arrived was only the beginning. In that new situation, far away from head office, the need for new blood, new ideas and new professionalism was all the more apparent.

In 1986 I came across a scampi factory in Kilkeel, Northern Ireland. Its turnover was just over £1 million, its book value £150,000; it employed fifty people. For a group the size of Inlaks, it was small beer. But I justified its acquisition to my head office by arguing that its managing director was a professional of many years' experience and with an excellent reputation in the seafood industry. It was a kind of headhunting, except that we acquired the whole company! My task was to integrate its managing director into the group. We had identified the major contribution he could make to our operation – and he's still contributing today and benefiting from his partnership in the group.

In Nigeria we made a similar acquisition when we bought out Alcan. Aluminium was an unfamiliar industry for Inlaks – but Alcan had very good professional management. We brought it into the group as a transfusion of skilled professionalism. What we got was, in effect, a reverse management takeover; Alcan had just a few hundred employees, but almost immediately its management was in key Inlaks posts. We learned from them things like how to formalise the acquisition of capital expenditure – a whole professional way of approaching, purchasing, buying and selling, recruitment and so on. Up until then we'd had no standardised way of assessing and evaluating requests for capital expenditure at group headquarters. A secretary would request my authorisation for expenditure on some item of office equipment like a £50 telephone, and I would reject it while at the same time authorising the purchase of a £3,000 computer.

Our new Nigerian colleagues introduced ways of looking at business decisions that we had been aware of, but had not made standard or integrated into our procedures. It was at that time that I picked up many useful analytical tools that I still use today in my work in the charitable sector. For example, when considering capital expenditure on equipment, in the Christmas Cracker charity of which I am Chairman, it would be easy, because of the enormous funds we raise, to not worry overmuch about making our capital expenditures as cost-effective as possible. But Christmas Cracker is a responsible charity with a duty to use its money wisely; and so I go back to the principles I learned in Inlaks, such as the ten essential questions to ask before making a capital purchase.

---

1. What? – What exactly is the proposed purchase?
2. Why? – Why are we doing this? (The rationale)
3. Why this? – What are the alternatives? Are there any?
4. Why now? – Is there a penalty for waiting? Is there a better time to buy – tax benefits, etc.?
5. How much? – What are the real costs?
6. With what resources? – How are we going to pay for it? (This includes part-exchange etc.)
7. By whom? – Whose budget will be debited for this purchase? Who therefore will be ultimately accountable?
8. By when? – (Timetable and critical path)
9. What are the consequences of proceeding?
10. What are the consequences of *not* proceeding?

This is an invaluable checklist when dealing with large numbers. Although we were already a large, prosperous multinational group we weren't used to such ideas and had to learn quickly. And we did.

Our new acquisitions were therefore also a means of on-the-job training. We developed a training strategy to help us manage change. We organised courses on subjects like 'The Creative Manager', 'Managing Corporate Culture', 'Communications' (the cost to companies of poor communication runs into billions of pounds) and 'Entrepreneurial Thinking in Action'. They were tailor-made to meet the challenge of winning over managers who were sceptical and gaining their ownership and support. All this had to be achieved without extinguishing the entrepreneurial flair and instinct of those managers – which, after all, was what had brought us to success so far.

PROFESSIONAL ENTREPRENEURISM

The Inlaks experience illustrates the key issue in bringing the South Asian business world fully into UK plc. The need is to harness the element of successful entrepreneurism and to combine it with professionalism. The issue is, **can 'professional entrepreneurism' really exist?**

For many British South Asians, trapped by the built-in limitations of their own entrepreneurial unorthodox flair, this is going to mean learning how UK plc works. It might mean that, as was the case in Inlaks, honoured members of the family who are not of the first quality in management will have to be sidelined or given a golden handshake. Many of the problems will be helped by the strong sense of family respect we have already discussed. But there will still be a sharp learning curve in modern business techniques with which South Asians will need help.

On the practical, internal day-to-day running of the business, much help can and is being given at the level I discussed in Chapter 11. For example, few South Asians place a high priority on business planning. Anuj Chande of Grant Thornton has found that seminars on the subject are often not well attended by the South Asian community. Asians, too, have the lowest take-up of pension schemes: partly because the family interdependence is so strong that they assume that when they are old the family will look after them, and partly because they have a strong faith (sometimes sadly disappointed) that at the end of the day the business will have generated a large pot of money from which all can draw for their future security. Similarly, many South Asian businesses have almost no personnel appraisal systems in place. There are no job specifications, no detailed attempt to fit candidates to posts, no staff evaluation or reviews. So there are very few ways, apart from looking at the cash piling up in the bank, of determining whether staff and company are achieving satisfactory goals and meeting targets optimally – in so far as targets exist at all.

When a professional adviser is consulted by such a firm, and proper analysis, forecasting, evaluation and methods are prescribed and implemented, the firm's productivity and profitability rocket. Not only does it acquire much greater day-to-day financial control and planning, the likelihood of future catastrophe is immediately reduced. It becomes much less likely that the accountant will have to break the bad news to elderly staff on the verge of retirement that the nest-egg they had assumed was waiting for them in the bank has long since dwindled away.

The question I want to address is: how can we achieve such results at the national level? How can we encourage appraisal at local business level, to institute some financial control on the wealth that is being produced (often haphazardly) by the South Asian entrepreneurs, and bring such entrepreneurs into the heart of British business?

MUTUAL ADVANTAGE

There will be plenty of benefits for all.

Productive diversity

The strengths of diversity are well understood these days. 'Many successful companies find that a mixture of age groups, races, religions, gender, educational and social backgrounds in the workplace can enhance organisational performance – if it is carefully managed.'[1]

The arguments for this echo many of the arguments I have included in this book. For example, in a 1996 White Paper on Competitiveness we find the following:

'The business case for harnessing diversity is that it helps a firm:
❑ attract better recruits
❑ understand the requirements of diverse markets and so develop more appropriate products and market them more effectively
❑ develop a culture that is more receptive to change and more innovative
❑ make more effective use of networking.'[2]

Every single requirement in this paragraph is amply met in the South Asian entrepreneurial culture. Are we harnessing this rich source of diversity in British business?

In the words of Sir Colin Marshall, Chairman of British Airways and of London First Centre (London's inward investment agency): 'Britain's cohesive mix of cultures is one of our most potent weapons in the battle to win inward investment for this country. We can offer a dynamic, flexible and multi-skilled workforce at ease and in tune with the global market. It is one of the reasons we are unquestionably the preferred gateway to Europe for most overseas companies, with all the economic benefits this brings.'[3]

An ethnic windfall bonus

A great deal has been said about the 'windfall tax' on which New Labour based much of its economic manifesto. The argument was that the utility companies were privatised on such advantageous terms that a one-off windfall tax would not jeopardise their financial survival and delivery of their business plans – nor cause a price rise, which would in effect be a tax on the consumer. This was essentially new money for the exchequer to finance the flagship Welfare to Work scheme. It didn't need spending cuts to finance it, or taxation in another area. It was raised by taxing windfall surpluses and it represented a windfall for the national economy.

It has been estimated by Business in the Community's Race for Opportunities Campaign that the black pound – the disposable income of the minority ethnic communities – is of the order of £10 billion, giving to the exchequer an annual, regular tax revenue of a similar size to the income from the one-off windfall tax on the privatised utilities. In addition, ethnic businesses have created jobs (albeit mainly for ethnic community members) of a magnitude not dissimilar to the Welfare to Work target of 250,000 jobs.

This means that, since the main immigration influx of twenty-five years ago, what has happened in practice is a self-implemented Welfare to Work strategy generating an *annual* ethnic windfall bonus to the exchequer, with the potential for much greater return and benefits if properly harnessed.

It can, of course, be argued that these calculations are on a gross basis, not taking account, for example, of the cost of educating children in state schools. But the essential question remains: are we harnessing this rich source of diversity in British business?

CURRENT INITIATIVES

There are a wide number of initiatives that have already been launched, and agencies already exist to achieve many of the objectives that I have identified so far. Let me mention three with which I am involved and know at first hand.

Training and Enterprise Councils (TECs)

The TECs were launched by the Conservative government in 1990 with the aim of improving Britain's skills base and encouraging business start-ups. They have had a controversial history, and it seemed at one time that they might be replaced by other organisations. But more recently they have defined their role and made strategic plans for the future. Described by a leader of the business community as 'valuable conduits from the government ... able to help local partnerships and implement a considerable range of things in the local economy',[4] TECs also have support from trade unions who were once suspicious of these private-sector-led organisations.

The TECs are investing effort and resources in a variety of schemes that benefit ethnic minorities. I have already mentioned SOLOTEC's pioneering research into the demography of the South Asian population. There are many similar initiatives among the TECs. West London TEC, for example, covers an area that includes Heathrow Airport and 200 company headquarters, and for thirty years has been the most prosperous area of the UK. The TEC has joined with local employers to form a Diversity Focus Group. This produces sound business policies and strategies to help companies develop the business opportunities that are going to arise within an ethnically diverse population. It also supports community projects, such as the Southall Youth Project, Action For Acton, two Prince's Trust Volunteer Schemes, the Education Business Partnership Compacts, West London Disability Partnership and Southall Opportunities Centre.

Business Links

The Business Link concept has been described as a 'small-business one-stop shop'. It aims to ensure that the business community is enabled to take full advantage of the wealth of available information, support, counselling and consultancy services. Business support services are proliferating at an ever-increasing rate, and many business people find it almost impossible to keep fully informed. But a telephone call to a Business Link puts a business in touch with help and advice.

Business Links are funded by the Department of Trade and Industry. They are aimed at small and medium-sized enterprises, which often find it difficult to obtain impartial advice and support. Businesses whose expansion will significantly benefit the local economy are especially targeted. Help is on two levels. Many queries can be, and are, handled over the telephone. More complex questions may call for the visit of a Personal Business Adviser (PBA). In 1996 it was reported that, of 500 PBAs so far appointed, 87 per cent had experience of running a small business and 93 per cent were graduates or had professional qualifications. The PBA works closely with the client to develop a package of support tailored to that business. Consultancy services employed by Business Link are given financial backing by the present and previous governments. The 1995 White Paper on Competitiveness, for example, announced a commitment of around £100 million for new high-quality services: in Manchester over £1.2 million was to be provided over three years to help improve the competitiveness of manufacturing, software and IT companies.

Business Links' investment in ethnic minority businesses is growing. In April 1996, for example, Business Link London West published a project report, *Reaching Out to Ethnic Minority Growth*

Businesses,[5] an invaluable compendium of solid research and also a rich source of analysis of the characteristics and circumstances of the ethnic minorities in London and indeed in Britain as a whole. In May 1996 the Business Link London network launched its Ethnic Minority Taskforce at the Queen Elizabeth Hall Westminster, with representatives from the Commission for Racial Equality, the London Research Centre, local authorities, London First and Business in the Community's Race for Opportunity.

Race for Opportunity

Race for Opportunity is organised by Business in the Community and led by a team of senior business people chaired by Robert Ayling, Chief Executive of British Airways. A national campaign to encourage business to invest in the diversity of Britain's ethnic minority population communities, it was launched in October 1995 after extensive consultations with a wide range of business, ethnic minority and public-sector organisations throughout Britain. Organisations committed to the campaign include Barclays, the BBC, McDonald's, NatWest UK and WH Smith. Commitment involves:

❑ reviewing current diversity policies and practices, using the Commission for Racial Equality's 'Racial Equality Means Business'
❑ agreeing an organisation-wide policy on diversity, endorsed at the highest level and linked to the organisation's business objectives
❑ committing the organisation to an action plan covering Race for Opportunity's four areas of focus
❑ evaluating progress and reporting annually on what has been achieved.

The 'four focuses' are:

❑ Employment – developing business skills and opportunities for ethnic minorities
❑ Purchasing – supporting the growth of ethnic minority owned businesses

❑ Marketing – marketing to ethnic minority customers and involving them in the planning, design and delivery of products and services

❑ Community involvement – building business support for educational and community organisations.

Other initiatives

There are many other initiatives and indications that the needs of the ethnic minority community are being taken seriously. Let me suggest at random the existence of the Public Appointments Ethnic Monitoring Unit; the various information programmes to explain funding, help etc.; commercial initiatives (for example, the UK is the major European investor in Asia as a whole); and the government (and royal) endorsement of the Asian community's achievements and values, symbolised by, for example, the presence of the last Conservative Home Secretary as speaker at an Asian dinner at London's Disraeli Club, and that of Prince Charles at a number of Asian celebrations. In 1997 the Prince was Guest of Honour at the launch of the celebrations for 50 years of Indian Independence at the Royal Albert Hall, organised by Asia House.

Pull and push

If these government and voluntary initiatives might be described as a pulling force, then it could be said that what we need to inculcate in the South Asian community are a desire and a need to push, to take their part in mainstream British life. As I have suggested already, the push for success has sometimes meant, for many Asian businesses, creating a bubble or a shelter that has survived recession and racism and negative legislation and attitudes.

But we have already observed that there is a danger that such success carries with it the seeds of disaster. The very entrepreneurial spirit that overcomes difficulties can lead to new difficulties. Recent research suggests that many Asian retail outlets are fighting for share of a diminishing ethnic market and the good times may not last for ever. And opting out of mainstream Britain can sometimes lead to personal fulfilment but the impoverishment of the business community. I know of a qualified tax inspector who recognised that because of the 'glass ceiling' he would never rise beyond a certain point in the civil service. Now he sells gift items in a shop in Ashford, Kent. I know of a chartered accountant who did the same thing. Likewise, Asian skilled graduates will not meekly stay around if no use is made of them. While Britain continues to fail to build on their success, this group of highly educated, highly motivated people are growing increasingly impatient with the bureaucracy and limitations of the traditional business world. They are being lost to overseas and other workplaces.

But if we get behind Asian entrepreneurs, who have often struggled with the in-built opposition to immigrant input, structural racism, glass doors and glass ceilings, and build on their success by providing opportunities for training and involvement in the business structures of UK plc, the economy can and will benefit.

In this book I have used the picture of the Asian subeconomy as a series of bubbles of security in a difficult economic climate, like air-conditioned domes on the surface of an alien planet. We can learn from such bubbles. But do those bubbles have the capacity to continue as a protecting force, or are there forces within the communities themselves that threaten a possibility that the bubbles may begin to burst?

Already many of these bubbles are dangerously vulnerable. We have seen that many Asian entrepreneurial businesses are now threatened by the very rivals they spurred into greater competitiveness. The corner-shop success of the 1970s and 1980s has drastically declined in the 1990s following the establishment of supermarkets and hypermarkets that are now competing with smaller South Asian businesses 24 hours a day, 7 days a week, 365 days a year.

We must build on success! Failure of the South Asians would be both a human and a business tragedy (and mean maintaining from the public purse many who have so far been major contributors to it).

So let me present you with a preliminary agenda of what is needed.

AN AGENDA FOR ACTION

Appointment of a government minister with a specific portfolio to monitor minority ethnic representation at all levels

The model is already in place: one of the first actions of the New Labour government was to appoint Harriet Harman as a cabinet supremo on the gender issue. Let's have a similar appointment to monitor minority communities' representation in government, civil service, quangos, public companies etc. – across the board.

Government-sponsored research into the limitations of and barriers to growth

What are the factors that hinder the growth of small owner-managed businesses? We have discussed a wide range of problems in this book and seen what some individual agencies are doing to help. But we also need a government-sponsored programme of research, nationwide, across the whole spectrum of business. It should pre-scribe cures as well as identify ills. It should be non-aligned with any political party or ethnic group, but be a truly independent body. It should be chaired by a figure respected by all the ethnic groups, and its recommendations should be widely distributed. And it should be backed up by a network of local spokespeople, local action groups, regional funding centres – indeed everything that is necessary to turn the vision into reality.

More relevant training opportunities

Over the next twenty years there is a danger that the pool of unem-ployed qualified graduates will increase. Young Asians who would have made a contribution to the national economy by engaging in economic activity won't do so. And in the under-25 generation there is structural unemployment – less among South Asians than among other ethnic minorities, admittedly – that represents an opportunity loss of the most serious kind.

Although there is a disproportionately high number of million-aires and achievers in the South Asian community, the wealth is not evenly spread. As generation succeeds generation, each one further removed from the first immigrants, there is less creation of economic wealth comparable to the levels of those early years. The younger generation is not motivated to go back to the corner shop and the high street retail business. The problem is that other opportunities are often not plentiful.

We need training schemes that are designed to help South Asians to maximise the opportunities they have and the skills they possess. For example, the Prince's Youth Business Trust is in the business of turning plans into reality. Many young and some not so young entrepreneurs from all backgrounds have been given grants that have enabled them to set up in business. We need apprentice schemes, assisted places at training institutions, training programmes with real jobs at the end, and help for the children of ethnic minorities to escape from the cycle of always having to over-achieve merely to maintain parity with the majority population. We need to equip the current generation of South Asians and other ethnic minorities with the skills and know-how to outperform the first generation. It must all be relevant. Relevant to who the South Asians are, for example; not to what we think they are, or should be.

More help for UK South Asians as they manage change

Change management has long been recognised as a major issue in Western business. Professional journals, seminars and conferences have grappled with the problems of a world that is developing at an unprecedented rate and technology that is accelerating so quickly that mastering technology at one stage in a professional career can still leave you badly out of date a few years later unless retraining, familiarising and refresher courses are built in to business structures. This is one reason, for example, for the success of Bharat Desai's Syntel Corporation: it offers to take over the strain of keeping the technological cutting edge and of constantly retraining staff.

For some businesses, the help needed will be in closing down and relocating, or even re-skilling. They will need consultancy and other advice to evaluate new directions and new possibilities, because for them the business that the family has successfully run until now cannot withstand competition. Maybe it is just in the wrong place; maybe it has outlived its natural span and the demand it once satisfied has died. For firms that continue, much help will be needed not only to adjust to change but to build good foundations, and make good plans, for the years to come. It may mean adding a facility such as an off-licence; it may mean changing to a different type of stock, like a shop selling 'everything under a fiver' – thus diversifying their product range and getting several types of use from the same site.

Information is crucial. External change can have devastating consequences for small businesses, but many South Asians are unaware of the help that is available. I know of an Asian bailiff, for example, who is employed to execute seizure orders and other drastic measures. He frequently finds that the South Asians on whom he is required to call have no idea of what avenues are available to them to avoid legal action. He will often sit down with them and show them how a simple form or a phone call can halt the legal process while things are sorted out.

Another example is that of a major pharmaceutical facility that closed in South London, making thousands jobless or relocating them elsewhere. The impact on the local community could have been devastating. The firm gave grants to organisations like SOLOTEC to fund, for example, Personal Business Advisers, relocation assistance, local community grants and retraining. I do not think that many Asians, if indeed any at all, benefited. They were simply unaware of the grants and the help that had been made possible. After all, after nearly thirty years in Britain, I didn't know companies did such things. I was unaware of it when I made the suggestion, at the time of the building of the Tesco store at Hammersmith (p. 12), that Tesco might wish to consider paying for retraining and relocation of affected local retailers.

The South Asian community has unique problems that make change management very complex. In this book I have outlined some of the characteristics which limit growth and which call for radical readjustment as the millennium approaches. Help in this process should be given by government and other agencies as a matter of urgency; both because the consequences of a failure to manage change will have severe consequences for the economy as a whole and because, as British citizens and British enterprises, it is their right. The way forward has been shown by some British organisations like British Coal, British Steel and some European initiatives.

More information on funding and sources of business advice and market intelligence

A restaurateur who is just starting out on an entrepreneurial ethnic food manufacturing business attended my March 1997 lecture at London's Royal Society of Arts, which was on the same subject as this book and was the seed of it. Afterwards he commented, 'That's all very interesting. But how can I get my hands on the funding you say should be available to me? And where do I go to for help and advice?'

There is a need for major publicity programmes going far beyond the publicity presently put out by TECs, Business Links and other agencies. It needs to be specifically targeted, for example using Asian languages and placed in Asian media. Banks that offer help to South Asian communities should have information desks where leaflets, addresses and other information can be found; local libraries and post offices are other places where this would be effective. These information points should be at least partly staffed, and banks particularly should offer surgeries – either by appointment or as a regular weekly or monthly service – at which local South Asian business people can be advised on sources of assistance.

It will be important to remember that many of these public institutions are not used by many in the South Asian community, or if they do use them, they leave the premises as quickly as they can. An effective alternative might be to provide the information as trailers to Asian videos, which would reach a majority of the South Asian population.

More ethnic awareness and expertise in funding bodies, banks etc.

There is a need for leaders and executives in the majority population to have a better awareness and understanding of Asian culture and background. Training programmes are needed to teach major British government departments, institutions and companies basic issues like the significance of names: what background a particular name signifies (for example, that Mr Singh is a Sikh, Mrs Patel is a Gujerati and Miss Khan a Muslim).

More South Asians on the boards of public companies

We need better representation, not just because that will help to represent South Asian interests, but because public company administration should reflect the constituency (the British public) that it serves. The representation of South Asians in British society is not reflected by its representation on public boards, which are dominated by old-boy and school-tie networks of which the South Asians are not part.

More South Asians on local authorities, NHS Trusts, TEC Boards, Business Link Boards etc.

More of the same! With major South Asian representation in the medical professions, in retail industries, in sport and in other sectors, there should be much greater representation than there is at present. The solution is not, as is sometimes suggested, to create special ethnic minority departments or black groups – that merely perpetuates at management level the ghettoising tendencies of our society. We need integration at key levels so that an integrated perspective can be brought to bear on the issues such bodies deal with every day.

As a Director of the Business Link National Accreditation Advisory Board, one of my major concerns has been to urge a reappraisal of the gender and ethnicity of Business Link Board membership. Out of the eleven that we've accredited, three have no women board members, let alone ethnic minority members. The Chairman of the Board has issued a directive to all Business Link Boards requiring them to ensure that their composition reflects the composition of the local community. If we exist to serve the community, is the community we are serving adequately represented?

And it's not just at board level that there is inadequate representation. At a national TEC conference shortly before this book went to press, around 800 delegates were present. At a very generous estimate, no more than two dozen of them were from the ethnic minorities. On the main platform there were none at all. The previous year a formal request had been made that a platform speaker be invited to address this issue. Instead, a fringe meeting was programmed – exactly what was not required. This has been a fringe issue for much too long.

More business exploitation of markets opened up by South Asian success

I've argued strongly in this book that South Asians bring to the national economy not merely entrepreneurial skill, hard work and dedication, but also a rich tapestry of international contacts and access to global markets throughout the diaspora. For example, the Madhvani family (p. 75) has unrivalled access to the Ugandan markets. Involved in rebuilding the country after the terrible years of Idi Amin's rule, they are brilliantly placed as a stepping stone for British companies to profit in the way that they have shown.

The same is true of much smaller firms with much less impressive turnovers. At local level, many Chambers of Commerce could be making much more use of the Asians in their midst. When one considers how town twinning has been used to exploit commercial and industrial opportunities between Britain and Europe, it is surprising that towns and cities with large Asian populations have not exploited more enthusiastically the fact that local people are importing from and exporting to the subcontinent. For years South Asians have been familiar with the ins and outs of dealing with endless bureaucracy, and with the best ways of promoting their goods and services overseas. Yet many British companies insist on re-inventing the wheel.

Of course, if this is to happen it means that South Asians in Britain will have to be treated as a resource, not a problem. The same is true in global terms. In previous centuries the Third World was plundered by the West. Raw materials and resources were taken from the subcontinent, turned into profitable commodities and sometimes even sold back to the subcontinent at exorbitant cost. Today, skills are as important as resources, and if the global village is going to function it will have to function as a partnership with dignity, not an empire. This may yet call for a great deal of re-thinking and re-adjusting – on both sides.

More government use of South Asians' unique skills and global trade links

As an extension of this, why not give leading British South Asians diplomatic and trade ambassadorial roles in overseas High Commissions and Embassies? Asia is a thriving area of British trade: UK companies are working hard to penetrate its new markets. In the last few years over 80 new commercial slots in Asian missions and nine new commercial posts have opened, from Lahore to Chiang Mai, Kuching to Nagoya. In 1997 there were big trade missions to Indonesia and the Philippines, Malaysia and Vietnam, and the biggest ever missions to Pakistan and China. Do British South Asians feature in these strategic initiatives?

More successful South Asian entrepreneurs to be encouraged to set up Soros-style charitable foundations for the benefit of UK and global communities

I hope that I have recorded adequately the fact that many of Britain's most successful entrepreneurs are extremely generous, and that the activities of some have been omitted from this book because they prefer not to publicise their charitable deeds. As an entrepreneur in the charitable sector I am very well placed to acknowledge the contribution that is being made already – one that does not benefit only the ethnic minorities.

I am sure, however, that there is even more scope for major

charitable foundations to be set up that will take their deserving causes from the whole spectrum of British society. It would not be an unusual development. George Soros, whose charitable activities are worth millions, is Hungarian. Paul Getty was an American, and the foundation from which many British causes benefit is based in the United States. Andrew Carnegie, whose gifts to Britain include major public library buildings, made his money in the United States. Nothing established the affection these people felt for Britain, nor their awareness that giving to the needy and the deserving leaps across all ethnic and geographical borders, so much as the foundations that bear their names. It will be surprising if in the next decades the deep affection many wealthy South Asians feel for Britain – the deep affection, and often the political commitment – does not manifest itself in similar foundations.

Often benefactors are geniuses at the work that made them rich but need help and advice in setting up foundations or selecting the causes they want to benefit. At local, regional and national level, the process ought to be already under way. I realise it is a British ethnic trait to be reserved and diplomatic – but often the people who are in a position to embark on this kind of initiative, and would dearly like to, need a nudge and a helping hand. The Association of Charitable Foundations has set up a subgroup specifically to debate this issue; and Trusts in Partnership has already held specific events to encourage such activities.

PUTTING IT ALL TOGETHER

This might seem a fearsome agenda – but it isn't. There are organisations already tackling many of these items. They have the know-how, they have the resources and, where neither know-how nor resources exist, they are creating them. Go to such organisations as South Asian Development Partnership, Business in the Community's Race for Opportunity campaign, Asian Business Initiative, the National Organisation of Asian Businesses, the Centre for Asian Entrepreneurial Research and many more. You will find statistics, analysis, programmes, surveys, publications, original research, guides to published research, contacts already established with key figures in government and industry, and much more.

Yet time is not on our side. There is a great deal to be done. Some parts of the South Asian community have taken a battering in recent years and need to be shored up. Others are beginning to disintegrate: for example youth programmes are needed, job-creation schemes that produce real jobs, training that develops skills that can be marketed, and much more. Some skills are being exported, never to return; some British institutions are losing South Asian customers to off-shore or other rivals, and there is only limited time to stem the flow.

If we do commit to a new investment in the South Asian community, the results will benefit the entire country. The ethnic minorities are not the only people who will prosper if growth and diversification are made possible. It's an investment well worth underwriting with the best efforts of government, agencies and individuals.

But we must put the matter in hand soon and as a matter of urgency. We must make it a priority instead of relegating it to 'Any other business' on our agendas – as sadly has often been the case for far too long.

Let's do it!

Appendix

South Asian Directories

Asian Who's Who Directory
Asian Observer Publications
47 Beattyville Gardens, Barkingside
Ilford, Essex IG6 1JW

Tel: 0181 550 3745
Fax: 0181 551 0990

The Asian Business Directory
486 Honeypot Lane
Stanmore, Middlesex HA7 1LQ

Tel: 0181 951 3838
Fax: 0181 951 5666

INTERNATIONAL SOUTH ASIAN PUBLICATIONS

Bharat Ratna International
TST P O Box 96410   Tel: 852 2376 2117
Tsimshatsui, Kowloon, Hong Kong   Fax: 852 2317 5110
Ms Sandee Harilela
http://www.bharat-ratna.com.hk

Little India
1800 Oak Lane   Tel: 610 396 0366
Reading, PA 19604, USA   Fax: 610 396 3367

The International Indian
PO Box 6573   Tel: 09714 366 464
Dubai, United Arab Emirates (UAE)   Fax: 09714 368 466
Mr Frank Raj

ORGANISATIONS AND COMPANIES

Asia House
105 Piccadilly   Tel: 0171 499 1287
London W1V 9FN   Fax: 0171 499 8618

Asian Business Association
London Chamber of Commerce & Industry
33 Queen Street   Tel: 0171 248 4444
London EC4R 1AP   Fax: 0171 489 0391

Asian Business Initiative Ltd/BreakOut
Enterprise House, 297 Pinner Road Tel: 0181 427 6188
Harrow, Middlesex HA1 4HS   Fax: 0181 861 5709

Blackstone Franks
26–34 Old Street   Tel: 0171 250 3300
London EC1V 9HL   Fax: 0171 250 1402

Centre for Asian Entrepreneurial Research
Roehampton Institute London   Tel: 0181 392 3487
Senate House, Roehampton Lane   Fax: 0181 392 3646
London SW15 5PU

Centre for Research in Ethnic Relations
University of Warwick   Tel: 01203 524956
Coventry CV4 7AL

Commission for Racial Equality
Elliot House, 10-12 Allington Street　　Tel: 0171 828 7022
London SW1E 5EH　　Fax: 0171 630 6664

Grant Thornton
22 Melton Street　　Tel: 0171 383 5100
London NW1 2DZ

High Commission of Bangladesh
28 Queens Gate　　Tel: 0171 584 0081
London SW7 5JA

High Commission of India
India House, Aldwych　　Tel: 0171 836 8484
London WC2B 4NA　　Fax: 0171 240 4338

High Commission for Pakistan
35 Lowndes Square　　Tel: 0171 235 2044
London SW1X 9JN

High Commission for Sri Lanka
13 Hyde Park Gardens　　Tel: 0171 262 1841
London W2 2LX

Indo-British Partnership
Department of Trade and Industry　　Tel: 0171 215 4825
Bay 444, Kingsgate House　　Fax: 0171 215 8626
66-74 Victoria Street, London SW1E 6SW

Leicestershire Asian Business Association
4-6 New Street   Tel: 01533 512300
Leicester LE1 5NT   Fax: 01533 517799

Midland Bank plc/South Asian Banking Unit
27/32 Poultry   Tel: 0171 260 3948
London EC2P 2BX   Fax: 0171 260 3953

National Organisation of Asian Businesses
100 Alcester Street   Tel: 0121 666 6157
Birmingham B12 0QB

Overseas Doctors Association
24 Melville Road   Tel: 0121 327 6423
Edgbaston, Birmingham B16 9JT   Fax: 0121 327 1674

Society of Asian Lawyers
Peer House, 8–14 Verulam Street   Tel: 0171 813 2400
London WC1X 8LZ   Fax: 0171 405 3870

Southern Asia Advisory Group (SAAG)
Kingsgate House, 66-74 Victoria Street Tel: 0171 215 4825
London SW1E 6SW   Fax: 0171 215 8626

South Asian Development Partnership
PO Box 43, Sutton   Tel: 0181 770 9717
Surrey SM2 5WL   Fax: 0181 770 9747

UK Pakistan Overseas Chamber of Commerce
5 Bathurst Street   Tel: 0171 262 7599
London W2 2SD

South Asian Media List

English:

The Asian Age – Media Asia (Europe) Ltd
Dolphin Media House
Spring Villa Park, Spring Villa Road   Tel: 0181 951 4878
Edgware, Middlesex HA8 7EB   Fax: 0181 951 4839
Editor: Mr Shekar Bhatia
(Daily published simultaneously in Bombay, Delhi and London with
Bombay Stock Exchange prices)

Asian Times
3rd Floor, Tower House,
141-149 Fonthill Rd.   Tel: 0171 281 1191
London N4 3HF   Fax: 0171 263 9656
Editor: Mr Araf Ali

Eastern Eye
148 Cambridge Heath Rd,   Tel: 0171 702 8012
Bethnal Green   Fax: 0171 702 7937
London E1 5QJ
Editor: Mr Sarwar Ahmed

India Mail
150A Ealing Road, Wembley   Tel: 0181 900 1757
Middlesex HA0 4PY

LIBAS Magazine
16 Connaught Street,   Tel: 0171 706 7766
London W2 2AF   Fax: 0171 706 7097
E-mail: 101571.473@compuserve.com

New World
234 Holloway Rd   Tel: 0171 700 2673
London N7 8DA   Fax: 0171 607 6706
Editor: Dhiren Basu

The Weekly Awam
37-39 Woodfield Road, Balsall Heath   Tel: 0121 446 4737
Birmingham B12 8TD   Fax: 0121 446 4388
Editor: A Hussain

Bengali:

Ananda Bazar Patrika Daily/Sunday Weekly Magazine
Wheatsheaf House,
4 Carmelite Street   Tel: 0171 353 1821
London EC4Y 0BN   Fax: 0171 583 5385
Editor: A Sarkar

The Daily Deshbarta
170 Brick Lane   Tel: 0171 377 1584
London E1 6RU   Fax: 0171 247 9299
Editor: Mr Shariful Hasan Khan

Janomot
Unit 2, 20B Spelman Street   Tel: 0171 377 6032
London E1 5LQ   Fax: 0171 247 0141
Editor: Mr Syed Samadul Haque

Notun Din
Rm 5 Brady Centre,
192-196 Hanbury Street   Tel: 0171 247 6280
London E1 5HU   Fax: 0171 247 2280
Editor: M Chowdhury

Gujarati:

Garavi Gujarat/Asian Trader
Garavi Gujarat House, 1 Silex St   Tel: 0171 928 1234
London SE1 0DW   Fax: 0171 261 0055
Editor: R C Solanki

Gujarat Samachar/Asian Voice/Asian Business
8-16 Coronet St, Off Old Street   Tel: 0171 729 5453
London N1 6HD   Fax: 0171 739 0358
Editor: C B Patel

Hindi:

Amar Deep Hindi
36 Trent Avenue   Tel: 0181 840 3534
London W5 4TL   Fax: 0181 579 3180
Editor: J M Kaushal

Navin Weekly
59/61 Broughton Rd, Fulham   Tel: 0171 385 8966
London SW6 2LA
Editor: Ramesh Kumar

Punjabi:

Awaze Quam International
Gate 2 Unit 5b Booth St,   Tel: 0121 555 5921
Smethwick, Birmingham B66 2PF   Fax: 0121 555 6899
Editor: Raghbir Singh

The Punjabi Guardian
129 Soho Road,   Tel: 0121 554 3995
Handsworth, Birmingham B21 9ST   Fax: 0121 567 1065
Editor: Inder Jit Singh Sangha

Punjab Times International
24 Cottonbrook Road   Tel: 01332 372 851
Sir Francis Ley Industrial Park South Fax: 01332 372 833
Derby DE23 8YJ
Editor: H S Mander

Weekly Des Pardes
8 The Crescent, Southall   Tel: 0181 571 1127
Middlesex UB1 1BE   Fax: 0181 571 2604
Editor: Mr Virk

Urdu:

The Daily Jang
Jang Publications Ltd.,
1 Sanctuary St   Tel: 0171 403 5833
London SE1 1ED   Fax: 0171 378 1653
Editor: Zahoor Niazi

RADIO STATIONS

Sunrise Radio
Sunrise House, Sunrise Road,   Tel: 0181 574 6666
Southall, Middlesex UB2 4AU   Fax: 0181 813 9800
Chief Executive: Avtar Lit

TV Stations

Asia Net Ltd
Elliott House,
Victoria Road, Park Royal   Tel: 0181 930 0930
London NW10 6NY   Fax: 0181 930 0546
Chief Executive: Dr Banad Viswanath

Zee TV
Unit 7
Belvue Business Centre, Belvue Road   Tel: 0181 841 5112
Northolt UB5 5QQ   Fax: 0181 841 9550
Head of News: Anita Anand

INTERNET: SOUTH ASIAN WEB SITES

Asia Business Connection
http://www.asiabiz.com

The Asian Age
http://www.asianage.com

Discovery of India
http://www.mahesh.com/india

ExploreIndia
http://www.exploreindia.com

India WWW Virtual Library
http://www.webhead.com/wwwvl/india

India Online
http://www.indiaonline.com

INDOlink
http://www.genius.net/indolink/

Little India
http://www.littleindia.com

Further Reading

This short bibliography is intended to be neither a comprehensive introduction to the literature of the subject nor a systematic listing of all the sources I have used in putting this book together. It is a selection of books that usefully develop some themes I have discussed in the book, and provide resource materials.

On the South Asian Diaspora

Ali, Ahmed, et al., *Pacific Indians: Profiles in 20 Countries* (Inst. of Pacific Studies University of the South Pacific, and Hanns Seidel Foundation, 1981).

Chaliand, Gérard, and Jean-Pierre Rageau, *The Penguin Atlas of Diasporas* (Penguin Viking, 1995).

Clarke, Colin, Ceri Peach and Steven Vertovec (eds), *South Asians Overseas: Migration and Ethnicity* (Cambridge University Press, 1990).

Fryer, Peter, *Staying Power: the History of Black People in Britain* (Pluto Press, 1984).

Helweg, Arthur W., and Usha M. Helweg, *An Immigrant Success Story: East Indians in America* (Hurst & Co., 1990).

Hiranandani, Popati, *Sindhis: the Scattered Treasure* (Malaah Publications, New Delhi, 1980).

Kotecha, Bhanubahen, *On the Threshold of East Africa* (Jyotiben Madhvani Foundation, 1995). On the Asian settlements in East Africa.

Seidenberg, Dana April, *Mercantile Adventurers: The World of East African Asians 1750–1985* (New Age International, Delhi, 1996).

Veer, Peter van de, *Nation Migration: The Politics of Space in the South Asian Diaspora* (University of Pennsylvania Press, 1995).

Visram, Rozina, *Indians in Britain* (Batsford, Peoples on the Move Series, 1987). This is a GCSE textbook and a useful, well-illustrated, short summary.

On British South Asian Culture

Chowdry, Pushpinder, *Women of Substance: Profiles of Asian Women in the UK* (Hansib Publications/Asian Women in Publishing, 1997).

Gidoomal, Ram, with Mike Fearon, *Sari 'n' Chips* (Monarch MARC/South Asian Concern, 1993).

Guptara, Prabhu, *Black British Literature: an Annotated Bibliography* (Dangaroo Press, 1986).

Robinson, Vaughan, *Transients Settlers and Refugees: Asians in Britain* (Clarendon Press, 1986).

Sachar, J. S. (ed.), *Asian Who's Who International* (Asian Observer Publications, 1997).

Sharma, Sanjay, John Hutnyk and Ashwani Sharma (eds), *Dis-Orienting Rhythms: the Politics of the New Asian Dance Music* (Zed Books, 1996).

On Social Issues

Research & Planning Department, Austin Knight, *Focus on Young Asians: Attitudes, Preferences and Experiences in Career Choice and Equality* (Austin Knight, 1997).

Drew, David, *'Race', Education and Work: the Statistics of Inequality* (Avebury, 1995).

Modood, Tariq, Richard Berthoud et al., *Ethnic Minorities in Britain: Diversity and Disadvantage: The Fourth National Survey of Ethnic Minorities* (Policy Studies Institute, 1997).

On UK (and International) South Asian Business, Entrepreneurism etc.

Cragg, Claudia, *The New Maharajahs: the Commercial Princes of India, Pakistan and Bangladesh* (Random House Century, 1996).

Dhaliwal, Spinder and Vijay Amin, *Profiles of Five Asian Entrepreneurs* (Roehampton Institute and Asian Business Initiative, 1995).

Hiscock, Geoff, *Asia's Wealth Club: Who's Really Who in Business – the Top 100 Billionaires in Asia* (Nicholas Brealey Publishing, 1997).

Srinivasan, Shaila, *The South Asian Petty Bourgeoisie in Britain: an Oxford Case Study* (Avebury, 1995).

Miscellaneous

Gersick, Kelin E., et al., *Generation to Generation: Life Cycles of the Family Business* (Harvard Business School Press, 1997).

Graves, Earl G., *How to Succeed in Business Without Being White* (Harper Business, 1997).
Gregory, Robert G., *The Rise and Fall of Philanthropy in East Africa: the Asian Contribution* (Transaction, 1992).

Notes

Introduction

1   Documented in Geoff Hiscock, *Asia's Wealth Club: Who's Really Who in Business: the Top 100 Billionaires in Asia* (Nicholas Brealey Publishing, 1997).

2   'Charity Work Takes Singer Frankie to the Palace', *Daily Telegraph*, 10 May 1997.

3   'Patels Put Cullens in their Shopping Basket', *The Times*, 10 May 1997.

4   'The Hills are Alive - With the Sound of Hindi', *The Independent*, 24 May 1997.

5   'Oxbridge Gets Asian Master', *Eastern Eye*, 11 June 1997.

6   *Eastenders* is transmitted on BBC1 at 8 p.m. on Mondays and at 7.30 p.m. on Tuesdays and Thursdays.

7   Tariq Modood and Richard Berthoud, *Ethnic Minorities in Britain: Diversity and Disadvantage* (Policy Studies Unit, 1997).

8   Quoted in 'Immigrants Swell Ranks of British Middle Class', *Daily Telegraph*, 22 May 1997.

Chapter 1

1   South Asian Development Partnership/SOLOTEC, *South Asian Population Report for Great Britain* (SASP/SOLOTEC, 1992), p. i.

2   Popati Hiranandani, *Sindhis: the Scattered Treasure* (Malah Publications, New Delhi, 1980), from the introduction by Ram Jethmalani, p. xi.

3   In Gerard Chaliand and Jean-Pierre Rageau, *The Penguin Atlas of Diasporas* (Penguin, 1995), the authors suggest four criteria for the definition of a diaspora: '1. Collective forced dispersion of a religious and/or ethnic group', '2. Collective memory, which transmits both the historical facts that precipitated the dispersion and a cultural heritage (broadly understood)', '3. The will to survive as a minority by transmitting a heritage', and '4. The time factor' (pp. xiv-xvii).

4   See Richard Crossman, *The Diaries of a Cabinet Minister 1966–68*, vol. 2 (Hamilton & Cape, 1976), p.526 ff.

5   By 1968 legislation was being tabled. See, e.g., 'Stem the Immigrants Say Tories', *Daily Mail*, 22 February 1968.

6   See Peter Fryer, *Staying Power: The History of Black People in Britain* (Pluto Press, 1984), pp. 372–3.

7   Malcolm Rifkind, 'New Opportunities in Asia', speech to the Royal Society for Asian Affairs (London, 21 February 1996).

8   'The Xenophobic Tendency', *Economist*, 4 May 1996.

9   Philip Beresford and Khozem Merchant, *Britain's Richest Asian 100: 1997* (Eastern Eye Publications with Caroline Banks Associates, 1997), p. 55ff.

10   Said in conversation with the author, Autumn 1997.

11   All quotations in this book that are not footnoted are taken
     from personal interviews conducted in early 1997.

12   Said in conversation with one of my researchers, 1996.

13   'The Europa Community', *Evening Standard*, 12 August 1996.

Chapter 2

1   Shaila Srinivasan, *The South Asian Petty Bourgeoisie in Britain:
     An Oxford Case Study* (Avebury, 1995), p. 136.

2   The effects and the often inefficient application of the rule were
     discussed in a letter to *The Times* of 31 May 1997 from Keith
     Best of the Immigration Advisory Service.

3   See e.g. H.E. Aldrich, J.C. Carter, T.P. Jones and D. McEvoy,
     'Business Development and Self-Segregation: Asian Enterprise
     in Three British Cities', in: C. Peach, V. Robinson and S. Smith
     (eds), *Ethnic Segregation in Cities* (Croom Helm, 1981).

4   T.P. Jones, D. McEvoy and G. Barrett, 'Labour Intensive Prac-
     tices in the Ethnic Minority Firm', in: J. Atkinson and D. Storey
     (eds), *Employment, the Small Firm and the Labour Market* (Rout-
     ledge, 1994).

5   Tariq Modood, Satnam Virdee and Hilary Metcalf, *Asian Self-
     Employment in Britain: The Interaction of Culture and Economics.
     Part 1: Theoretical Approaches to Asian Business* (Policy Studies
     Institute, 1996).

6   Ram Gidoomal with Mike Fearon, *Sari 'n' Chips* (Monarch, 1993).

7   Richard Crossman, *The Diaries of a Cabinet Minister: Volume 1, Minister of Housing 1964-66* (Hamilton & Cape, 1975), p. 270.

8   Harold Wilson, *The Governance of Britain* (Weidenfeld & Nicolson, 1976), p. 52.

9   Information kindly supplied by Midland Bank.

10 Said in conversation with the author, Summer 1997.

11 Information kindly supplied by the deputy headmaster, Mr C. W. Field.

12 Information kindly provided by Shell.

13 Information kindly provided by Professor Raman Bedi, Eastman Dental Institute, London.

14 Adrian E. Platts, Jennifer Tann and Zahid Chisti, *Ethnic Minority Pharmacy Practice* (unpublished, 1997).

15 Barclays Review, *Cultural Change and the Small Firm* (Barclays, Small Business Service, 1997), p. 3.

16 Modood and Berthoud (1997), p. 65.

17 See discussion in 'Integrated but Unequal', *The Economist*, 8 February 1997.

18 Modood and Berthoud (1997), pp. 76–77.

19 Ibid.

Chapter 3

1   Sir Herbert Maxwell, *Sixty Years a Queen: The Story of Her Majesty's Reign* (Eyre & Spottiswoode, 1897), p. 101.

2   James Morris, *Pax Britannica: The Climax of an Empire* (Penguin, 1979), p. 323.

3   Laxmishanker Pathak (Obituary), *The Times*, 15 April 1997.

Chapter 5

1   Press release from Syntel.

2   Syntel IntelliSourcing, *Helping You Build.*

3   Janice Castro, 'Come on Down! Fast!', *Time*, 27 May 1991, p. 38.

4   John Greenwald, 'The Job Freeze', *Time*, 1 February 1993, p. 52.

5   Mohul Pandya, 'Speeding on the Information Highway', Little India (electronically published by ASIANET), vol. 6, 2 February 1996.

Chapter 6

1   Myrtle Langley, *World Religions* (Lion Publishing, 1981), p. 63.

Chapter 7

1   'Integrated but Unequal', *The Economist*, 8 February 1997.

2   Information from Zee TV quoted in 'Parties Break New Ground with TV Appeal to Asians', *The Times*, 12 April 1997. I am indebted to that article for the substance of this paragraph.

Chapter 8

1   See articles in *Business Life*, October 1997, pp. 32, 69.

2   Matthew Bond, 'Light Entertainment and Serious Money', *The Times*, 1 November 1995.

3   Michael Syrett and Jean Lammiman, 'Britain's Own Tiger Economy', *Director*, January 1997, p. 34.

4   The advertisement promoted the book and travelling exhibition *Roots of the Future* (CRE, 1997).

5   This is usefully expanded in Spinder Dhaliwal and Vijay Amin, *Profiles of Five Asian Entrepreneurs* (Roehampton Institute and Asian Business Initiative, 1995), p. 17ff.

6   'Bringing Investors to Book', *Sunday Times*, 11 May 1997.

7   'Double Fantasy Fund Winner Invests in Real World', *Sunday Times*, 29 October 1995.

Chapter 9

1   Quoted in Alex Wijeratne, 'Asian Wave', *The Times*, 23 August 1997.

2   Research and Planning Department, Austin Knight. *Focus on Young Asians: Attitudes, Preferences and Experiences in Career*

Choice and Equality (Austin Knight 1997), p. 3.

3   'Asian Influence colouring Different Shades of Blue', *Daily Tele-graph*, 9 April 1997.

4   Prabhu S. Guptara, *Black British Literature* (Dangaroo Press, 1986).

5   Raminder Kauer and Virinder S. Kalra, 'New Paths for South Asian Identity and Musical Creativity', in: Sanjay Sharma, John Hutnyk and Ashwan Sharma (eds), *Dis-Orienting Rhythms: The Politics of the Asian DAnce Music* (Zed Books, 1996). p. 219.

Chapter 10

1   'Crisis Ahead for London Corner Shops', *Breakout*, (issue 4, Winter 1997), p. 1.

Chapter 11

1   Philip Beresford and Khozem Merchant, *Britain's Richest Asian 100*, p. 7.

2   P. Narayan Pant and Vasant G. Rajadhyaksha, 'Partnership with an Asian Family Business – What Every Multi-National Corporation Should Know', *Long Range Planning*, 29:6, 1996, pp. 818–20.

3   White Paper: Competitiveness: Creating the Enterprise Centre Of Europe (presented to Parliament to the Deputy Minister and First Secretary of State, June 1996).

4   'Asians Can't Bank on Help', *Guardian*, 7 January 1997.

5   Quoted in 'Asians Can't Bank on Help', *Guardian*, 7 January 1997.

6   Ibid.

7   Barclays Review: *Cultural Change and the Small Firm* (Barclays Business Sector, 1997).

Chapter 12

1   A theme usefully developed in P. Iles and E. Wilson, *The Business Benefits of Diversity* (Liverpool, John Moores University, 1996).

2   White Paper: Competitiveness: Creating the Enterprise Centre of Europe (presented to Parliament by the Deputy Minister and First Secretary of State, June 1996).

3   'Ethnic Diversity Attracts Inward Investors', *Financial Times*, 11/12 October 1997.

4   'Industry Tide Starts to Turn for the Tecs', *Sunday Times*, 7 July 1996.

5   Asian Business Initiative, for Business Link London West and West London TEC, *Reaching out to Ethnic Minority Growth Businesses* (Business Link London West, April 1996).

Index

A

accountancy 207–9
Action For Acton 223
advisers 195–200, 206–7
Ahmed, Ajaz 145
Ahmed, Nizan 152
Ahmed, Shami 14, 31, 116,
    143, 145–54, 195, 205, 210
Akhter 31
Alcan 92, 217
Amin, Ali 142
Amin, Idi 7, 65, 76, 77, 232
Amin, Nidish 28
Amin, Vijay 206, 209
Amstrad 150–1, 152
Arthur Andersen 208
Ashdown, Paddy 73, 142
Asian Business Initiative 206,
    209, 234
Aston Hotels 209
Audio Marketing 31
Ayling, Robert 224

B

Babylon Zoo 176
Bagri, Lord Raj 16, 140, 142

Bahl, Kamlesh 11
Bangalore phenomenon 109
Bank of Ireland 210
banking 42–3, 147–8
Barclays 42, 210, 224
BBC 224
Berthoud, Richard xvi, 46
Bird's Eye 67–8
Blackstone Franks 196, 204,
    207, 208, 213
Blair, Tony viii
Bombay Halwa 66, 67, 71
Bose Corporation 49
British Airways 44, 57, 66, 221,
    224
British Coal 230
British Dental Association 45
British Steel 230
Brookside 179
Brown, Gordon 104
BT 30
bureaucracy, minimising 52–4
Business in the Commu-
    nity 221, 224, 234
business integrity 25
Business Link 205, 206, 223–4,

Business Link (*cont.*) 230, 231–2

C

Caparo Group 14, 140
Care First 162, 165
Centre for Asian Entrepreneurial Research 234
Chabbria 49
Chambers of Commerce 232
Chande, Anuj 196, 208, 219
Christmas Cracker 179, 217
City Tote 121–2
Clarke, Kenneth 104
Colonial Dominion Overseas Bank 42
Commission for Racial Equality 224
Cook, Robin 126
Cosby Show, The 179
Court Cavendish 14, 162, 164–5, 166
Crossman, Richard 39
Cullens xiv
culture 175–6
Cunningham, Jack 126

D

Dattani, Dina 37, 129, 135–9
Datwani, Kumar 16, 85, 100–7, 159, 185
Daver, Berjis 119–28, 172
Deep Wouhra, Tony 205
Desai, Bharat 14, 31, 51, 85, 107–17, 228

Desai, Lord Meghnand 140
Desai, Neerja 111, 116
Dewan, Ramesh 142
Dhiri, Amita xv
Dholakia, Lord Navnit 16, 140
discrimination 188–9
diversity 220–1
divorce 26
Domino's Pizza 144
Dulwich College 44

E

EastEnders xv, 179
Echobelly 176
education 44–7
Education Business Partnership Compacts 223
Elizabeth Emanuel 150
Ethnic Minority Taskforce 224
Europa Foods xiv, 29

F

family firms 181–4, 187–92, 211–14
family
  change within 180–7
  extended 24
  importance of 17–22, 200
Festival of Spiritual Unity 83
'Fine Fashions' 211–14
Flather, Baroness Shreela 11, 16, 140–1
Foley, Ronnie 210
Fourth Party 142
Framjee, Pesh 208

G

Gidoomal family 6–7, 17, 20,
    24, 35–7, 40–1
Gidoomal, Ravi 50–1
Gohil, Vinod 182
Grant Thornton
    International 196, 197,
    208, 213, 219
Grindlay Ottoman 42
Guptara, Prabhu 175

H

Harilela 49
Hart's the Grocers xiv, 28
Hasan, Ayesha 129–30
Heseltine, Michael 73
Highland Seafoods 3
Hinduja brothers 13
Hong Kong and Shanghai
    Bank 43, 148
Hussain, Tony xiv

I

India, Partition of 6, 121
Indo-British Partnership 27
Inlaks Group xiv, 3, 14, 21, 28,
    85–99, 216–19
Integrated Advisory Group
    International 196
integration 172, 173

J

Johnson, Sir Garry 43
Jumbo Electronics 49

K

Kalra, Virinder S. 176
Kapoor, Shobu xv
Kaur, Raminder 176
Keillers 12
Kelly, Tom 126
Kenya, independence 6
Kenyatta, Jomo 6, 39, 76, 77
Khabra, Piara 139
Khan, Imran 74, 174
Khan, Ustad Ali Akhbar 176
Kind Edward's School 45
Kirpalani's Store 174
Kotecha, Paresh 209
Koureshi, Hanif 175
Kumar, Ashok 140
Kureishi, Hanif 180–1

L

Ladbrokes 14, 20–6
Lara, Brian 149
Lawrence Jones 138
legal profession 129–39
Legendary Joe Bloggs 31,
    145–54
Lehman Brothers Kuhn
    Loeb 164
Leisuresoft 31
London First Centre 221, 224
London Research Centre 224

M

Maas, Robert 196
Macdonald, Malcolm 39
Madhvani, Jayant Muljibhai 76

Madhvani, Manubhai 14, 15,
    75–83, 172–3, 232
Madhvani, Muljibhai P. 76
Major, John 27, 73, 142, 185
Malik, Art 175
Manek, Jayesh 14, 106, 155–62
Mann, Jas 176
marriage 26–7, 186–7
Marshall, Sir Colin 221
McDonald's 224
media 175–6, 178–80
Merrill Lynch 164
Midland Bank 43, 148
Mishra, Jyoti 176
Mittal, Lakshmi 13
Modood, Tariq xv–xvi, 46
Mombasa Silk Emporium 20
Monteluce, Nicolo Sella de 91
Muggeridge, Malcolm 181
Mughal, Humayan 31
Museveni, Yoweri 77–8
Musquaan Trading 31
My Beautiful Laundrette 180–1

N
National Organisation of Asian
    Businesses 234
National Westminster
    Bank 148, 224
Nehru, Jawaharlal 60
networks 47–9
New Media 145
Noon Products 48, 68–73, 189
Noon, Gulam 13, 14, 29, 48,
    57–74, 80, 112, 142, 174

North London TEC 127
North West London TEC 125

O
One Nation forum 81

P
Paper, Print and Products 63
Patel brothers xiv, 28, 29
Patel, Chai 14, 162–7, 184
Patel, Peter 142
Pathak, Laxmishanker 60
Paul, Lord Swarj 14, 16, 140,
    142
Pearce, Nazreen 129, 141
Pennywise 147, 149
politics 139–41, 142
Popat, Surendra 141
Powell, Enoch 39
Prashar, Usha 130
Prescott, John 126
Prince's Youth Business
    Trust 223, 228
professionalising 202–4,
    216–20
Public Appointments Ethnic
    Monitoring Unit 225

R
Race for Opportunity 44, 221,
    224–5, 234
Razahussein, Jessa 31
religion, influence of 23–4
role models 50–1, 173–4
Royal Sweets 61–2, 64–5, 67, 69

Rushdie, Salman 175–6

S

S & A Foods xiv
Sainsbury's xiv, 57, 69
Sainsbury, David 69, 71
Sarwar, Mohammad 140
Savine, John 1
second generation 143–4,
    171–2, 174–6, 202
Sen, Amartya xv
Shankar, Ravi 176
Shankar, Ricky 116
Shankardass, Arun 207
Shell 45
Sheth, Pranlal 141
Shivdasani, Azad 14, 85–99,
    144, 216
Shivdasani, Indurkumar
    (Indoo) 86–9
Shivdasani, Sonu 99, 144
Singh, Anurag 45, 173
Singh, Judge Mota 112, 130–5,
    183–4, 188–9
Singh, Marsha 140
Singh, Rabinder 141
Singh, Reuben 143
Singhvi, His Excellency Dr L.
    M. 3, 35, 73
SKD Pacific 100–7
Smethwick 38
social problems 172, 183–4
SOLOTEC 10, 222, 229
Somerfield 57, 69
Soneva Pavilions 144

South Asian Advisory
    Group 28
South Asian Development Part-
    nership 10, 234
Southall Opportunities
    Centre 223
Southall Youth Project 223
success gene 44–52
Sugar, Alan 150–1, 152
survival mechanisms 33–44
Suterwalla, Taherbhai 64
Syntel 14, 31, 49, 51, 107–17,
    228
Syrett, Michael 210

T

Taj International Hotel Group
    66
Takare 162, 165
Taneja, Meera 31
Tata Consultancy Services 110
Tata Foundation 127
Taylor, Ashok 31
Tebbit, Lord vii, 175
Training and Enterprise Coun-
    cils (TECs) 125–6, 127–8,
    222–3, 230, 232
Tesco 12, 229
Thakrar, Subhash 196, 201,
    207
Thatcher, Lady 81
This Life xv, 137
Thomas Goode 144
TRS 64
Tulsiani, Vashi 31

U

Uganda, expulsion of Asians 7,
    36, 65, 75–7

V

Vaz, Keith 139
Verjee, Rumi 144
Verma, Deepak xv

W

Wadia, Jim 208
Wagh, Mark 45, 173
Waitrose 57, 69
Warsi, Perween xiv

Watford Electronics 31
Watford Football Club 144–5
Welcome Break 69
Welfare to Work 221
West London Disability Part-
    nership 223
West London TEC 222
WH Smith 30–1, 224
White Town 176
Wilson, Harold 39
windfall tax 221

Z

Zee TV 142